Rob Nijskens • Melanie Lohuis • Paul Hilbers •
Willem Heeringa
Editors

Hot Property

The Housing Market in Major Cities

Editors
Rob Nijskens
De Nederlandsche Bank
Amsterdam, The Netherlands

Melanie Lohuis
De Nederlandsche Bank
Amsterdam, The Netherlands

Paul Hilbers
De Nederlandsche Bank
Amsterdam, The Netherlands

Willem Heeringa
De Nederlandsche Bank
Amsterdam, The Netherlands

https://doi.org/10.1007/978-3-030-11674-3

Foreword

Amsterdam: the city with the highest house price rises in the Netherlands and, in 2017, also in the Eurozone.[1] I live in this city, so I have witnessed these soaring prices at first hand. Like many capital cities, Amsterdam has led the rebound in the Dutch housing market, which started in 2013. Prices here began to take off and within a few years were growing at annual rates of over 15%. A similar story can be told about other large cities in the Netherlands. And more recently the rest of the country has followed this trend, albeit at a slower pace, which means that house prices are now rising everywhere.

My work takes me all over the globe to the world's major cities, so I have seen similar housing market dynamics in London, Paris and Berlin, but also Washington, Seoul and Sydney. The book you are about to read comprises views on these developments by leading academics, central bankers and policymakers from across the globe. They delve into some serious questions: Do we agree on the analysis of the problems in this field? Could we learn from each other's best practices? Is there one solution?

As an urban resident, as central bank president and of course as an economist, I see both opportunities and challenges. While the increased popularity of cities worldwide may be good news for these places, and for homeowners, it also creates issues. Demand for urban housing is strongly outstripping supply. This leads to the surge in housing prices that we are seeing. At the same time, it also puts pressure on rental markets. And although supervisors, central banks and governments have strengthened mortgage regulation since the financial crisis, the risk of a credit-driven boom always looms. After all, homeowners are often willing to take on more debt to be able to live in the city. In the Netherlands, we haven't yet seen a credit boom, but in countries such as Norway, Sweden, Belgium and Finland, house price growth has been accompanied by strong mortgage growth.

---

[1] In real terms, as of 2017: see ECB Financial Stability Report, May 2017.

Strong price increases are making urban housing affordability a pressing issue everywhere in the world. For central bankers, who are mainly responsible for financial stability, affordability may not always be the most important concern. However, extreme examples show this can become a problem for broader economic well-being: think of the San Francisco Bay Area, Silicon Valley in particular, where the average house costs €1.5 million by now. As these areas are booming, many workers cannot afford to live there anymore. An increasing literature is documenting these consequences of decreasing affordability, social as well as economic. Indeed, urban demographics are changing as a result. Young, well-educated people are drawn to cities, often chasing a limited supply of housing. Due to the housing shortage, middle-income households are put at a disadvantage: too rich to qualify for social housing, not rich enough to buy a house. They have to rely on the rental market. However, if this market does not function well, as is the case in many cities, middle-income families are forced to move out of the city. Moreover, the rise of major cities also leads to increasing divergence between these cities and more peripheral regions. At the same time, spillover effects cause prices to rise in areas surrounding major cities. This ultimately affects the structure of economic development, which increasingly shifts to urban areas and away from the periphery.

Major supply shortages in cities, and to a lesser extent in other parts of the country, are a main driver of current price rises. And as we know from past experience, strong house price rises can lead to overshooting, often followed by a correction. This price volatility does not remain confined to the housing market. In countries like the Netherlands, Sweden and the UK, with a high rate of home ownership and dependence on mortgage lending, house price volatility feeds into the real economy. The link between house prices and private consumption is strong here, and this symbiotic relationship causes economic booms to grow larger and busts to be deeper.

A more balanced and suitable supply of housing is thus needed. This does not only mean owner-occupied housing but also private rental, especially for middle-income households. As a 2017 study by De Nederlandsche Bank (DNB) pinpointed, they are put in a tight spot on the housing market.[2] A larger mid-market private rental segment is the key first step to creating a housing market that is free of such imbalances, especially in cities. However, a lack of planning and building capacity, as well as zoning restrictions, is still impeding new-build developments in and around cities. Moreover, lower-tier governments like municipalities lack effective incentives to develop the private rental sector. The Dutch national government is currently taking a more proactive, leading role to overcome these impediments and ensure an appropriate supply of new houses.

For central bankers with a financial stability mandate, these housing market developments pose new challenges for risk analysis and possible policy responses. Other policymakers are struggling with these challenges as well. And that is why DNB, in May 2018, organised a seminar that brought together speakers from different countries and divergent backgrounds. This has helped to avoid groupthink

[2]"The housing market in major Dutch cities", DNB Occasional Study, May 2017.

and to promote a healthy exchange of views from different perspectives: central banks and public bodies, academia, the private sector and representatives from major cities themselves.

During the seminar, four questions were addressed, which are also reflected in the chapter of the book that lies before you. The first question is why big cities are so popular, and whether this popularity is here to stay. Is there a fundamental demand for urban housing, and will it last for the years to come?

Subsequently, the bubble question pops up: do we see a housing bubble in the big cities and how do you measure this? If there is anything the financial crisis has taught us, it is that there is most cause for concern when this bubble is fuelled by excessive credit provision. Credit-driven bubbles are the most detrimental to financial stability. Curiously, in the Netherlands, the current housing market recovery does not seem to be credit driven: house prices are surging, but mortgage growth is near zero. I cannot help but notice that this atypical development is driven by today's low interest rates. As private investors do not find sufficient return in savings accounts or other safe investments, they turn to the housing market, driving up prices.

After considering housing demand, the supply side of the housing market also needs to be taken into account: what role do supply frictions play in the current environment? Cities are notoriously dense, and expanding supply is thus difficult in urban areas. Therefore, even more than in peripheral areas, supply issues and policy options in cities should be studied in detail.

This brings us to the last topic: which policy actions are needed to effectively address these issues? Until recently, macroprudential policymakers focused mainly on restricting demand. Measures like LTV limits, LTI restrictions and capital requirements should keep mortgage growth, and thus price growth, in check. However, current developments seem less driven by credit and more by fundamentals like population growth and supply shortages. It is thus likely we need to look further than our standard housing market toolkit.

The seminar participants have produced a rich collection of papers that will surely add to our collective knowledge on urban housing markets. I hope you enjoy reading their insights and that this book provides inspiration to tackle the housing market challenges ahead.

De Nederlandsche Bank, Klaas Knot
Amsterdam, The Netherlands
July 2018

Preface

Cities are booming, as are their housing markets. All over the world, people are flocking to cities for the job opportunities, educational facilities and cultural provisions they offer—and these people all need a place to live. In many cities, this has caused demand for housing to outpace supply, leading to a sharp increase in housing prices and pressures on rental markets. This development is often accompanied by subdued activity in countries' more peripheral regions. For central banks and other policymakers with a responsibility for financial stability, this trend towards urbanisation and the resulting divergence between cities and other regions poses challenges for both analysis and policy.

In order to address these challenges, De Nederlandsche Bank organised a high-level seminar on the housing market in major cities in Amsterdam on May 24–25, 2018. This seminar has yielded many useful insights into the issues at hand, their impact on society, the economy and financial stability and possible policy responses. The following 18 chapters, written by the seminar speakers, elaborate upon these insights. In this preface, we identify 10 key takeaways from the seminar and the chapters in this book.

Key Takeaways

1. **Cities are becoming more and more popular all over the world, leading to a surge in demand for urban housing.**
   The housing boom in big cities is universal and is largely attributable to the lure of big cities. Cities have transformed themselves: heavy investments have been made in infrastructure and in cultural and recreational facilities. They have become the economic powerhouses of the countries they are in. People are drawn to the cities as cities offer education, jobs, cultural events, creativity, recreational opportunities and of course the presence of other people. Particularly highly educated young people are migrating to urban centres. Immigrants in search of work and education are also focusing on the cities, where they can

connect with communities of the same origin. It is expected that by 2100, no less than between 80% and 90% of the population will live in cities (see Chap. 1 by Lisette van Doorn et al.).

2. **Capital is currently finding its way to residential property in the cities, spurred by low interest rates and a search for yield.**
   The demand for housing as an investment good, from domestic as well as foreign investors, contributes to the increasing demand for urban housing. Investors see the buy-to-let market as a favourable investment option, as the yield of a buy-to-let investment is relatively high compared to alternatives. This attracts different sorts of investors, including high net worth individuals, institutional investors and foreign investors. House prices in the cities thus not only reflect the local factors such as supply constraints, regulations and zoning, but also global trends like the growing role of foreign investors. This phenomenon is called "glocalisation" (see Chap. 7 by Hites Ahir and Prakash Loungani).
3. **Housing supply is lagging behind the growing demand for homes in the cities.**
   Supply is only increasing slowly. Suitable land for residential development in city centres is notoriously scarce, leading to larger increases in house prices (see Chap. 12 by Bahar Öztürk et al.). The lack of suitable land is also caused by administrative building restrictions and the *Not In My Backyard* (NIMBY) syndrome that is surfacing around the world. Building requires long planning processes, in which many different stakeholders and interests are involved. The governance of new housing construction is complex: cities are subject to different layers of public administration, each with its own authority. Owner-occupied and rental markets cannot be viewed in isolation: demand for rented accommodation is rising, partly owing to flexible millennials and expats, while supply is lacking. Rental regulations play a role here. In Sweden for example, rents in the regulated market are low, which hampers the turnover of apartments as people continue to live in their rented accommodation (see Chap. 11 by Kjersti Næss Torstensen and Kasper Roszbach). In the Netherlands, the non-regulated rental sector is underdeveloped: the supply of mid-market private rental housing falls short of demand in large cities, which is partly because social rental and owner-occupied housing are subsidised (see Chap. 3 by Rob Nijskens and Melanie Lohuis). In the discussion about lagging supply, it's good to keep in mind that there is a difference between short-term and long-term supply (see Chap. 9 by Albert Saiz). Short-term supply is very inelastic, leading to rising prices when demand is increasing. Often, real house prices are expected to continue rising permanently, which is irrational as supply will catch up with demand in the long term.
4. **These factors together are causing affordability problems for middle-income earners.**
   Rising house prices and rents in the major cities are putting ordinary inhabitants, who live in a private rental house or are trying to buy their first homes, in a tight spot. In Amsterdam, it's difficult for families with children to find an affordable

larger home, which is why these families leave the city. Meanwhile, young people often turn to shared homes or small studios to live in (see Chap. 10 by Laurens Ivens). In London, huge affordability problems have arisen (see Chap. 2 by Jamie Ratcliff): more than one-quarter of Londoners live in poverty if their housing expenses are included.

5. **House prices in the cities are often leading the rest of the country.**
House price fluctuations in capital cities tend to be more volatile and stronger than in the rest of the countries and have a tendency to overshoot. Cities are often experiencing house price changes ahead of other regions. Such a ripple effect can be observed in London and Paris (see Chap. 5 by John Muellbauer). In the Netherlands, this is the case as well: whereas house prices in the major cities are soaring, the housing market in the regions surrounding these cities is now gaining strong momentum as well.
6. **Next to similarities, there are also differences between countries, among others in structural housing market characteristics.**
Countries for instance show different political and cultural preferences: in some countries (e.g. Germany) people prefer renting to buying. Rules, regulations and policies also differ between countries, for example with respect to the rental market. While there is virtually no rental protection in the USA and the UK, tenants in the Netherlands are well protected. In addition, in Australia, Canada and London, foreign investors play a large role, whereas their role in Paris and Amsterdam is less significant. Other structural characteristics that differ are for example taxation (e.g. property taxes, stamp duty taxes, mortgage tax deductibility), the preference for fixed or floating rate mortgages and the liquidity of the housing market. These kinds of differences continue to play a significant role in shaping house price dynamics and can explain differences in the amplitude of housing cycles between countries (see Chap. 6 by Laurent Clerc).
7. **In some countries, the house price boom is accompanied by booming lending, but certainly not everywhere.**
In Australia, price-to-income and debt-to-income ratios are increasing, and interest-only loans are popular. In addition, a substantial growth in investor lending can be observed there, which raises concerns about procyclical behaviour of housing investors (see Chap. 17 by Michele Bullock and David Orsmond). Not in all countries rising house prices are accompanied by a surge in lending. In the Netherlands for example, mortgage lending growth has remained subdued to date. Whereas there might be little danger of bubbles and crises in the absence of lending growth, possible future bubbles continue to be difficult to identify.
8. **Macroprudential policies aimed at the housing market definitely have an impact, but are insufficient on their own.**
Since spillover effects from the cities to the rest of the country can be observed, one might think of implementing macroprudential policy to address vulnerabilities. Macroprudential policies may contribute towards curbing price rises and debt accumulation, but will often not be sufficient to counter imbalances. This is because the vulnerabilities on the housing market in the major cities are

fundamentally a supply-and-demand issue, which cannot be resolved with demand-oriented macroprudential policies.

9. **Targeted big-city macroprudential policies are a mixed blessing.**
Several countries, including South Korea, Norway and New Zealand, have tried to implement targeted big-city macroprudential policies. House price fluctuations in capital cities tend to be more volatile and stronger than in other parts of the countries, warranting more targeted measures at the local level (see Chap. 15 by Grégory Claeys et al.). Calibrating these measures is, however, even more difficult than calibrating national measures (see Chap. 4 by Stijn Claessens and Jochen Schanz). The effectiveness of targeted macroprudential policy is hampered by potential leakages: buyers will probably be inclined to look just beyond the regions affected by the policy, which may lead to spillover effects to nearby regions. Macroprudential measures may also lead to unwanted effects: for example, first-time buyers might be pushed off the market (see Chap. 14 by Marco Lo Duca and Sergio Nicoletti-Altimari). Macroprudential policies need to be fairly drastic to be effective. In 2017, South Korea for instance lowered its loan-to-value limits to 40% from 70% and increased transaction taxes to 20% from 10%. House prices in Seoul nevertheless continued rising for a little while longer; the effects of the implemented policies have become more visible in 2018 (see Chap. 16 by Ho Soon Shin and Hyun Chang Yi).
10. **A broader package of measures is necessary: we need to increase supply and build smarter.**
To solve vulnerabilities on the housing market in major cities, a multidisciplinary analysis and approach is needed. The supply of homes is crucial, however. A massive increase in housing supply is needed, as part of a coherent housing and planning policy approach (see Chap. 13 by Kajsa Ollongren and Chap. 18 by Christian Lennartz et al.). Large housing supply growth can be achieved with the use of only a limited amount of land, and with little disturbance of historic city centres, as long as higher rise dwellings can be built (see Chap. 8 by Edward Glaeser). It is essential to increase the housing supply in a manner that matches the requirements of the future occupiers. This can be achieved by applying the principles of "good density": creating mixed use environments with high-quality green and public space that are well connected to each other, suitable for several income and population groups and pleasant to live in (see Chap. 1 by Lisette van Doorn et al.). In addition, by using modern methods of housing construction and off-site manufacturing, the speed of construction can be increased.

Conclusion

The subject of urban housing markets is a timely, many-faceted issue that will be on the minds of policymakers for some time to come. It has become clear that housing markets in major cities are not only just part of a national housing market. They are markets with their own characteristics, which are sometimes even more connected to other foreign urban areas than to their own domestic market. Indeed, we see that major city housing markets are attracting attention from would-be residents, investors and policymakers all over the world.

Much more than before, policymakers, but also academics, are conducting analyses and devising policy options particularly tailored to the needs of major cities. This type of policies will gain in importance in the future, as urbanisation continues and cities will play an increasingly larger role in domestic and global economic development. Naturally, we do not know how exactly this development will unfold. But we have one certainty: there is no easy, one-size-fits-all solution. Tackling the challenges on the housing market in the major cities will prove to be a marathon, not a sprint.

Amsterdam, The Netherlands

Rob Nijskens
Melanie Lohuis
Paul Hilbers
Willem Heeringa

Contents

Part I
The Rise of Major Cities: Causes and Consequences

Chapter 1
In the Age of Cities: The Impact of Urbanisation on House Prices and Affordability

Lisette van Doorn, Amanprit Arnold, and Elizabeth Rapoport

1 Introduction

Global megatrends are re-shaping the world economic order. From urbanisation, to the rise of the global middle classes, ageing population and technological trends, these changes all pose major implications for the built environment and demand for housing in the short- and long-term. According to the latest projections by the United Nations, the world's population is expected to grow by 2.9 billion in the next 33 years and potentially another three billion by the end of the century. At the same time, the move towards cities is expected to continue, driven by economic, climate change and conflict motivations, as a result of which, 80–90% of people are expected to live in cities by 2100 (United Nations 2017).

As population growth and urbanisation continue, cities are faced with a number of challenges such as air pollution, congestion, social issues and pressure on housing markets. The pressure on housing markets can be analysed from different perspectives. Looking at the issue from a financial market perspective, the issue of financial market stability is a key element. However, when addressing the issue from a social and economic perspective, the focus lies more on risks like affordability, city competitiveness and social segregation.

This paper examines the role of urbanisation and current megatrends we are seeing in today's world, as well as the implications of the growing popularity of residential property as a real estate investment class, on the housing market in major cities. Unintended consequences of rising house prices, housing shortages and unaffordability are explored followed by potential solutions. In order for cities to be successful, careful consideration needs to be given to managing and resolving housing affordability challenges. This is a step towards creating a balanced housing

L. van Doorn (✉) · A. Arnold · E. Rapoport
Urban Land Institute, London, UK
e-mail: lisette.vandoorn@uli.org; amanprit.arnold@uli.org; elizabeth.rapoport@uli.org

R. Nijskens et al. (eds.), *Hot Property*, https://doi.org/10.1007/978-3-030-11674-3_1

market, as seen from both a financial market as well as economic and social perspective.

2 The Popularity of Major Cities

At the start of the industrial age, large urban centres in the United States and Europe were often crowded and crumbling. The emergence of car ownership started to mobilise urban populations as travel beyond the cities and towns got easier. This also helped the middle-class to improve the quality of lives with access to fresh air, green space and spacious affordable homes. Not only citizens left the cities, also companies moved to suburban office parks and retail concentrated in car-accessible out of town shopping centres. Continued sprawl in the 1980s further increased residents' reliance on cars along with pollution, congestion and pollution. People living farther from urban centres spent more time commuting. Objections to urban sprawl arose slowly and urban planners began rethinking policies and developers started to encourage regeneration and mixed-use developments in city centres, in line with a growing focus on sustainability and carbon emission reduction.

The transition, in many advanced economies, from an industrial to a service-led economy, has had profound implications for cities. Many formerly industrial cities have transformed themselves. Older industrial zones have become the focus of strategies to foster the development of the service, tourism, knowledge and creative economies. Polluted waterfronts have been regenerated, market squares have become public spaces again and railway station districts are renovated. This has been supported by a wave of investment in infrastructure, and cultural and recreational amenities.

Consequently, cities are increasingly popular as locations to live, work, play and invest. Cities have become magnets for economic, cultural and social activities. They now attract not only a new generation of city dwellers, and a previously suburban generation that rediscovered the appeal of city living and urban lifestyle, but also businesses and institutional investors that are focusing exclusively on urban areas. Impacted by the rise of the sharing economy, and a demand for greater flexibility, in many cities the proportion of residents who prefer to rent rather than buy their homes is rising.

At the same time, urban demographics are rapidly changing. In 2015, the International Organization of Migration (IOM) recorded in excess of one million arrivals in Europe, with migrants arriving from more than 100 countries (McKinsey Global Institute 2016). Many of these people settle in cities. In Europe, 25% of the population is already aged 60 years or over and that proportion is projected to reach 35% in 2050 and 36% in 2100 (United Nations 2017). As a result of this, we now have many different generations living in cities. While previously, families tended to move out when children came, more and more are staying in the city, with older people also remaining in, or returning to cities when they retire.

3 Consequences of the Rise of Major Cities: Housing Affordability and Its Challenges

One of the consequences of the growing popularity of cities, particularly in large, global cities, has been a strong increase in demand for housing. As shown in Fig. 1.1, during the financial crisis of the late 2000s, in many cities, especially in the Netherlands, the housing market came to a complete standstill. The resulting mismatch between supply and demand intensified due to inflows of people in cities and rapidly changing demands. When construction resumed, it could not pick up quickly enough to satisfy the demand for housing. As a result, house prices and the overall cost of living in many cities have increased quickly. This has not only led to financial market risks, but also to a housing affordability crisis that drives both lower skilled workers and talented young professionals out of major cities.

Recent research by MSCI found that out of 97 countries analysed, only four had affordable rental real estate available that covered at least 50% of their urban populations, and only six countries had affordable mortgage conditions for middle-income populations. This 'unaffordability bubble' for median income residents, estimated to be more than 50 million households by 2020, could potentially be left out of affordable options within some of the biggest cities in the world (Lopez-Alcala 2016). In many cities, high rents and house prices mean that young people are not able to save enough to put down the deposit required to qualify for a mortgage and purchase a property, leading to the rise of "generation rent".

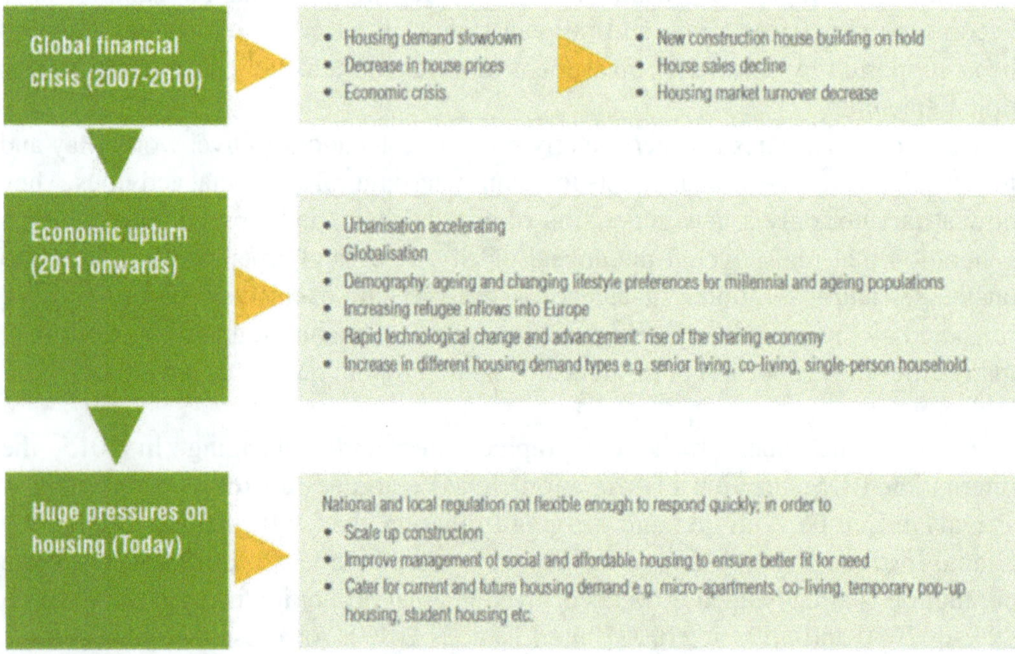

Fig. 1.1 Timescale of contributing factors to the current housing market picture (ULI 2018)

ULI Housing Affordability Research—Preliminary Findings
Despite media and political attention on ever-rising housing costs, ULI members have also observed that institutional investors lacked a consistent global measure of housing affordability. The ULI European Residential Council, in partnership with Savills, looked at housing affordability across five European cities: Amsterdam, Barcelona, Berlin, London and Warsaw. The research analyses the experience of different types of households with lower, median and upper quartile disposable incomes, and the percentage of income spent on housing, whether rent or mortgage. Initial findings are that affordability issues vary depending on household and tenure type. Using a single average income to rent/mortgage ratio for a city, as is commonly done, does not reflect the true costs, and challenges, faced by different types of households. The short-term costs of renting are lower than owning, but the lifetime costs of owning outweighs this. People are paying 20% less on mortgage payments than in rent in most cities. The working paper with findings will be available in 2019 (ULI 2018).

3.1 *Causes of the Housing Affordability Crisis*

Figure 1.2 below sets out some of the causes of the affordability crisis in major cities, which are discussed in more detail below.

Increased Investment in Real Estate and Residential in Particular
Global capital and foreign real estate investment into cities is more and more focused on investing in residential, which puts pressure on house prices. However, investors can also play a role in maintaining a more stable housing market through the different cycles. More information about the impact of institutional investors on the housing market can be found in Sect. 4.

Limited Land Supply and Complexity of Delivery
In many cities, land supply for new developments is very limited. In order to develop in the urban core and prevent further urban sprawl, in many European cities new housing is created through large, complex urban regeneration projects. These projects involve a wide range of actors, large sums of capital and a combination of infrastructure and real estate development. As a result, they usually take a long time from initiation to completion.

Rising Costs
Due to the lack of available land in combination with the strong demand, land values have increased rapidly which is an obstacle to affordable housing. On top of expensive land costs in cities, construction costs are largely determined by market forces including a shrinking labour force, rising material and resource costs and the market expectation of low-density housing. These all influence house prices and what people can afford to rent and buy.

Cause	Global	Europe	National	City
Global capital flows and investment into local cities	x	x		
Mobility and migration to cities	x	x	x	
Megatrends i.e. demographics and disruptive technology	x	x		x
Social preferences and change i.e urban vs. suburban lifestyle	x		x	x
Limited land supply			x	x
Housing shortage and demand			x	x
Commodity prices i.e. Construction material and labour costs	x		x	
Regulation				
• Planning and land use			x	x
• Building		x	x	
• Environmental		x	x	
• Tax and subsidies			x	
• Monetary and mortgage			x	x
• Private rental market				x

Fig. 1.2 Multi-layered geographic causes of housing affordability (ULI 2018). Note: x symbolises the geographical level that creates the cause for housing unaffordability

Inflexible Regulation

Accommodate to changing demands created by demographic shifts requires new types of housing. These include flexible micro-living spaces, affordable housing with more space for families, and housing tailored to the needs of elderly people. In many cities, regulations do not permit new and innovate housing typologies, or slow down the process of developing these. Overall, Urban Land Institute (ULI) members have found that in the European cities where they operate, regulation appears to react slowly to the changing demands of the housing market. This then leads to low rates of new construction, slow delivery of new housing stock, and higher prices for new units. The overall impact of all these factors is low elasticity of housing supply, and high housing costs. If applied in the right way, regulation can help to control the housing market such as capping rents to make housing affordable and appropriate for everyone.

ULI Affordable Housing Game initiative

In 2017, ULI in partnership with a city gaming company, Play the City, brought ULI members and partners together to develop innovative, and collaborative approaches to increase a city's supply of affordable housing. Members played the game three times, twice in Dublin and once in Amsterdam. A common theme in all three games was that affordable housing is not just about

(continued)

housing but a wider range of issues, including high-quality placemaking, cultural, educational and transport infrastructure, and collective work places. It also found that current regulation is not suitable for solving housing affordability issues among these cities. Players often spoke about the need for public space and amenities to create good density for mixed-income residents. Infrastructure improvement would make other affordable housing areas within a city more desirable. In areas such as the city centre where land is scarce, players recommended strategies to manage the existing stock in a way that will create a greater diversity of housing options, so that it is easier for residents to move when their needs change (ULI and Play the City 2018).

4 The Impact of Institutional Investment on the Housing Market

Global investors increasingly recognise the benefits of investing in real estate as a means to diversify their portfolios and focus on income return. Recent INREV research (see Fig. 1.3) shows that globally, real estate makes up 8.9% of institutional investors' total assets. Approximately half of the institutional investors expect their allocations to real estate to increase over the next 2 years (INREV 2018). This may have a significant impact on the real estate market. With more capital seeking real estate to invest in, prices might be pressured even further. However, on the other hand, the presence of long-term institutional investors in the market can help to make real estate cycles less volatile, as these types of investors tend not to overbid for properties at the peak of the market, and do not have to sell in a downturn (INREV 2013).

Until about 5–10 years ago, investors made investment decisions based on the overall attractiveness of a country or region. Today, many are increasingly focusing on well performing cities. Cities are evaluated through a combination of top down and bottom up analysis. Cities' performance in renowned international city indices are key inputs for these kinds of analyses. While in the past, the governance

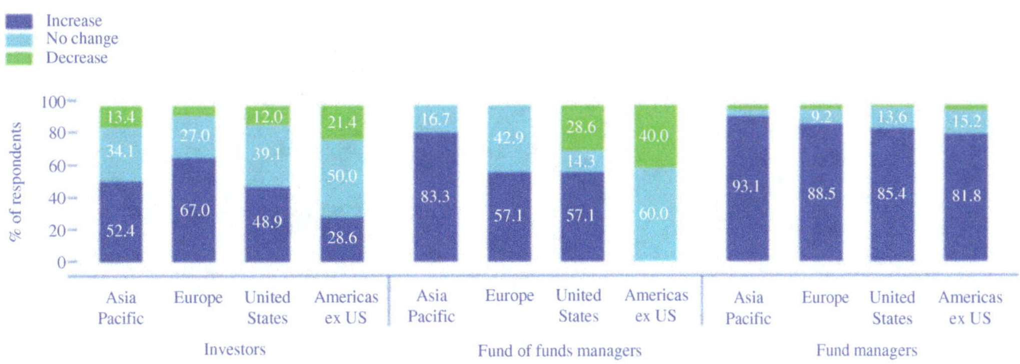

Fig. 1.3 Expected changes to real estate allocations by region over the next 2 years (INREV 2018)

framework, competitive climate and economic performance were key indicators, today investors tend to focus more and more on 'softer' factors such as connectivity, quality of life, the capability to attract talent and innovative businesses.

This focus is clearly visible in the preferences of institutional investors regarding the type of cities where they see the best development and investment opportunities. Cities in the top 10, as shown in Fig. 1.4, reflect cities which score high on elements such as connectivity, sustainability and quality of living.

In some countries such as the Netherlands, France and Germany, residential housing has been a key real estate investment sector for investors for many years. However, in many other countries in Europe, until about 5–10 years ago, institutional investors concentrated almost exclusively on commercial real estate, such as offices and retail. The lack of scale and the burden of intensive property management were often cited as reasons not to invest in residential real estate.

However, following the financial crisis, many investors looked to diversify their portfolios. They recognised the huge opportunity given the demand and supply characteristics of residential property in cities and began expanding into residential real estate, which is known for having a non-cyclical character, continuing to perform even in a downturn, as people always need somewhere to live (see

Fig. 1.4 Cities ranking 2018 (PwC and ULI 2017)

Overall ranking	Cities
1	Berlin
=2	Copenhagen
=2	Frankfurt
4	Munich
5	Madrid
6	Hamburg
7	Dublin
8	Stockholm
9	Luxembourg
10	Amsterdam

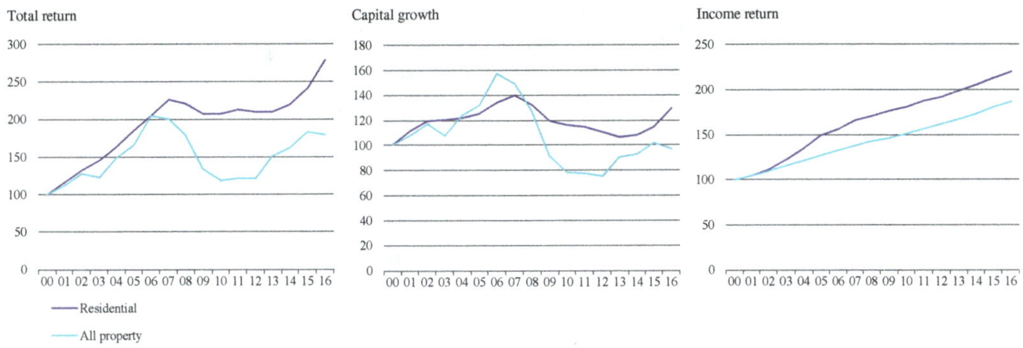

Fig. 1.5 Indexed long term return perspective (2000 = 100) for residential versus all property (Europe) (INREV 2018)

Fig. 1.5). Today there is a growing amount of institutional capital, both international and domestic, flowing into the residential sector. Over time the percentage of international capital being investing in residential has grown in particular. This shift was also influenced by changing demographics and the emergence of new products, such as student housing.

This shift can be seen in the change in the way respondents to the annual ULI/PwC Emerging Trends in Real Estate® Europe report have ranked the investment prospects of residential real estate (Fig. 1.6). While in 2009, only one of the sectors ranked in the top ten for investment prospects was residential, in the 2018 report, five of the sectors ranked in the top 10 were related to residential, including private sector residential, student housing, retirement living, housebuilding for sale and serviced apartments (PwC and ULI 2017).

Products such as retirement living, student accommodation, build-to-rent and high-quality housing close to workplaces can all offer long-term, stable returns, which are attractive to investors, including pension funds who are looking to increase the real estate component of their portfolios. This increase in investment adds to the overall housing supply and variety of options available provided in a transparent and professional way.

5 Potential Solutions

There is no single solution to the rising house prices and housing affordability challenge in cities; what is required is a multi-faceted approach including actions by the public, private and not-for-profit sectors. And while the housing prices and affordability issue can be analysed from many different perspectives, the fundamental factors for solving the issue require a significant increase in the supply of housing and ensuring a better fit between the house and the resident.

There are a number of key elements which should be taken into consideration when aiming to speed up construction and delivery of housing.

2018

Overall ranking	Sector
1	Logistics facilities
=2	Self-storage facilities
=2	Private rented residential
4	Student housing
5	Retirement/assisted living
=6	Housebuilding for sale
=6	Shared/serviced offices
8	Healthcare
9	Serviced apartments
10	Data centres

2009

Overall ranking	Sector
1	Central city office
2	Street Retail
3	Retail
4	Shopping centres
5	Hotel
6	Mixed Use
7	Apartment residential (rental)
8	Warehouse distribution
9	Office
10	Retail parks

Fig. 1.6 Sector prospects in 2018 and 2009 (PwC and ULI 2008, 2017)

Good density: Previous ULI research, and conversations with members have identified some of the most important changes required to enable an increase in housing supply that aligns with the principles of good density; mixed-use, well-connected environments with high-quality green and public space (Clark and Moir 2015). By densifying cities in the right way, ensuring mixed use, green space and good connectivity, we create the business case and critical mass to provide sufficient public transport and amenities for people to enjoy them in their neighbourhood. This creates vibrant, liveable and sustainable communities, while also reducing energy consumption and emissions and decreasing the infrastructure costs per resident.

Streamline regulation: National polices do not always address housing affordability challenges in cities as individual cities have their own set of specific circumstances and market structure that are unique to the city, that it requires standalone city-level policies and regulation whether it would be planning or the rental market. However, there has been a recent focus on the role of the planning system to boost housing supply through a faster planning process and flexible planning and building regulations. We are also seeing a slow change in regulation where minimum unit sizes are required to make housing liveable.

Public private collaboration: Delivering adequate housing in major cities is a complex process and requires close collaboration between the public and private sectors. Productive collaborations are essential to attract investment, particularly from international and institutional investors that are increasingly interested in the residential sector and for projects that have clear risk sharing components. Working together, the public and private sectors can combine their respective areas of expertise to ensure that projects deliver the housing, and supporting infrastructure, that citizens require. In particular, as ULI has learned through playing our affordable housing game in Dublin and Amsterdam, the public and private sectors will need to work together and involve citizens to develop creative solutions to creating an adequate supply of social and affordable housing.

Speed up construction: Modern methods of housing construction and off-site manufacturing can be viewed as a solution to help speed up the delivery of homes and at an affordable level. With technological change, new innovative housing approaches are happening and there are some early signs of manufacturing-led foreign companies overcoming traditional barriers to market entry through use of pre-manufactured construction products as opposed to traditional construction methods (Farmer 2016).

6 Conclusions

Cities can be viewed as both the source of and solution to many of today's economic, social and environmental challenges and they are evolving as places for people to live, work and play and for investors to invest in. However, many cities across the world increasingly experience housing as being one of the most critical urban challenges in cities today. Despite the rise of cities, along with it comes a number of unintended consequences including rising house prices, affordable housing shortages and inflexible housing stock. These problems in turn threaten not just financial market stability, but also quality of life and integration, as well as city competitiveness on the national and international scale.

In response, ULI recommends that cities should focus on creating more housing, including a more diverse range of options so that the housing stock can better meet the needs of different household types and income levels. By applying the principles of "good density"—mixed, use, well-connected environments with high-quality placemaking, integrated urban environments can be created that cater to a range of income and population groups and contribute to the vibrancy and authenticity of a city.

Cities require continuous management and flexible planning policies and regulations is one way forward. There is also a new wave of investment in affordable housing as it offers long-term returns and a broader societal impact. Solving housing affordability challenges is part of a bigger task in creating great cities that remain competitive and where people can afford to enjoy urban lifestyles.

References

Clark, G., & Moir, E. (2015). *Density: Drivers, dividends and debates*. London: Urban Land Institute.

Farmer, M. (2016). *The farmer review of the UK construction labour model*. Accessed April 23, 2018, from http://www.constructionleadershipcouncil.co.uk/wp-content/uploads/2016/10/Farmer-Review.pdf

INREV. (2013). *Real estate as a long-term investment: The impact of regulatory change on long-term investing strategies and on the real economy*. Amsterdam: INREV.

INREV. (2018). *Investment intentions survey*. Amsterdam: INREV.

Lopez-Alcala, M. (2016). *The crisis of affordability in real estate*. London: MSCI.

McKinsey Global Institute. (2016). *People on the move: Global migrations' impact and opportunity*. Accessed April 23, 2018, from http://www.mckinsey.com/global-themes/employment-and-growth/global-migrations-impact-and-opportunity?cid=other-eml-alt-mgi-mgi-oth-1612

PwC and ULI. (2008). *Emerging trends in real estate Europe 2009*. London: PwC.

PwC and ULI. (2017). *Emerging trends in real estate Europe 2018*. London: PwC.

ULI. (2018). *European housing affordability*. London: Urban Land Institute.

ULI and Play the City. (2018). *Amsterdam affordable housing game report*. London: Urban Land Institute.

United Nations. (2017). *World population prospects: The 2017 revision, key findings & advance tables* (Working Paper No. ESA/P/WP/248). New York: United Nations.

Chapter 2
Tackling London's Housing Crisis

Jamie Ratcliff

1 Defining the Crisis

The origins of London's housing crisis can be traced to a failure over decades to provide the number and types of homes that people working in London's growing economy require. London is an incredibly successful global city but the pace of homebuilding has fallen far behind demand. Between 1997 and 2016, London's housing stock grew by just 15% (470,000 homes) (GLA 2017a), at the same time London's jobs increased by 40% (1.6m net additional jobs) and its population by 25% (1.7m more people). London's housing delivery is constrained by a reliance on private home-builders, with a homogenous business model.

If London's housing stock had grown at the same rate as its population since 1997, there would have been an extra 700,000 homes by 2016 (4.2m compared to 3.5m). The latest city-wide assessment found that London now needs 66,000 new homes a year, of which around 65% should be affordable to fully meet needs (GLA 2017b). Just 33,000 homes a year were built between 2013/14 and 2016/17 (GLA 2017c), resulting in a backlog of unmet need, and the worsening of affordability in the intervening years.

This shortage of homes means that Londoners are being forced sharing less space with more people. After a century of reductions in the average number of people in each household in London, it was 2.3 in 1991, but it has now started to rise. According to one survey London's average household size is now up to 2.7 (GLA 2017d). There is a rapidly growing number of unrelated people sharing accommodation contributing to this rise. The number of households containing two or more distinct family units rose from around 300,000 in 1996 to around 470,000 in 2016 (GLA 2017a). Contrary to some beliefs, the number of empty homes in London is at an historic low level (GLA 2017a).

J. Ratcliff (✉)
Greater London Authority, London, UK
e-mail: Jamie.Ratcliff@london.gov.uk

R. Nijskens et al. (eds.), *Hot Property*, https://doi.org/10.1007/978-3-030-11674-3_2

The failure to build the homes that Londoners need has also resulted in rapidly rising prices and rents. Once housing costs are taken into account more than a quarter of Londoners are now living in poverty (DWP 2017). Whilst housing in London has long been comparatively expensive, in 2016 the gap between average house prices in London and the rest of England reached the widest ever recorded. The average private rent for a three-bedroom home in every other English region is now less than the average for a one-bedroom home in London. Since 2010, average private rents in London have risen more than three times as fast as average earnings (GLA 2017e), and around a quarter of privately renting households in London spent more than half of their income on rent in 2015/16 (GLA 2017f). Perhaps unsurprisingly, given these trends, more than half of households in London's private rented sector have little or no savings (GLA 2017g).

The number of Londoners in the private rented sector who receive regular financial support from the Government through Housing Benefit to help pay their rent, more than doubled from 2000 to 2017 (from 100,000 to 230,000) (GLA 2017h). Since 2011, government reforms to the welfare system have reduced the amount of this support, in spite of increasing rents, resulting in increasing affordability problems for these tenants, highlighting the pressing need of those on low incomes for genuinely affordable homes.

Pressure on the housing stock is increased by the fact that Londoners are moving less often. This is likely to be due to the rising costs of moving house. Buyers have to pay Stamp Duty Land Tax, at a high level, on purchase, whereas renters face high tenancy deposits and agent fees. In every tenure the rate at which Londoners move has fallen over the last 20 years (GLA 2017i).

2 Building Homes for Londoners

The only way to solve London's housing crisis over the long term is to build significantly more new homes, especially genuinely affordable homes. This cannot be achieved by doing more of the same. Building significantly more homes needs substantial diversification in terms of what homes are being built, who builds them and where. For too long London's housing supply has been dependent on a homogenous business model of developers, large complicated development sites in expensive areas and a relatively narrow range of types of homes. The Mayor has expanded and strengthened his Homes for Londoners team to relentlessly pursue this agenda. He has tasked them with taking a much more proactive role in getting land into development for new housing, developing new funding and policy approaches and working in partnership with other levels of government and the housing industry (GLA 2017j).

London's current land use policies, and its land market, have failed to bring forward the sites the city desperately needs to be used for building new homes. There is a need to increase land supply by supporting more intensive use of London's available land, and by the public sector proactively intervening in the land market.

Public investment plays a central role in sustaining and supporting homebuilding. It helps to speed up build-out rates, unlock stalled schemes, and make more land available for housing. The Mayor has funding programmes to invest in homes and infrastructure, including through: his Affordable Homes Programme; the Housing Infrastructure Fund; targeted investment in areas where delivery of new and genuinely affordable homes can be maximised; and supporting access to finance for home builders. Targeted investment in new transport schemes can support new homes—whether through major new rail lines like Crossrail 2, high quality rapid bus transit, or more local investment to make cycling and walking easier.

London will not increase its levels of homebuilding unless more of the homes built can be accessed by more Londoners, and until more homes are built by a wider group of organisations including councils. In order to build many more homes in London, new players must enter the market to complement the work of traditional private sector developers. New purpose-built private rented homes can provide a more stable and well-managed supply of homes at a range of rent levels. Small- and medium-sized builders are more likely to build on smaller sites and in outer London, where homes can be built faster and at more affordable prices. Housing associations (not-for-profit housing providers) are showing strong ambition to deliver many more affordable homes—mixed in with private homes to create profit for their purpose. Support for ambitious councils could help them access the resources they need to boost their plans to build new council housing.

At present, there are not enough people who have the right skills and who want to work in London's construction industry, and relying on traditional building methods alone will make it hard to significantly increase the number of new homes. There is a need to improve London's construction skills training system, and support the industry through the risks posed by leaving the European Union. Leadership and coordination is needed to improve the image of construction, including by supporting a shift to more of the components of London's homes being precision manufactured, in factories.

3 Beyond Building

The Greater London Authority's analysis of London's housing requirement is that we need to build 66,000 homes every year for the next 25 years. Action to help Londoners cannot wait that long. More immediate actions to mitigate London's housing crisis are needed, alongside a recognition that not all manifestations of the housing crisis will be solved by supply alone.

3.1 Genuinely Affordable Homes

The clearest immediate action is ensuring that as many of the new homes built as possible are genuinely affordable. As stated above affordable homes can accelerate the rate of home-building overall but they are also a valuable resource in and of themselves. Social housing enables Londoners on low incomes from a fantastically varied range of backgrounds to live here, contributing to London's vibrancy and economic success. Yet for many years London has failed to build sufficient new affordable homes (GLA 2017k) resulting in net reductions to London's overall social housing stock (Wellman 2018).

Londoners have become suspicious of the term 'affordable housing' in recent years. Clearer definitions of what homes are affordable for Londoners on low and middle incomes to rent and buy are needed. The Mayor of London is investing in homes based on social rent levels for Londoners on low incomes, in London Living Rent homes for middle income Londoners struggling to save for a deposit, and in shared ownership homes for Londoners who cannot afford to buy on the open market.

The Mayor is committed to a long term strategic target for half of new homes built to be genuinely affordable. To achieve this, he will ensure the planning system secures more affordable homes as part of new developments, including through fast tracking developments that deliver a set level of affordable housing (currently 35%). Further increases in the levels of new affordable homes can be delivered through investment, including London's funding of £4.82 billion to support starts of 116,000 affordable homes by 2022. London's surplus or underutilised publicly-owned land can also be used to support the delivery of more genuinely affordable homes.

3.2 London's Private Rented Sector

There are two million private renters in London, who face a range of challenges including rising rents and other costs, a lack of security and stability, and, in some cases, unacceptable conditions. To visitors from most other jurisdictions London's private rented sector would appear strange. The majority of landlords are individuals, typically only owning one or two homes as an amateur business. The sector is incredibly lightly regulated with no controls on rent setting or increases, limited quality standards for properties and landlords and almost no security of tenure. After an initial period of 6 months a landlord can near automatically end a tenancy for any reason or none, with almost no legal protections for tenants.

London's high rents impact upon a wide range of people from young people unable to save for a home of their own, to low-income Londoners whose rent is no longer covered by welfare payments, to families with children struggling with the high costs of living in the capital. In 2017, around 550,000 London children lived in the private rented sector. The Mayor believes there is an urgent need to offer greater stability and tenant rights, balanced with the legitimate interests of landlords, to make the legal system underpinning London's private rented sector fit for the 21st Century (GLA 2017j).

3.3 *Homelessness and Rough Sleeping*

London is one of the richest cities in the world. Yet in recent years homelessness has been increasing due to the high cost of housing, and lack of support for those who need it. One in 50 Londoners is now homeless, according to a recent study, including around 8000 people who last year were seen sleeping on the streets (GLA 2018a). The Mayor believes that it is unacceptable that in one of the richest and most successful cities in the world thousands of people are sleeping rough on the streets every year. He has called it our basic moral responsibility as a society to right this wrong (Khan 2018).

More and more Londoners have been finding themselves without a place to call home. Fundamentally this is due to the shortage of affordable homes, the insecurity of private renting, and changes to the welfare system, but immediate action can have an impact. There is a need to invest in places for homeless Londoners to live, better coordination between councils when accommodating homeless Londoners and focus on homelessness that is caused by violence against women and girls.

It is unacceptable that anyone has no choice, or feels they have no choice, other than to sleep on London's streets. The Mayor's aim is to ensure there is a way off the streets for every single rough sleeper in London (GLA 2018b). This will be achieved through coordination with councils, charities, Government, and others to boost services beyond the £8.5 million a year he has committed toward support for rough sleepers. The Mayor has also made available funding to invest in improving and expanding London's network of hostels and refuges (GLA n.d.).

4 Devolution

Whilst the Mayor has been clear with Londoners that tackling London's housing crisis will be a marathon and not a sprint, there have been significant successes in his first 2 years including record levels of funding, ambition from housing providers, construction starts of genuinely affordable homes and radical policies to drive homebuilding faster. The Mayor is doing all he can within his existing powers and resources, but to effectively tackle the housing crisis more support is needed from national government.

The UK remains a highly centralised state, which means that devolution or national government action is needed to support the Mayor. It is not feasible to deliver the right level of affordable homes and infrastructure with the current level of funding on offer. Life for London's private renters cannot be transformed through existing regulations alone. Homelessness will not be solved if its root causes are ignored.

The planning system can identify capacity for new homes, but there is now consensus that planning policies and consents alone cannot be relied upon to ensure sufficient land comes forward to support the housing targets we have set, with too much developable land lying empty or poorly used. The Mayor needs effective powers that can be used proactively to support land assembly and incentivise more efficient use of scarce land. This includes radical reform of land assembly rules, including the reform of compulsory purchase powers and the introduction of new land assembly mechanisms and resources, and a long term commitment to a more progressive system of land taxation. The Mayor also needs much stronger powers over publicly-owned land earmarked for new homes, particularly central government land.

London government lacks the funding it needs to provide adequate numbers of the right types of affordable homes, or to invest in the infrastructure that will underpin more homebuilding. Funding deals are negotiated with Government periodically, or for specific schemes, on terms that tend to change with each iteration. This makes long term and joined-up thinking very challenging. There is a need for an immediate boost in funding for affordable homes alongside a commitment to negotiating a substantial and long-term affordable housing and infrastructure settlement, underpinned by fiscal devolution.

London's private rented sector is amongst the most poorly regulated in Europe. The Mayor is calling for a radical overhaul of regulation of standards and conditions in the private rented sector, alongside a commitment to work with him to implement a new model of private renting aiming to provide much more stability for tenants, and to explore options for addressing high rents and unacceptable rent increases.

References

DWP. (2017). *Households below average income: An anlysis of the income distribution 1994/95 to 2015/16*. Retrieved from https://www.gov.uk/government/uploads/system/uploads/attachment_data/file/600091/households-below-average-income-1994-1995-2015-2016.pdf

GLA. (2017a). *Housing in London 2017: The evidence base for the Mayor's housing strategy*. Retrieved from https://files.datapress.com/london/dataset/housing-london/2017-01-26T18:50:00/Housing-in-London-2017-report.pdf

GLA. (2017b). *The 2017 London strategic housing market assessment*. Retrieved from https://london.gov.uk/sites/default/files/london_shma_2017.pdf

GLA. (2017c). *Analysis of provisional London development database data for 2013/14 to 2016/17* Retrieved from https://files.datapress.com/london/dataset/housing-london/2017-01-26T18:50:00/Housing-in-London-tables-2017.xls

GLA. (2017d). *Analysis of census and labour force survey data, 1996 to 2016*. Retrieved from https://files.datapress.com/london/dataset/housing-london/2017-01-26T18:50:00/Housing-in-London-tables-2017.xls

GLA. (2017e). *Analysis of ONS data on earnings and private rents.* Retrieved from https://files.datapress.com/london/dataset/housing-london/2017-01-26T18:50:00/Housing-in-London-tables-2017.xls

GLA. (2017f). *Analysis of English housing survey data, 2015/16.* Retrieved from https://files.datapress.com/london/dataset/housing-london/2017-01-26T18:50:00/Housing-in-London-tables-2017.xls

GLA. (2017g). *Analysis of family resource survey data, 2015/16.* Retrieved from https://files.datapress.com/london/dataset/housing-london/2017-01-26T18:50:00/Housing-in-London-tables-2017.xls

GLA. (2017h). *Analysis of DWP StatXplore database.* Retrieved from https://files.datapress.com/london/dataset/housing-london/2017-01-26T18:50:00/Housing-in-London-tables-2017.xls

GLA. (2017i). *Analysis of English housing survey and survey of English housing data. Trends in the rates of overcrowding and under-occupation are reported in GLA, Housing in London, 2017.* Retrieved from https://files.datapress.com/london/dataset/housing-london/2017-01-26T18:50:00/Housing-in-London-tables-2017.xls

GLA. (2017j). *London plan annual monitoring report 2015/16.* Retrieved from https://www.london.gov.uk/sites/default/files/amr_13.pdf

GLA. (2017k). *Mayor's housing strategy: City Hall to buy land for affordable homes.* Retrieved from https://www.london.gov.uk/press-releases/mayoral/mayor-launches-housing-strategy-for-london

GLA. (2018a). *Rough sleeping in London (CHAIN reports).* Retrieved from https://data.london.gov.uk/dataset/chain-reports

GLA. (2018b). *Mayor launches new help for rough sleepers.* Retrieved from https://www.london.gov.uk/press-releases/mayoral/number-falls-in-london-for-first-time-in-a-decade

GLA. (n.d.). *Funding for supported and specialist housing.* Retrieved from https://www.london.gov.uk/what-we-do/housing-and-land/increasing-housing-supply/funding-supported-and-specialist-housing

Khan. (2018). *We have a moral duty to end rough sleeping – Here's how we make it a thing of the past.* Retrieved from https://www.huffingtonpost.co.uk/entry/rough-sleeping-london_uk_5b33aed8e4b0cb56051e439a?guccounter=1&guce_referrer_us=aHR0cHM6Ly93d3cuZ29vZ2xlLmNvbS8&guce_referrer_cs=81dqf6SsSuDQJbTo783ykQ

Wellman, P. (2018). *London sees net loss to social housing stock.* Retrieved from https://www.egi.co.uk/news/london-sees-net-loss-to-social-housing-stock/

Chapter 3
The Housing Market in Major Dutch Cities

Rob Nijskens and Melanie Lohuis

1 Introduction

The Dutch housing market is recovering strongly from the crisis, with major cities leading the housing price growth. Prices have risen by over 25% since the post-crisis low in 2013 and have returned to their 2008 record levels. Annual transaction volume has increased from 100,000 in 2013 to over 240,000 in 2017. Figure 3.1 shows that house prices in the four major cities have recovered more strongly than in the rest of the country, and were on average already 22% above pre-crisis levels at the beginning of 2018. Transaction volumes also recovered more quickly in the cities. Recently, these developments have been spilling over to regions surrounding major cities (DNB 2018).

A similar pattern, of faster price increases in major cities than in the rest of the country, can be seen abroad. In fact, prices in some foreign cities have risen even faster over the past 3 years than in Dutch major cities (Fig. 3.2). In Canada, for instance, house prices have appreciated by 9% nationwide versus 15% per year on average in Vancouver. For China the difference is even larger: house prices rose by 6.5% in the whole country, but 15% in Beijing. The United Kingdom demonstrates spillover effects, as house price growth outside London has caught up and is now even higher than in the British capital.

This chapter asks why prices have risen so rapidly in the four major Dutch cities and what consequences this may entail for financial stability. We investigate whether

---

The views presented in this chapter are those of the authors and do not necessarily represent the views of De Nederlandsche Bank. This chapter is based on M. Hekwolter of Hekhuis, R. Nijskens and W. Heeringa (2017), The housing market in major Dutch cities, *DNB Occasional Study, 15-1* and DNB (2018), *Financial Stability Report*, Spring.

R. Nijskens (✉) · M. Lohuis
De Nederlandsche Bank, Amsterdam, The Netherlands
e-mail: r.g.m.nijskens@dnb.nl; m.s.lohuis@dnb.nl

R. Nijskens et al. (eds.), *Hot Property*, https://doi.org/10.1007/978-3-030-11674-3_3

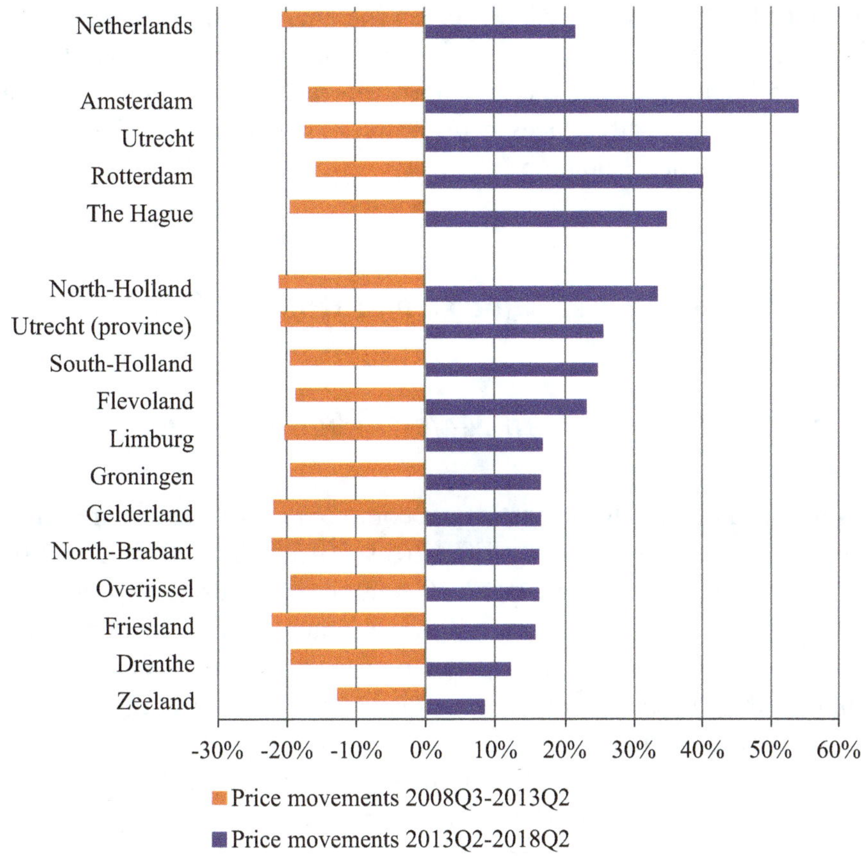

Source: Statistics Netherlands (2016)

Fig. 3.1 Dutch regional house prices since the previous peak (*Percentage change from 2008 levels*). Note: The price movements in this chart are shown in percentages of the 2008 level to enable a fair comparison between the two periods considered

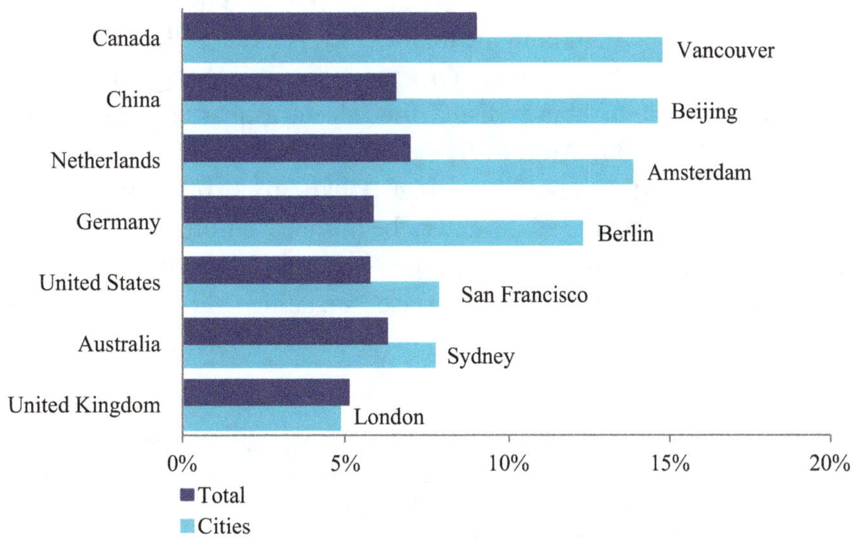

Source: National statistical offices (between 2018Q1 and 2018Q2)

Fig. 3.2 House price increases in selected cities and countries (*Three-year average annual growth rate*). Note: The last reference period is 2018Q2 for all countries except Australia (2018Q1)

a credit-driven bubble is forming in the cities and analyze differences between cities and the rest of the Netherlands in the mismatch of demand and supply. Then, we will set out the consequences that rising prices can have for the position of middle-income earners and the differences between renters and buyers. The chapter ends with some policy recommendations.

2 Price Movements in Major Urban Housing Markets Dissected

2.1 Signs of Overheating in Major Urban Housing Markets

Price-to-income and price-to-rent ratios are commonly used to measure price movements and the degree of overheating (ECB 2011, 2015; ESRB 2015; IMF 2016). The price-to-income ratio is a benchmark for affordability: if house prices rise faster than incomes, owner-occupied properties will, given interest rates, become less affordable. The price-to-rent ratio is, at a given interest rate level, a benchmark for the degree of equilibrium between owner-occupied and rental housing. This equilibrium should be achieved through arbitrage: if house prices rise much more sharply than rents, potential house buyers will be inclined to rent instead of buy.[1]

Alongside price benchmarks, transaction-related indicators can thus help to determine the degree of overheating. Overheating stems from increasing scarcity in the housing market: when more properties are sold than come on the market, supply shrinks, potential house buyers have less choice and the market tightens. This drives up prices. Another factor is the time it takes to sell a house: quickening house sales could point to overheating. Finally, when selling prices are structurally higher than asking prices, this may indicate the market is overheating.

Figure 3.3 shows that major urban housing markets are indeed showing signs of overheating. The housing market in the major cities is a real seller's market: demand is surging ahead of supply. In all major cities, the ratio between the transaction volume and the number of houses listed for sale in a quarter greatly exceeds the pre-crisis average (Chart 3a). Moreover, the time it takes to sell a property has more than halved compared to the pre-crisis average (Chart 3b). In other words, the housing market in the cities has become a lot tighter: the number of homes for sale in the cities is now 65% lower than in 2007–2008. In the Netherlands as a whole, there are 35% less homes for sale. In addition, far more houses are being sold above the asking price than just before the crisis: in Amsterdam and Utrecht, this amounts to nearly three

[1]The effect of interest rates is not fully factored into these benchmarks. Interest rates influence both the price and the financing cost of housing: lower mortgage rates lead to higher house prices but lower financing costs. The price-to-income and price-to-rent ratios do include the impact of interest rates on prices, but not the effect on financing costs (Himmelberg et al. 2005). Our own calculations show, however, that in recent years financing costs have followed a similar pattern to the price-income ratio.

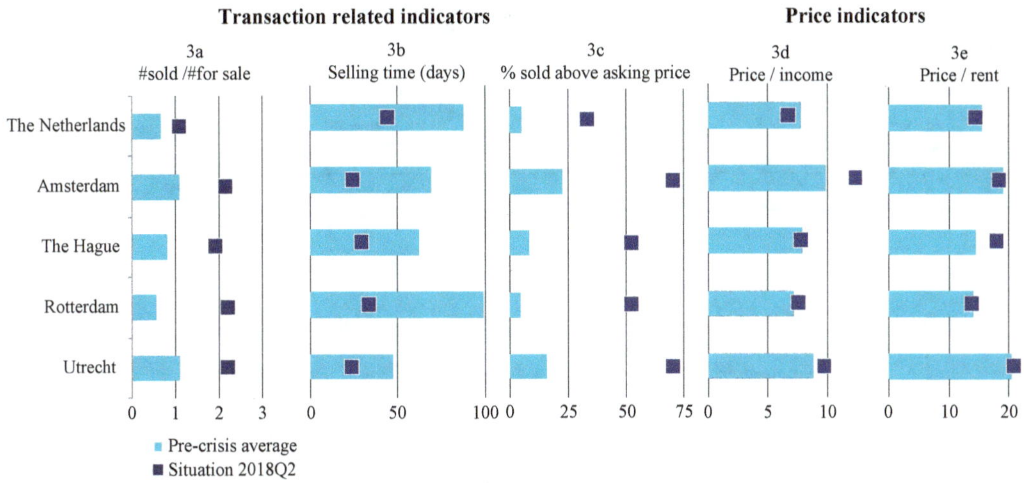

Source: Statistics Netherlands (2016), Dutch Real Estate Agents Association (NVM)

Fig. 3.3 Indicators for overheating in the Dutch housing market. Note: The prices for price/income (3d) and price/rent (3e) are for all existing owner-occupied properties, sold and unsold. Income is average disposable income. Asking and selling prices (3c) exclusively relate to sold properties. Rents (3e) relate to newly rented properties in the private sector. Average pre-crisis levels cover the periods 2007 Q1 to 2008 Q3 (house sales and supply, 3a, 3b), 2006 Q1 to 2008 Q3 (asking prices, 3c), 1995 Q1 to 2008 Q3 (price/income, 3d) and 2000 Q1 to 2008 Q3 (price/rent, 3e)

quarters of all transactions (Chart 3c). The housing market is also rapidly tightening in medium-sized cities such as Groningen and Eindhoven. In the rest of the Netherlands, houses are sold less quickly and less often above the asking price.

Price-to-income and price-to-rent ratios confirm this overheating, as they are both substantially above pre-crisis average in the major cities. This is particularly visible in Amsterdam and Utrecht (Charts 3d, 3e); this level has not yet been reached in the rest of the Netherlands. The sharp decline in mortgage rates is an important contributing factor here, and it suggests that prices of owner-occupied properties are rising faster than rents in the private rental sector.

2.2 *As Yet no Indications of a Credit-Driven Bubble*

The traditionally strong link between mortgage lending growth and house prices is weakening in major cities. Figure 3.4 shows that overall Dutch mortgage debt has grown only very slightly since 2013. The four major cities initially see mortgage debt rising in tandem with house prices, but since early 2016 a divergence between the two can be noticed: house prices continue to climb while mortgage lending starts to slacken. One reason is the surge in voluntary repayments, which is an attractive option for home-owners because of low interest rates on savings. Accordingly, extra repayments since 2013 amounted EUR 70 billion. However, even when controlling for this factor, the picture of relentlessly rising house prices and limited mortgage growth in the major cities remains intact.

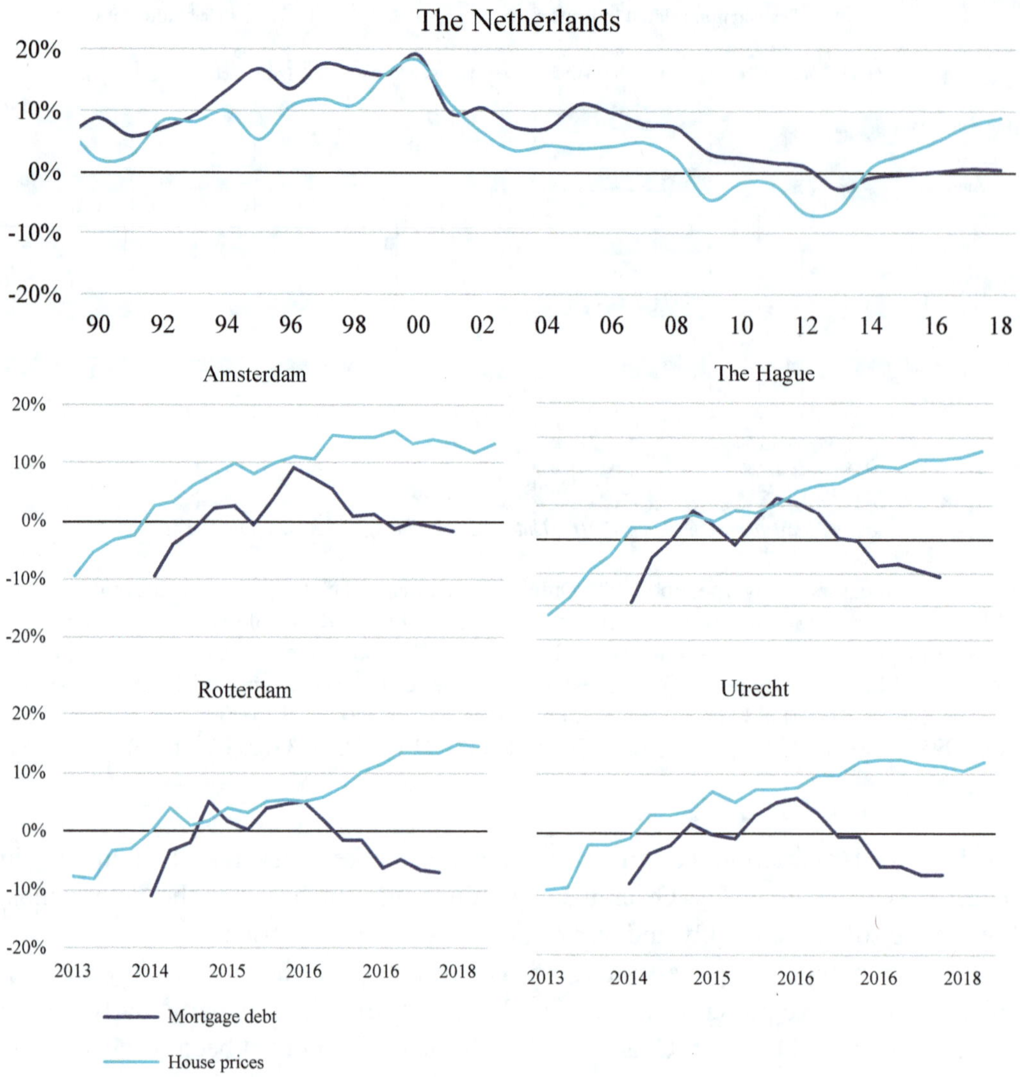

Source: DNB mortgage loan level data (2018), Statistics Netherlands (2016)

Fig. 3.4 Growth of mortgage debt and house prices. Note: The top part of the chart shows all Dutch household mortgages. The rest of the chart illustrates the picture for the four major cities based on some 90% of all mortgages extended by Dutch financial institutions

Another reason for the lower growth in mortgage credit is that more buyers in major cities are using own funds to help finance their home purchase. Land Registry figures indicate that house sales without an accompanying mortgage in the Netherlands have more than doubled from 8% in 2008 to nearly 17% in 2017. These non-mortgage sales are more common in the major cities. For instance, over a quarter of the transactions in Amsterdam since 2013 were financed without a mortgage at all. The relaxed tax exemption for gifts used for house down payments or mortgage repayments, which was in effect until the end of 2014 (and again since January 2017), has probably contributed to this trend. The number of first-time buyers who did not take out a mortgage peaked in December 2014, while tax records show that gifts made under the relaxed gift tax exemption topped EUR 10 billion in

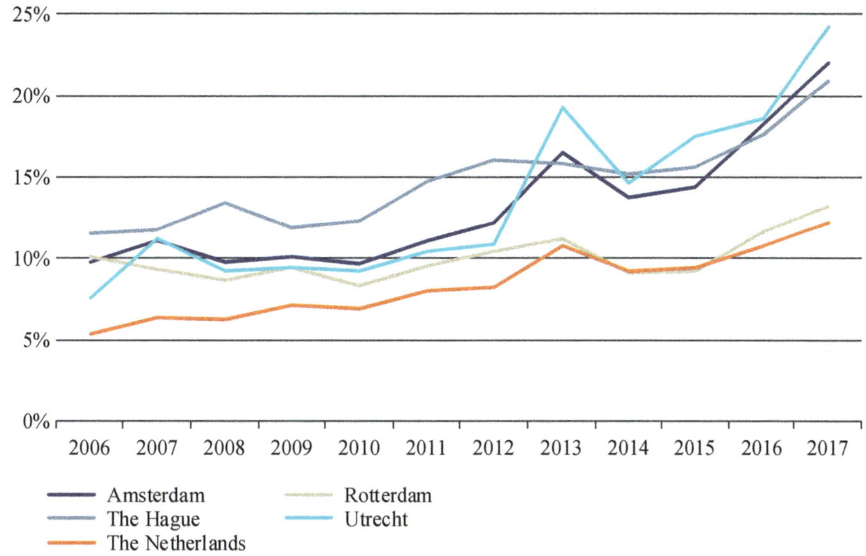

Source: Kadaster

Fig. 3.5 Share of private investors in owner-occupied market *(Percentage of all private housing transactions)*

2013 and 2014. Low interest rates on savings, of course, are another persuasive reason for using personal or family savings to buy a house.

Moreover, the number of properties purchased for private rental, often without a mortgage, has recently increased in the major cities. A Land Registry study shows that since 2014 the share of private rental or buy-to-let transactions in the cities has risen steadily to over 20% (see Fig. 3.5). These transactions also account for a large part (43%) of all transactions without a mortgage. Investors see the buy-to-let market as an alternative to low returns on other investments. According to experts, both professional parties and smaller private investors are queuing up to enter the non-rent regulated rental sector in the cities. Private investor interest can help to expand the private rented segment, although it also means more competition for home-seekers in the owner-occupied market, driving up prices.

Despite the rising house prices, the share of households borrowing close to or at the maximum allowed is lower in the cities than in the rest of the Netherlands (Fig. 3.6). Indeed, the percentage of Dutch households borrowing more than 90% of the Debt-Service-to-Income (DSTI) limit[2] has been hovering between 35% and 40% for the past 2 years, and is not higher in the major cities. The average Loan-to-Value ratio (LTV) for new mortgages is even lower in cities: in Amsterdam and Utrecht, it lay around 90% in 2016 versus 95% nationwide, for instance. This is mainly due to the larger number of buyers with an LTV below 80%, confirming the earlier observation that home buyers in major cities are contributing more own funds.

[2]This limit is based on the financing costs standards of the National Institute for Family Finance Information (NIBUD).

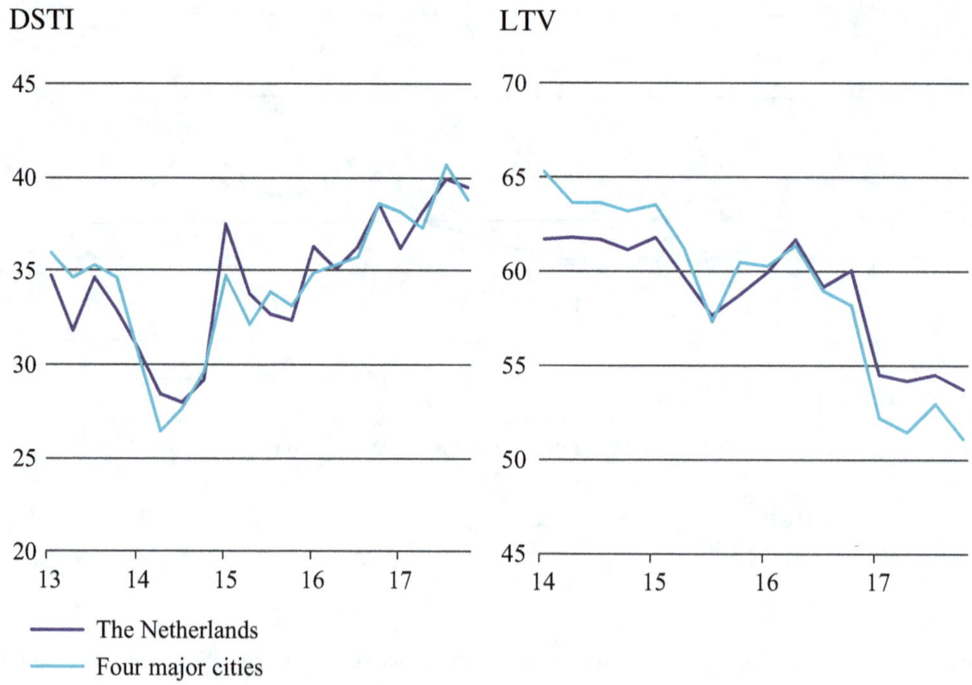

Source: DNB mortgage loan level data (2018)

Fig. 3.6 Share of households borrowing more than 90% of their DSTI and share of households with an LTV above 90%. Note: The calculation of the financing costs standard in this chart takes into account income differences between house buyers and the decline in interest rates over that period. The LTV limit has been decreasing from 105 in 2013 to 100 in 2018. First-time buyers cannot be perfectly identified, but are approximated by looking at all new mortgage borrowers younger than 35. The four major cities are Amsterdam, The Hague, Rotterdam and Utrecht

In sum, housing markets in major Dutch cities are showing signs of overheating, but there are no strong indications of a credit-driven bubble as of yet. Despite the tightening urban housing markets, credit indicators currently do not point to a credit-driven bubble. Even after adjusting for repayments, mortgage lending growth is limited and home-buyers are not borrowing closer to the maximum permitted amount than before. Interestingly, the LTV ratios in the cities are in fact lower than in the rest of the Netherlands. Therefore, it seems that price increases are mainly driven by the tightness in the housing market in the major cities.

3 Differences Between the Major Cities and the Rest of the Netherlands

3.1 Demand for Housing

Demand Drivers

An important factor driving housing demand in major cities is urbanisation, which is a strong international trend. In the past 25 years, the share of the population living in

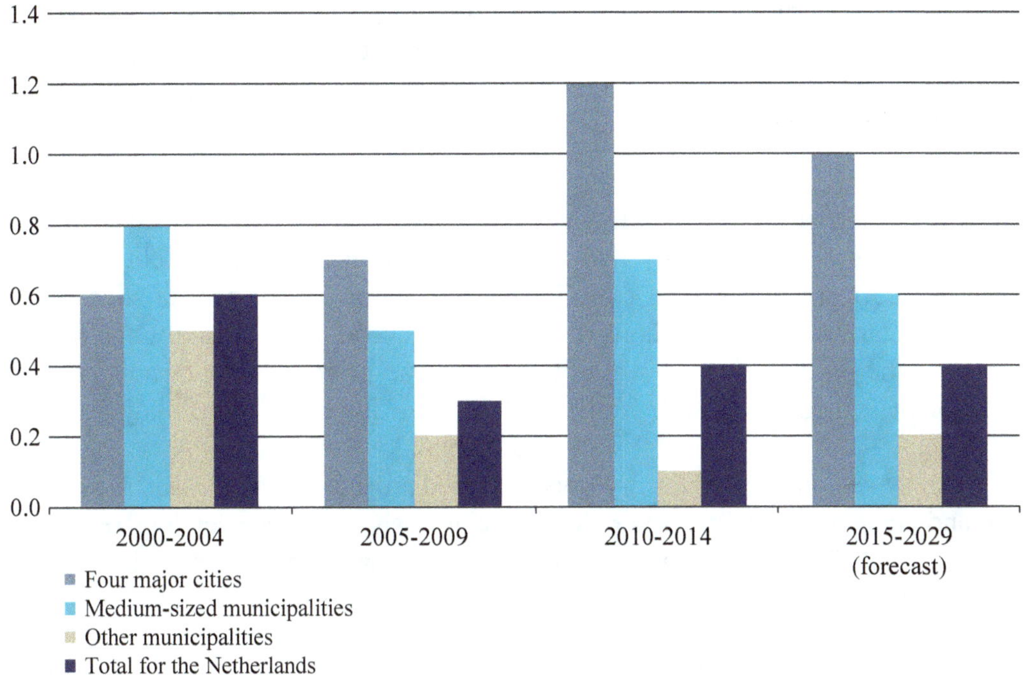

Source: PBL Netherlands Environmental Assessment Agency/Statistics Netherlands regional population and household forecast (2016)

Fig. 3.7 Annual population growth (*Percentage growth per year*). Note: Municipal boundaries in effect in 2015. Four major cities: Amsterdam, Rotterdam, The Hague and Utrecht. Medium-sized municipalities: other municipalities with more than 100,000 inhabitants in 2015. Other municipalities: all other municipalities

urban areas has steadily grown all over the world. In the Netherlands too, the population in the four major cities has grown proportionately faster than in the rest of the country since 2005 (Fig. 3.7). And since 2010, the urban population growth rate has been nearly three times higher than the nationwide average (PBL Netherlands Environmental Assessment Agency/Statistics Netherlands 2016). Forecasts show that this trend will continue in the Netherlands. The large cities and medium-sized municipalities are expected to continue seeing the strongest population growth in the future (Fig. 3.7). At the same time the number of households, which determines more precisely the demand for housing, is also growing: in the Netherlands as a whole by 9%, Rotterdam 5% up to 20% in Utrecht.

Mainly young people are flocking to the city to study or work, and because of cities' cultural and recreational offerings. The migration of young people to the cities is partly caused by the higher number of students enrolling in universities and colleges (PBL Netherlands Environmental Assessment Agency 2015). Another reason is that, between 1999 and 2013, the percentage increase in the number of jobs for highly educated persons was many times higher in the cities) than in the rest of the country (Brakman et al. 2015). This has to do with the rise of the service economy and technological developments in logistics and ICT (Parlevliet et al. 2016). In addition, natural growth also plays an important role: the presence of many young people in cities also means that a relatively large number of children are born. Finally, immigration is increasingly driving population growth in the four major cities, as many immigrants go to the large cities in search of work and education, and to connect with communities of the same origin (PBL Netherlands Environmental Assessment Agency/Statistics Netherlands 2016).

Buy or Rent?

Buying is financially more attractive than renting in the Netherlands. Due to mortgage interest deductibility and the current low interest rates, debt servicing costs are currently lower than rents in the private sector. By way of illustration: middle-income households who own their house spend approximately one fifth of their income on debt service, while middle-income private sector tenants spend a third of their income on rent (Netherlands Bureau for Economic Policy Analysis 2016).

But not everyone can live in an owner-occupied property, so there is also a growing demand for rental housing. After the financial crisis, mortgage lending regulation (LTV and DSTI) has been tightened, which means that homebuyers need to muster more own funds. This can be a hurdle for first time buyers, who usually do not have large savings. A more flexible labor market contributes to this growing demand for private rental housing. In 2009, 5% of all home-seekers wanted a rented home in the private sector; by 2015, the figure had risen to 12% (Ministry of the Interior and Kingdom Relations 2016). This flexibility is particularly important for self-employed people and flexi-workers. Evidence suggests that flexi-workers are indeed more likely to prefer rental housing compared to households in permanent employment (Boumeester and Dol 2016). Finally, the limited accessibility of the social rental segment for middle-income earners is also spurring demand for private sector rentals.

3.2 *Housing Supply*

The Structure of the Dutch Housing Market

The Dutch social rental sector is relatively large (particularly in major cities), also compared with other European countries. Figure 3.8 shows that the housing association sector makes up around 30% of the total Dutch housing stock, and more than 40% in Amsterdam and Rotterdam; moreover, most privately owned homes are rented out in the regulated segment instead of the private sector. The Dutch social rental sector is one of the largest in Europe and considerably bigger than its counterparts in France (19% of the total), the UK (15%) and Germany (only 5%) (BPD 2016; Whitehead et al. 2016).

The supply of mid-market private rental housing, therefore, falls short of demand in large cities. The non-rent regulated sector throughout the Netherlands has contracted steadily since the 1970s to less than 10% of all homes. This is partly because social rental and owner-occupied housing are subsidized (Whitehead et al. 2016; PBL Netherlands Environmental Assessment Agency 2017). Most Dutch rental housing is owned by housing associations and falls largely within the social

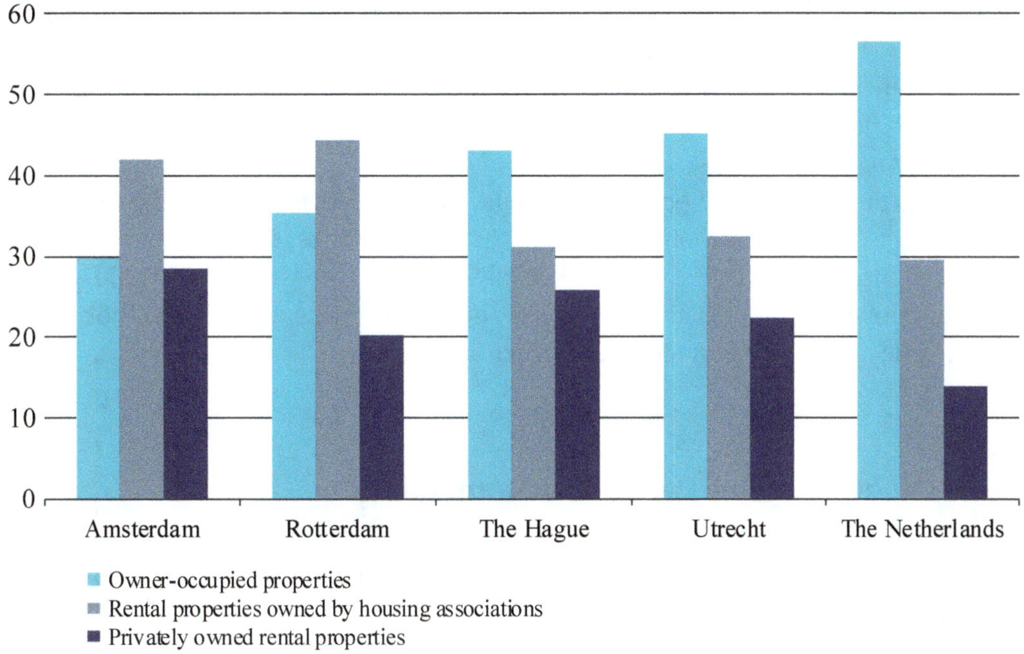

Source: ABF Research (2018)

Fig. 3.8 Housing stock ownership ratio in major cities and the Netherlands *(Percentage of total housing stock, 2017)*

segment. The result is a shortfall in the mid-market segment (monthly rent between EUR 700 and EUR 1000), particularly in Amsterdam and Utrecht (Schilder and Conijn 2015).

Obstacles to Increasing Housing Supply

The price elasticity of the housing supply in the Netherlands is very low in an international perspective (OECD 2011; Swank et al. 2002). Saiz (2010) and Hilber and Vermeulen (2016) demonstrate that geographical restrictions constrain the elasticity of supply, and urbanisation leads to price increases. This is the case in the Randstad conurbation: much of the land surface is already built up, and the expansion of some large cities in the Randstad conurbation is impeded by their location on the coast or near green belts shielded by nationally determined zoning restrictions on construction.

Municipalities lack effective incentives for developing private rental housing, partly because they depend on revenues from land development. This makes municipalities reluctant to grant building permits for land they do not own. Moreover, due to mortgage interest relief, land purchased for owner-occupied properties fetches more than land for rental housing. The land price is often determined on the basis of residual value, i.e. the difference between sale proceeds and construction costs. As buying a house is subsidized, owner-occupied housing fetches a higher price than rental housing and thus (assuming comparable construction costs) land prices are also higher for owner-occupied housing. Municipalities must lower the land price in order to make construction of the non-rent regulated housing profitable. However, they will not be keen to sell land for less than the relatively high price they paid themselves (PBL Netherlands Environmental Assessment Agency 2017). Moreover, municipalities will also want to keep existing residents satisfied, who may see new-build developments as contrary to their interests: the so-called NIMBY (*not in my backyard*)-effect.

Lastly, new-build development has only slowly recovered since the crisis due to capacity constraints. Both builders and municipalities reduced their capacity after the onset of the crisis. By way of illustration: in 2010 still 377,000 people were employed in the construction sector, but since then nearly 80,000 jobs have been lost leading to a shortage of construction workers.

4 Conclusions and Policy Recommendations

The strong house price rises in major cities signal a three-way divide in the Dutch housing market: an overheated housing market in major cities, a buoyant housing market in surrounding municipalities and a lagging housing market in shrinking regions. Indeed, spillovers from major cities put increasing pressure on satellite communities and cause price rises there. And the departure of young people from shrinking municipalities is creating a supply surplus in peripheral housing markets, worsening their plight.

Middle-income earners threaten to become stranded: living in the city is increasingly inaccessible for these groups. Their income is too high for social housing, they face fierce competition in the private rental market and they are not always able to buy a house in the city. As a result, prospective first-time buyers in particular are more or less forced to choose between relatively expensive rental housing in the city and buying or renting a more affordable place outside the city.

Housing supply shortages abound in and near major Dutch cities, and local governments do not always have the right incentives to ensure the right type of housing to be built. Municipalities are constrained by cuts in planning capacity and focus on owner-occupied instead of rental properties. Housing associations, playing a major role on the Dutch housing market, mainly focus on social housing. Therefore, the necessary increase in private rental housing supply does not take off.

The government can encourage municipalities to provide more private rental housing by setting minimum targets and through arrangements about the inclusion of a minimum percentage of mid-market rental housing in their zoning plans. But this is only possible if the land prices charged by municipalities are sufficiently low to make mid-market rental housing profitable. And to ensure that landlords also receive effective incentives, clear arrangements must be made about long-term rental and rent increase caps. Moreover, housing associations can contribute to a larger supply of private rental housing by renting out their more expensive homes in the private sector.

Finally, accelerated phasing out of mortgage interest relief is vital to ensure a long-term level playing field between owner-occupied and rental properties. Social rental housing and owner-occupied properties are both subsidized. Private rental housing is not, which makes it relatively expensive and often unaffordable for highly educated young people and middle-income earners (who are also ineligible for the social segment). In addition, mortgage interest relief means that people can pay more for owner-occupied properties than for rental housing. This gives property developers and municipalities an incentive to concentrate on the owner-occupied market. In 2017, the Dutch government has lowered interest deductibility from a marginal rate of 52% to 37%, effective 2023. While this is a necessary first step, a further phasing out of mortgage interest relief would reduce the subsidy on owner-occupation. This would make it more attractive to build for the private rental market and give municipalities an incentive to include mid-market private rental in their zoning plans.

References

ABF Research. (2018). *Syswov ownership housing stock*. Accessed July 1, 2018, from https://syswov.datawonen.nl/jive?workspace_guid=66f5bd0d-bb2b-4cb4-ab86-ecc24fe6c312

Boumeester, H., & Dol, K. (2016). Eigenwoningbezit en flexibilisering van de arbeidsmarkt. *Real Estate Research Quarterly*. March.

BPD. (2016). *Duitsland, Frankrijk, Nederland; Woningmarkten in perspectief 2016.*

Brakman, S., Garretsen, H., & Marlet, G. (2015). *Het verdwijnende midden in Nederlandse steden? Mogelijke gevolgen van fragmentatie voor de werkgelegenheid*. Pre-advice of the Royal Dutch Economic Association 2015.

DNB. (2018). *Financial stability report*. Spring.

European Central Bank. (2011). *Financial stability review*. June.

European Central Bank. (2015). *Financial stability review*. November.

European Systemic Risk Board. (2015). *Report on residential real estate and financial stability*. December.

Hilber, C. A. L., & Vermeulen, W. (2016). The impact of supply constraints on house prices in England. *The Economic Journal, 126*, 358–405.

Himmelberg, C., Mayer, C., & Sinai, T. (2005). Assessing high house prices: Bubbles, fundamentals and misperceptions. *Journal of Economic Perspectives, 19*(4), 67–92.

International Monetary Fund. (2016). *Global housing watch report*. November.

Ministry of the Interior and Kingdom Relations. (2016). *Wonen in beweging, de resultaten van het WoonOnderzoek Nederland 2015.*

OECD. (2011). Housing and the economy: Policies for renovation. In *Economic policy reforms 2011: Going for growth.*

Parlevliet, J., Doll, M., Vermeulen, R., & De Winter, J. (2016). Perspectief op groei: de Nederlandse economie in beweging. *DNB Occasional Studies, 14*(4).

PBL Netherlands Environmental Assessment Agency. (2015). *De stad: magneet, roltrap en spons.*

PBL Netherlands Environmental Assessment Agency. (2017). *Perspectieven voor het middensegment van de woningmarkt. Verkenning van maatregelen ter bevordering van het aanbod.*

PBL Netherlands Environmental Assessment Agency/Statistics Netherlands (CBS). (2016). *Regionale bevolkings- en huishoudensprognose 2016–2040: sterke regionale verschillen.*

Saiz, A. (2010). The geographic determinants of housing supply. *The Quarterly Journal of Economics, 125*(3), 1253–1296.

Schilder, F. & Conijn, J. (2015). Middeninkomens en het middensegment. De ontbrekende schakel op de woningmarkt. *ASRE Research Paper 2015-10*. Amsterdam: Amsterdam School of Real Estate.

Swank, J., Kakes, J. I., & Tieman, A. F. (2002). The housing ladder, taxation, and borrowing constraints. *DNB Research Memorandum 2002-9/688*.

Whitehead, C., Scanlon, K., Monk, S., Tang, C., Haffner, M., Lunde, J., Andersen, M. L., & Voigtlander, M. (2016). *Understanding the role of private renting: A four country case study*. Copenhagen: Boligokonomisk Videncenter.

Part II
Is There a Bubble in Major Cities?

Chapter 4
Regional House Price Differences: Drivers and Risks

Stijn Claessens and Jochen Schanz

1 Why Might Regionally Concentrated House Price Booms Raise Concerns?

Housing markets have often had policy makers' attention, most notably during the latest financial crises when prices plummeted in many economies. In recent years, rapid increases in house prices have again come into focus. In some countries, such as Sweden and Australia, these increases are widely spread, with real house prices surpassing levels seen before the 2007–2009 crisis. In others, such as the Netherlands, aggregate statistics may not signal similarly lofty valuations. But large discrepancies exist at the regional level, frequently involving booming markets in major cities and more subdued price developments in the rest of the country.

This chapter focuses on the effects of residential house price fluctuations for macroeconomic and financial stability, specifically in relation to house price increases concentrated within large cities. Large countrywide fluctuations in house prices and associated credit are known to amplify macroeconomic fluctuations and to impair financial stability. House price fluctuations that are concentrated within large cities can have qualitatively similar effects. These effects might become quantitatively important for macroeconomic or financial stability if the city is large and tightly integrated with the rest of the country's economy, via real or financial links. In this case it might be appropriate to use macroprudential policy to address regionally concentrated house price fluctuations. Measuring the systemic importance of such fluctuations and assessing the effect of regionally targeted measures is, however, not straightforward, arguably setting a high bar for regulatory invention.

S. Claessens (✉) · J. Schanz (✉)
Monetary and Economic Department, Bank for International Settlements, Basel, Switzerland
e-mail: stijn.claessens@bis.org; jochen.schanz@bis.org

R. Nijskens et al. (eds.), *Hot Property*, https://doi.org/10.1007/978-3-030-11674-3_4

After reviewing house price developments, we discuss how risks emerging from regionally concentrated house price fluctuations might be assessed and present some implications for using macroprudential policy to address them.

2 House Price Developments

House prices have increased in many countries since the financial crisis, and rapidly so in some. One reason is that economic activity has picked up. Another are unusually low mortgage interest rates. The co-movement of house prices in particular among major cities with large and comparatively liquid housing markets could be driven by institutional investors searching for yield across housing markets in a low-interest-rate environment (IMF 2018; Gauder et al. 2014). House prices may also have increased as the memory of the 2007–2009 crisis is starting to fade and as households put doubts behind them regarding the safety and profitability of housing investments.

While the broad background is one of globally rising house prices, important differences remain between national markets (Fig. 4.1). These are likely driven by population and income growth; cost and availability of credit; and national public policy (land policy, tax policy, and prudential policy).

Differences exist not only between countries, but also within them. In particular, house prices in metropolitan areas have typically grown faster than in rural areas

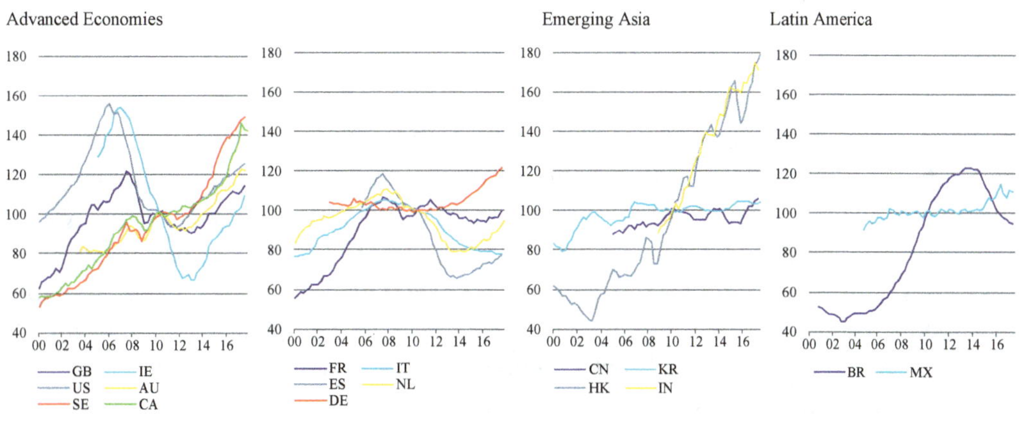

Sources: BIS and National data, BIS calculations (2018)

Fig. 4.1 International differences in real residential property price growth. CPI deflated; rebased 2010 = 100. AU = Australia; BR = Brazil; CA = Canada; CN = China; DE = Germany; ES = Spain; FR = France; GB = United Kingdom; HK = Hong Kong SAR; IE = Ireland; IN = India; IT = Italy; KR = Korea; MX = Mexico; NL = Netherlands; SE = Sweden; US = United States. For US, seasonally adjusted

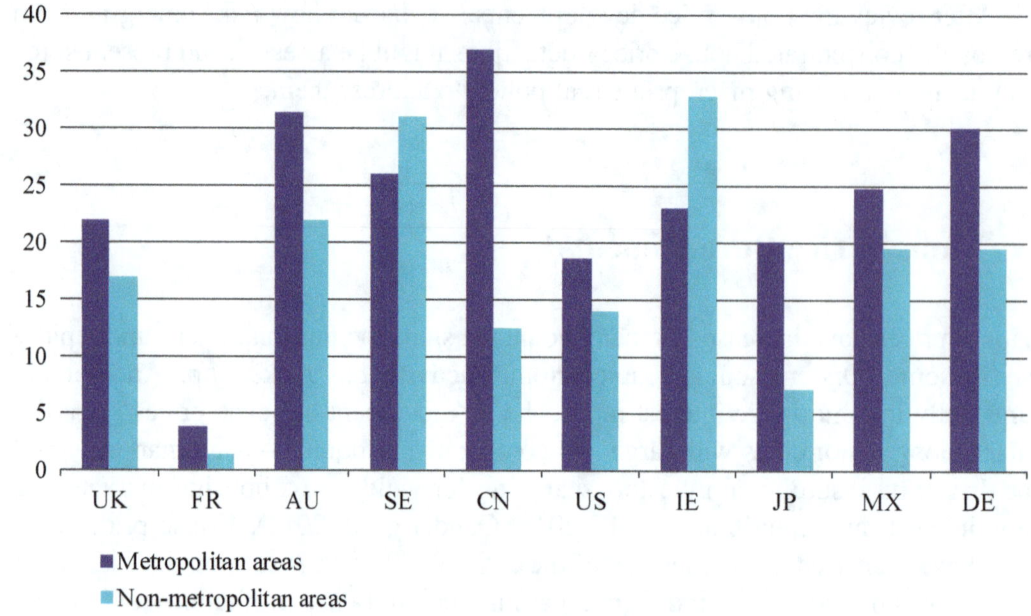

Sources: Nationwide.co.uk (2018), FHFA.gov (2018), CEIC (2018), National data and BIS calculations (2018)

Fig. 4.2 Regional house price differences. Cumulative nominal price growth (2014–2017). UK: London vs all other regions. FR: Île-de-France vs. Province (INSEE). AU: Sydney vs a weighted average of Sydney, Melbourne, Brisbane, Adelaide, Perth, Hobart, Darwin, and Canberra. SE: simple average of Stockholm, Malmö and Göteborg vs a simple average of the other regions of the country (SCB). DE: 7 largest cities vs the whole country (Bundesbank). CN: simple average of Beijing, Shanghai, and Guangzhou (CEIC) vs an average of 70 cities. US: metropolitan areas vs non-metropolitan areas (FHFA). IE: Dublin vs the rest of Ireland. JP: Tokyo vs entire country. MX: Mexico City vs entire country. For DE, cumulative nominal price growth over the period 2012–2015

(Fig. 4.2).[1] Urbanisation is likely to be the key driver, in turn driven by factors such as growing labour productivity in agriculture and the emergence of technologies and industries that come with larger network externalities.[2] Regional deviations have therefore shown a large degree of persistence. Beliefs, to the extent that they are based on regional developments, can reinforce this persistence. But prices have also co-varied with more volatile changes in regional economic conditions. For example, in Canada, residential house prices fell in Calgary from their peak in 2014, following a downturn in the local energy sector, while house prices in Toronto, Montreal, and Vancouver, continued to increase. In addition, regions may influence land planning regulations, driving differences in the supply for housing. Such regulations often add to supply constraints linked to geographical factors.

[1]Constrained by availability of comparable data, the figures refer to different types of residential housing for different countries.

[2]The literature on urbanisation has discussed a large number of other factors driving the population growth of cities. For an overview, see e.g. Glaeser and Gottlieb (2009), and Storper (2011).

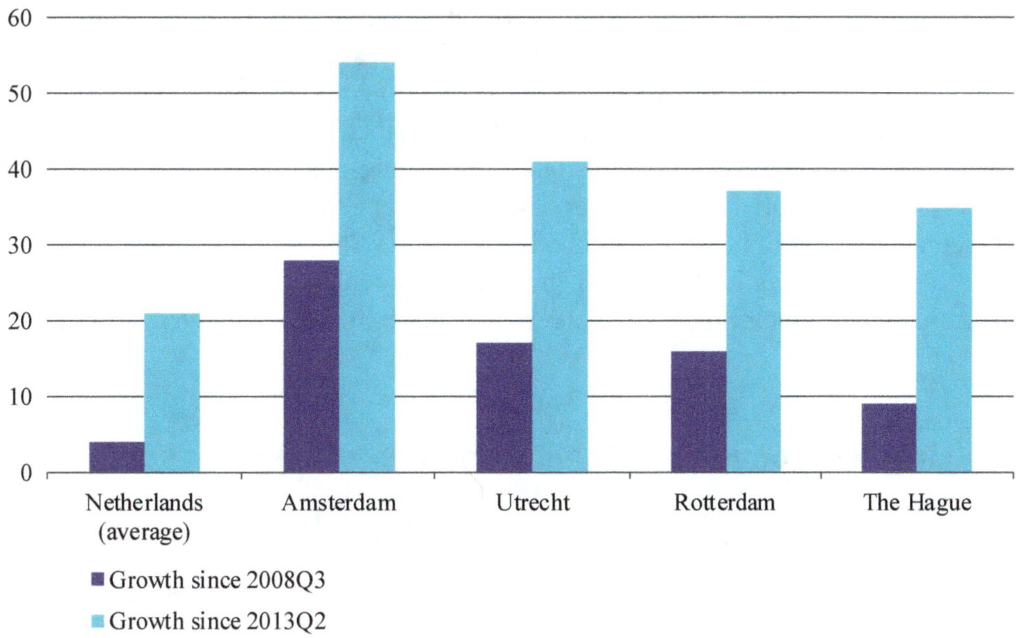

Sources: Statistics Netherlands (CBS) (2018) and BIS calculations (2018)

Fig. 4.3 Regional house price differences in the Netherlands *(Cumulative nominal price growth. Data as of 2017 Q4)*

Table 4.1 Regional housing markets in the UK

	Cumulative nominal growth		First-time buyer affordability indicators			
	Since 2007 Q3 (%)	Since 2009 Q1 (%)	Average loan (GBP)	Income multiple	LTV (%)	Debt service ratio (%)
UK	15	41	138,000	3.6	85	17.3
London	57	95	262,242	4.0	73	17.6
Scotland	−5	10	108,000	3.1	85	16.0
Wales	−1	23	111,788	3.3	88	16.6
Northern Ireland	−39	0	96,375	3.0	85	15.3

Data as of 2018 Q1. Income multiple is the ratio of loan size to income. Debt service ratios are in percent of monthly gross household income. Source: Nationwide (2018), UK Finance and BIS calculations (2018)

For the Netherlands, regional house price developments resemble those in most other countries. Average house prices have risen by 21% since their trough in June 2013 while regional discrepancies have widened (Fig. 4.3). In the major cities, the recovery has been speedier and firmer than elsewhere and house prices are above levels seen before the crisis. Amsterdam stands out, arguably showing signs of overheating. Higher prices in Amsterdam are, however, partly attributed to structural migration to cities and increasing interest shown by private investors (De Nederlandsche Bank 2017; Hekwolter of Hekhuis et al. 2017).

For the UK, Table 4.1 provides some detail on how leverage of first-time buyers co-varies with regional differences in house prices. House prices have grown rapidly since their post-crisis trough (2009 Q1) on average, and are now exceeding their pre-crisis peak (2007 Q3). But regional differences are large. Within London, economically the most important region, average income is almost double that in other regions. House prices are about 2.8 times higher than in other regions of the UK, as are average loan sizes, illustrating the strong positive correlation between house prices and mortgage credit. For first-time buyers, the ratio of average loan size to income is higher in London than in other regions. With income multiples high, the loan-to-value ratio is lower though in London, arguably offsetting the risks that banks incur from their borrowers' larger exposure to increases in interest rates.

3 Macroeconomic and Financial Stability Risks Assessments

Rising house prices typically go hand in hand with an expansion of mortgage credit. The associated increase in leverage, both among new home owners and banks, can influence macroeconomic and financial stability. The importance of leverage among households and banks for amplifying house price moves, and indeed for causing macroeconomic and financial instability, has been discussed in depth following the financial crisis (Jordà et al. 2013; Duca et al. 2010). Effects arise in the boom phase, as increasing house prices, growing credit, and greater economic activity feed on each other. When the cycle turns, the impact on macroeconomic and financial stability is largest when falling house prices and high debt interact in a downward spiral (Borio and Lowe 2002; Crowe et al. 2013).

Even if outright financial stress is avoided, house price developments matter for the macroeconomy: while housing booms can have a significant positive effect on output in the short run, they tend to have a negative impact in the longer term.[3] When leverage is high, consumption and investment respond more to changes in wealth caused by housing price fluctuations.[4] Effects are larger the greater the amplitude of the fluctuations (because of larger wealth effects) and the longer their duration (because consumption and lending respond more strongly to persistent changes in wealth; see Claessens and Kose (2018) for a review). House price fluctuations that are concentrated within large cities can have qualitatively similar effects; these can be quantitatively significant for macroeconomic and financial stability if the city is tightly integrated with the rest of the country's economy.

[3]For the financial stability and macroeconomic implications of house price changes see e.g. Aldasoro et al. (2018), Claessens et al. (2012), Crowe et al. (2013), Drehmann and Juselius (2012), Drehmann et al. (2017), Jordà et al. (2016), Lombardi et al. (2017) and Mian et al. (2017).

[4]Bunn and Rostom (2015) show that between 2007 and 2009, spending cuts by UK households with debt ratios above 400% were 10 times higher than those of households with ratios below 100%.

In order to assess risks emerging from regional housing price developments, it would therefore appear useful to have two sets of indicators. In the first set are those describing the likely persistence of house price changes and the size of reversals once the tide turns, as well as resilience indicators for households and banks, such as leverage. (Regional differences in the *level* of house prices are not necessarily relevant: limited supply and greater demand for housing are always likely to lead to higher house prices in cities.) In the second set are indicators capturing the external effects that a regional house price crash might have on the rest of the country. Aside from those measuring resilience, such indicators largely remain to be developed. In the following sections, we therefore qualitative describe factors that determine risks where indicators are, as yet, unavailable.

3.1 Persistence, Reversals and Resilience

Persistence Persistence of house price fluctuations is determined by both supply and demand for housing. Indicators for supply-related determinants of persistence include the amount of newly built housing to be available within the next few years and restrictions to the number of floors of new buildings. Indicators for demand-related determinants of persistence appear to be more difficult to construct. The emergence of new or the decline of old industries, which alters the importance of agglomeration benefits and hence the attraction of cities to labour, may be a drawn-out process lasting decades but is harder to quantify. Where immigration is a source of persistent demand, the existence of areas in which there is already some immigrant population may be a sign of persistent demand as such areas tend to attract new immigrants (Bartel 1989).

Indicators capturing whether market forces tend to reduce or increase persistence would also appear useful. Market forces help reduce demand for housing in expensive areas by inducing people to move out to other regions. For example, an estimated net 1.2% of those aged 60 or older migrated out of London each year between 2000 and 2015 (Gordon et al. 2017, Table 5.2). And, in 2015, 869,000 people employed in their main job in London lived outside London, up from 665,000 10 years earlier (Office for National Statistics 2016). As a result, free transport capacity and an elastic supply of housing in the regions surrounding cities would tend to reduce the persistence of regional house price divergences. Persistence might also be lower if other regions have a high-quality infrastructure, and if labour is sufficiently mobile (e.g. a large proportion of renters), such that firms can relocate production away from more expensive metropolitan areas.[5]

However, market forces might lose their power to attenuate regional housing imbalances if agglomeration benefits are large. Agglomeration benefits arise because

[5]See Oxford Economic Forecasting (2004) for examples of lower-value-added jobs being outsourced to UK regions outside London.

densely populated areas can facilitate matching in labour markets, reduce transportation cost, and provide a fertile environment for spreading ideas and fostering innovation. This means that agglomerations might continue to attract labour and investment even when residential house prices are comparatively high. For example, while the number of inward commuters to London increased between 2005 and 2015, that of people living *and* working in London increased by even more, from 3.1 million in 2005 to 3.8 million in 2015. Indicators describing agglomeration benefits are difficult to construct: indeed, in estimations, agglomeration benefits have typically been identified as a residual component capturing movements in productivity unexplained by other factors, such as human capital, geography, and institutions (Gennaioli et al. 2013).

Reversals The likely possibility and size of reversals in house price developments may depend on whether house price trends are driven by fundamental or speculative elements. House price booms driven by buyers hoping to benefit from future price increases, without paying much attention to fundamentals, are arguably destined for particularly strong reversals. The reason is that once speculative beliefs change direction, the typically high leverage in such markets tends to reinforce the decline in house prices, such that beliefs become self-confirming. But there are no tried-and-tested policy tools to affect beliefs systematically. Policy makers have used communication to affect housing markets by raising risk awareness, but the impact of such communications has proved difficult to predict (CGFS 2016).

Surveys of house price expectations, that collect information about the reasons underlying them, can provide useful indicators that help determine to what extent such expectations appear to be based on fundamentals. In addition, the rental market provides information for constructing estimates of fundamentals-based house prices, which can be compared with observed values. Developments in other regions can provide useful benchmarks since intra-regional comparisons are robust against common factors driving rents and house prices across regions, such as changes in mortgage interest rates, interest deductibility, and tenant protection.

While house price trends driven by speculation may experience particularly strong reversals, it is useful to keep in mind that fundamentals do change, and sometimes quickly and by a substantial amount—for example, a decline in oil prices rapidly changed the economic fortunes of the region of Alberta in Canada and ended the regional house price boom. Accordingly, one might construct indicators capturing the dependence of the economic fortunes of a region on specific sectors or industries. More generally, indicators capturing resilience to income shocks and to changes in house prices can inform the strength of reversals.

Resilience Finally, among indicators describing resilience, loan-to-value and debt service to income ratios have proven to be particularly useful to assess the risk that house price fluctuations cause macroeconomic and financial instability.[6] What

[6]See, e.g. Aldasoro et al. (2018) and the literature cited therein.

level of debt is sustainable may depend on structural features of the housing market (e.g. fixed vs. floating rate mortgages, recourse vs. non-recourse, liquidity of the housing market) and on the design of the social safety net as it determines, for example, the degree of support households would receive if they become unemployed.[7] Aldasoro et al. (2018) show that the level of debt relative to income is most important for predicting banking crises, but the extent to which debt is denominated in foreign currency appears to matter as well.

3.2 *Externalities*

The second set of indicators, those attempting to capture the externality effects of regional house price crashes, remains to be developed. Such indicators are key, because concerns for countrywide financial and macroeconomic stability arise only if externality effects on other regions are sufficiently large. Put differently, only if the regional housing market is systemically important, should there be specific macroeconomic or financial stability concerns.

One indicator of a region's macroeconomic importance is clearly its contribution to national GDP. For example, the metropolitan region including Dublin generates around half of Ireland's GDP; that including London about a third of the UK's GDP; but that including Berlin only 5% of Germany's GDP.[8] Another is the extent to which a city's economy is integrated with that of other regions, such as through supply chains or income transfers by workers commuting from one region to the other. For example, London-based companies and residents were estimated to source about a third of their supplies from other regions in the UK.[9] And around 15% of those working in London live in the surrounding regions, where they are likely to spend most of their salaries.

Regional shocks can also spill over to the rest of the country via financial links. These links can arise, for example, because of concentrated funding, interbank exposures, or an undiversified investor base. Indeed, as past crises have shown, the mere suspicion of the existence of exposures can create stress for lenders without any direct links to the region experiencing a downturn. For example, in 2009, regional housing market shocks had nation-wide effects; earlier U.S. crises (Texas, New England) had also some spillovers. Multiple channels were at play: the real estate bust in Texas in the late 1980s, related to a drop in oil prices, was a contributor to the savings and loan crisis, which in turn required federal government support to resolve. At times, changes in sovereign risks can give rise to links via the bank-

[7]See Zabai (2017) for an overview of key features of mortgage markets. Auclert (2017) shows that the greater the interest rate sensitivity—or duration—of a household's liabilities relative to that of its assets, and the shorter the maturity of these liabilities, the larger the impact on consumption.

[8]Eurostat (2017), Fig. 6.2.

[9]London Development Agency (2003), Table 9.7.

sovereign nexus if the government's support for struggling banks in one region exhausts its capacity to provide future support for banks in other regions. For example, the real estate related banking crises in Ireland and Spain affected the whole euro area: the final response involved a regional support mechanism with fiscal backing from other euro area countries. Moreover, it led to stresses among banks in other countries, which in turn affected local credit provisions.

4 Implications for Macroprudential Policy

Macroprudential policy has been shown to be generally effective in increasing resilience to housing price declines (Claessens et al. 2012). Against the background of large costs of housing market crashes, and a conjunctural environment that encouraged demand for property, policymakers have relied extensively on macroprudential tools to address financial risks associated with country-wide housing market imbalances.

Even if macroprudential measures apply uniformly to the entire country, they can affect different regions to different extents: an LTV ratio cap might well bind only in regions in which house prices are high. Nevertheless, some countries that experienced large regional imbalances have chosen to deploy region-specific measures, partly in order to reduce compliance costs in regions in which housing markets did not pose risks to stability.[10] For example, in New Zealand, restrictions on high-loan-to-value (LTV) mortgage lending were put in place in October 2013, with a cap of 80% applying for most mortgage borrowers. As the Auckland market started to accelerate while house prices in the rest of the country moderated, LTV requirements were tightened in Auckland in November 2015 and somewhat relaxed elsewhere: the share of mortgages banks were allowed to grant at LTVs exceeding the cap was raised from 10% to 15% for owner-occupied properties outside Auckland (Spencer 2015). This appeared to somewhat reduce house price inflation in Auckland (Spencer 2016). When housing market risks continued to grow nationwide, the regional differentiation was abandoned, with LTV restrictions being tightened somewhat in Auckland and more significantly elsewhere in 2016.

As the preceding discussion on indicators has shown, the bar to using macroprudential policy to target regional housing market imbalances is currently high. Calibrating such policy measures appears even more difficult than calibrating those measures targeting fluctuations at the national level. Externalities of regional housing market cycles have to be assessed and the impact of interventions on migration and agglomeration benefits should be taken into account. Economic models designed to calibrate regional macroprudential policies are more difficult to build and solve than those for national measures, because they require additional dimensions (capturing heterogeneity between regions) and additional non-linearities

[10] Fáykiss et al. (2017) discuss which macroprudential instruments might be effective when applied regionally.

(arising from agglomeration externalities). A suitable avenue for future research would be to identify and quantify externalities that link cities with the rest of the country, and to consider how regulation can address specific risks emerging from regional house price fluctuations.

References

Aldasoro, I., Borio, C., & Drehmann, M. (2018, March). Early warning indicators of banking crises: expanding the family. *BIS Quarterly Review*.

Auclert, A. (2017). *Monetary policy and the redistribution channel* (NBER Working Papers, no 23451).

Bank for International Settlements. (2018). *Residential property prices*. Accessed April 1, 2018, from https://www.bis.org/statistics/pp_selected.htm?m=6%7C288%7C596

Bartel, A. (1989). Where do the new U.S. immigrants live? *Journal of Labor Economics, 7*(4), 371–391.

Borio, C., & Lowe, P. (2002). *Asset prices, financial and monetary stability: Exploring the nexus* (BIS Working Papers, no 114).

Bunn, P., & Rostom, M. (2015). *Household debt and spending in the United Kingdom* (Bank of England Staff Working Paper, no 554).

CEIC. (2018). *House prices growth*. Accessed April 1, 2018, from https://www.ceicdata.com/en/indicator/house-prices-growth

Claessens, S., & Kose, M. A. (2018). *Frontiers of macrofinancial linkages* (BIS Papers, no 95).

Claessens, S., Kose, M., & Terrones, M. (2012). How do business and financial cycles interact? *Journal of International Economics, 87*(1), 178–190.

Committee on the Global Financial System. (2016). *Objective-setting and communication of macroprudential policies*. Basel.

Crowe, C., Dell'Ariccia, G., Igan, D., & Rabanal, P. (2013). How to deal with real estate booms: Lessons from country experiences. *Journal of Financial Stability, 9*(3), 300–319.

De Nederlandsche Bank. (2017). *Financial stability report*. Autumn.

Drehmann, M., & Juselius, M. (2012, September). Do debt service costs affect macroeconomic and financial stability? *BIS Quarterly Review*.

Drehmann, M., Juselius, M., & Korinek, A. (2017). *Accounting for debt service: The painful legacy of credit booms* (BIS Working Papers, no 645).

Duca, J., Muellbauer, J., & Murphy, A. (2010). Housing markets and the financial crisis of 2007–2009: Lessons for the future. *Journal of Financial Stability, 6*(4), 203–217.

Eurostat. (2017). *Regional yearbook*.

Fáykiss, P., Márton, N., & Szombati, A. (2017). Regionally-differentiated debt cap rules: A Hungarian perspective. In: *BIS (2017): Macroprudential frameworks, implementation and relationship with other policies* (BIS Papers, no 94).

Federal Housing Finance Agency. (2018). *House price index*. Accessed April 1, 2018, from https://www.fhfa.gov/DataTools/Downloads/pages/house-price-index.aspx

Gauder, M., Houssard, C., & Orsmond, D. (2014, June). Foreign investment in residential real estate. *Reserve Bank of Australia Bulletin*.

Gennaioli, N., La Porta, R., Lopez-de-Silanes, F., & Shleifer, A. (2013). Human capital and regional development. *Quarterly Journal of Economics, 128*(1), 105–164.

Glaeser, E., & Gottlieb, J. (2009). The wealth of cities: Agglomeration economies and spatial equilibrium in the United States. *Journal of Economic Literature, 47*(4), 983–1028.

Gordon, I., Champion, T., McDonald, N., & Whitehead, C. (2017, September 3). *Migration influences and implications for population dynamics in the wider South East*. Report to the

East of England Local Government Association, London School of Economics and Political Science.

Hekwolter of Hekhuis, M., Nijskens, R., & Heeringa, W. (2017). The housing market in major Dutch cities. *DNB Occasional Study, 15*(1), 7–59.

International Monetary Fund. (2018, April). House price synchronization: What role for financial factors? *Global Financial Stability Report* (pp. 93–133).

Jordà, Ò., Schularick, M., & Taylor, A. (2013). When credit bites back. *Journal of Monetary Credit and Banking, 45*(2), 3–28.

Jordà, Ò., Schularick, M., & Taylor, A. (2016). The great mortgaging: Housing finance, crises and business cycles. *Economic Policy, 31*(85), 107–152.

Lombardi, M., Mohanty, M., & Shim, I. (2017). *The real effects of household debt in the short and long run* (BIS Working Papers, no 607).

London Development Agency. (2003, December). *The London annual business survey*.

Mian, A., Sufi, A., & Verner, E. (2017). Household debt and business cycles worldwide. *Quarterly Journal of Economics, 132*(4), 1755–1817.

Nationwide. (2018). *House price index*. Accessed April 1, 2018, from https://www.nationwide.co.uk/about/house-price-index/headlines

Office for National Statistics. (2016). *London jobs by commuting pattern: 2004 to 2015*. Ad-hoc request, Reference number 005564. Accessed from https://www.ons.gov.uk

Oxford Economic Forecasting. (2004). *London's linkages with the rest of the UK*. Oxford, UK.

Spencer, G. (2015, August 24). *Investors adding to Auckland housing market risk*, speech delivered to The Northern Club, Auckland.

Spencer, G. (2016, July 7). *Housing risks require a broad policy response*, speech delivered to New Zealand Institute of Valuers, Wellington.

Statistics Netherlands. (2018). *House price index per region*. Accessed April 1, 2018, from https://opendata.cbs.nl/statline/#/CBS/en/dataset/83913ENG/table?dl=F8A5

Storper, M. (2011). Why do regions develop and change? The challenge for geography and economics. *Journal of Economic Geography, 11*(2), 333–346.

Zabai, A. (2017, December). Household debt: Recent developments and challenges. *BIS Quarterly Review*.

Chapter 5
A Tale of Two Cities: Is Overvaluation a Capital Issue?

John Muellbauer

1 Introduction

Since the global financial crisis, there has been a great deal of research on links between credit growth, especially if real-estate linked, the overvaluation of house prices and financial stability. Cerutti et al. (2017), analysing an (unbalanced) panel data set of 50 countries for 1970–2012 find that house-price booms are more likely in countries with higher loan-to-value ratios and mortgage funding models based on securitization or wholesale sources. They find that most house-price booms end with a recession, and that such downturns are predicted to be deeper and longer when preceded by booms in both residential mortgages and other private debt, and in reliance on non-retail deposit funding that fuel duration mismatch problems on lenders' balance sheets. Muellbauer (2012) considered links between house price overvaluations and financial instability and suggested ways in which empirical evidence could be used to detect episodes of overvaluation. Muellbauer (2018a) spelled out further the amplifying and sometimes stabilising feedback loops in real

Paper prepared for the DNB conference Hot Property: the Housing Market in Major Cities, May 24–25, 2018 Amsterdam. Part of this paper builds on a research project pursued at the ECB during John Muellbauer's tenure of a Wim Duisenberg Visiting Fellowship, and in particular on a paper co-authored with Valerie Chauvin of Banque de France. Thanks are due for advice on French data from Guillaume Chapelle, Jacques Friggit, Andrew Goodwin and Clara Wolf, to James Wyatt on prime central London house prices, and to John Duca for helpful discussions. Longer term research support from the Open Society Foundation via INET at the Oxford Martin School is gratefully acknowledged.

J. Muellbauer (✉)
Nuffield College, Oxford, UK

Institute for New Economic Thinking at the Oxford Martin School, University of Oxford, Oxford, UK
e-mail: john.muellbauer@nuffield.ox.ac.uk

R. Nijskens et al. (eds.), *Hot Property*, https://doi.org/10.1007/978-3-030-11674-3_5

estate booms accompanied by credit booms. These can vary greatly between countries. In the short run, there can be strong positive feedbacks via consumption, where down-payment constraints are loose, access to home equity loans is easy and rates of owner occupation are high. The UK and the US offer a sharp contrast here to Germany and France. Another feedback is via residential investment, which boosts employment and household income. In the UK, where the housing supply elasticity is low, such a feedback would be weaker than in the US, Ireland or Spain. There can also be pronounced macroeconomic effects of an overshooting of house prices induced by a series of strong positive shocks and amplified by extrapolative expectations of capital gains. This is so particularly in economies where high levels of leverage are possible, such as the UK and US (but not Germany or France), since leverage amplifies returns and risks. As Geanakoplos (2009) has argued, an endogenous leverage cycle can simultaneously drive growth in debt and in asset prices.[1]

One rapid stabilising feedback loop, in countries where down-payment constraints are strong, is in the higher saving for a housing down-payment of those hoping to enter the housing market. Other negative feedbacks, such as the higher burden of debt on spending or of an expanded housing supply on house prices, would be stabilising if they acted quickly enough. They could, however, make a crisis still worse if they coincided with the above amplifying mechanisms deepening a downturn in housing and credit markets.

This discussion makes it clear that empirical evidence on variations between countries and over time, for example on the response of aggregate consumption to house prices, on the importance of extrapolative expectations in amplifying house price dynamics, and on differences in housing supply elasticities can be very helpful in assessing risks to financial stability. Understanding what drives house prices is important. In many countries, house price movements in major cities such as the capital are more extreme and often seem to lead the rest of the country. A framework for analysing prices at a regional level is therefore useful and Sect. 2 sets out a simple one: a two-region version in which the capital city is one, and the rest of the country the other. The example of London is used to illustrate the leading role of London house prices and the apparent ripple effect seen in the other regions. These make one suspect that early indications of over-valuation might be seen first in the London market. The special role of wealthy international investors in the top end of the market is a major issue for many world cities and London is no exception. Section 3 examines house prices in Paris vs France and summarises some empirical findings. Section 4 draws brief conclusions.

[1]Evidence, see Duca et al. (2016), is consistent with an asymmetry, a stronger response in a downturn—a credit crunch due to bad loans arising from negative housing equity—than in the upswing of the cycle.

2 A Framework for Regional House Price Modelling: The Case of London

We begin by illustrating general issues of supply and demand with a simple log-linear 2-region model. Consider a two region economy (j = 1,2) with log-linear housing demands. One can think of region 1 being the capital city and region 2 the rest of the country. Because households have migration and commuting options affecting their location decisions, the demand for housing in region j depends not only on house prices at j but also on the relative price vis-à-vis the other region r (j ≠ r). Let h be the log housing stock per head, y be log real income per head, ph be the log real house price index and z be a demand shifter capturing other influences. Then the log-linear demand function at location j is:

$$h_{jt} = -\alpha_j ph_{jt} - \alpha_{jr} \left(ph_{jt} - ph_{rt}\right) + \beta_j y_{jt} + \beta_{jr} y_{rt} + z_{jt} \tag{5.1}$$

Note that relative house prices in regions j and r influence demand in region j, as does income in region r as well as in region j. Reversing subscripts r and j gives the corresponding housing demand function in region r. Solving the two equations for ph_{jt} and ph_{rt} as a function of incomes, housing stocks and demand shifters in the two regions, defines the inverse demand functions.[2] These answer the question: given housing stocks, incomes and other influences in the two regions, what house prices will equilibrate demand and supply? Partial adjustment dynamics around these long-run solutions will generate equations suitable for estimation. Demand shifters in z_{jt} should include credit conditions, interest rates, user cost and demography, not necessarily confined to region j: for example, relative expected appreciation dependent on lagged house price dynamics affects regional migration, see Cameron and Muellbauer (1998), Cameron et al. (2006a), and is part of regional house price dynamics in the UK, Cameron et al. (2006b).

An alternative formulation has the same long-run solution but allows a lagged, rather than instantaneous, response to relative house prices:

$$h_{jt} = -\alpha_j ph_{jt} - \alpha_{jr} \left(ph_{jt-1} - ph_{rt-1}\right) + \beta_j y_{jt} + \beta_{jr} y_{rt} + z_{jt} \tag{5.2}$$

These equations can be generalised to more than two regions. The strengths of the spill-over effects α_{jr} and β_{jr} are likely to be greater for contiguous locations and for pairs of locations otherwise economically connected. To reduce the complexity of such models, apart from selecting a small number of strategic alternative locations, national average data can be used to summarise the remainder of alternative locations.

---

[2] See Deaton and Muellbauer (1980), pp. 56–57 and Theil (1976) on inverse demand functions and, for an empirical application, Barten and Bettendorf (1989). For simplicity, (5.1) omits the demand shifter in region r.

Solving for ph_{jt}, Eq. (5.2) implies a positive coefficient on ph_{rt-1} because of the lagged effect of substitution. However, it is unclear whether, once incorporated in a dynamic adjustment process, this sign will be preserved in the equilibrium correction form of the equation for the change in ph_{jt} (Δph_{jt}). The reason is that excess demand in one region can spill over into the other(s). In other words, Δph_{jt} may increase not just with excess demand in region j but also with excess demand in region r. If excess demand is represented by the deviation between fundamentals and respectively ph_{jt-1} and ph_{rt-1}, Δph_{jt} would depend negatively on lagged house prices in both locations. This could overwhelm the effect of lagged substitution, leaving the overall sign ambiguous.

Such formulations give content to the spatial correlations often picked up in equation residuals. Some studies use complex estimation methods to 'correct' models developed for single locations—'islands'—for spatial correlations that reflect omitted variables arising from the spill-over effects discussed above, e.g. Oikarinen et al. (2018). US studies of metro areas adopting the 'islands' view include Hwang and Quigley (2006) and Follain and Velz (1995); Abraham and Hendershott (1996), Malpezzi (1996), Capozza et al. (2004) and Green et al. (2005) examine equilibrium correcting behaviour of house prices in MAs. The most influential recent study is Glaeser et al. (2008).

One area in the literature where spatial coefficient heterogeneity has been seriously considered in modelling the dynamics of regional house price change, is in the so-called ripple effect, where a leading location, experiences house price changes ahead of other regions. UK studies, where the leadership of London ahead of other regions has been evident for some time, include Meen (1999), Cook (2003, 2012) and Cook and Watson (2015). US studies include Gupta and Miller (2010, 2012), Holmes et al. (2011), Barros et al. (2012), and Chiang and Tsai (2016). Teye et al. (2017) find ripple effects from Amsterdam.

Cameron et al. (2006b) follow the theoretical framework set out in Eq. (5.1) above to incorporate between-region spill-overs between London and seven other UK regions using annual data from 1972 to 2003. The house price equations control for mortgage credit conditions and for expectations of house price appreciation from reduced form forecasting equations incorporating data of which households are likely to have been aware. Credit conditions influence house prices directly but also indirectly by shifting more weight onto real interest rates and less on nominal interest rates as credit conditions ease. Regional heterogeneity includes a response of London given its role as financial centre (and to a lesser extent the South East region around London), but not other regions, to the stock market. But the effect is asymmetric, probably because negative stock market returns make relative returns in housing look better. Downside risk in housing induces another asymmetric response, namely to past changes in house prices: prospective home-buyers appear to have a memory of up to 4 years for negative returns in housing. This delayed the recovery of house prices after the crisis of the early 1990s, which was triggered by interest rate rises. Negative returns were particularly pronounced in interest-sensitive London. London also responds more strongly to shocks in income and interest rates than other regions.

London is the only region not influenced by lagged house price changes in other regions. Regions near London are strongly affected directly by the London spill-over effect; regions further away, are influenced by spill-over effects from nearby regions, and hence indirectly by London. There is thus a clear picture of a ripple effect spreading out from London. National shocks from the stock market, interest rates and income and population growth, including growth in the adult population aged under 40, drive London and eventually feed through to other regions, together with the direct regional impact of interest rates, incomes, housing stocks, demography and population. The results suggest that, since 1997, mortgage credit liberalization, lower interest rates and financial sector leadership via London have been important factors increasing real house prices. Higher per capita income growth and population growth, driven by net foreign immigration, contributed to a rise since 1997 in house prices in Greater London compared to other regions.

With data up to 2003, Cameron et al. (2006b) found no signs of overvaluation in UK regional house prices, provided fundamentals of income, interest rates, credit conditions and lack of housing supply remained broadly within range. Short-term dynamics did not point to significant extrapolative over-shoots of house price expectations. Subsequently, as the Turner (2009) report for the Financial Stability Authority showed, lending became more risky, especially after 2005. For example, low-documentation loans accounted for about half of new mortgages in 2006–2007 and lenders increasingly resorted to money markets to fund short-term, incurring serious maturity mismatch. When the global financial crisis hit, unprecedented monetary policy easing, bank rescues and increased help for borrowers with payment difficulties were needed to stabilize the financial system.

Post-sample, the model helps to explain why, given the sharp falls in interest rates in the global financial crisis, London has outperformed other regions. However, it seems likely that a more explicit treatment of global investment in the top end of the London market would be needed to fully account for London's outperformance in the UK. Badarinza and Ramadorai (2018) have found evidence of safe-haven demand for London property, linked with foreign political and economic crises.

Figure 5.1 shows logs of the real UK house price index excluding London, the index for Greater London and for prime Central London. Since 1970, house prices in Greater London have outpaced house prices in the UK excluding London by a large margin, and particularly since 1997 as noted above. The UK's local property taxes are probably another factor in London's outperformance: uniquely in the OECD, they are highly regressive and based on valuations unchanged since 1991, with zero marginal tax rates on expensive properties disproportionately found in London. Since 1976, when the prime Central London data begin, this market has outpaced the Greater London market. However, this is not so taking 1985 as the base. After the global financial crisis, prime Central London prices recovered more rapidly than Greater London. This is probably due to low interest rates, foreign demand and lower sensitivity to credit constraints, which were relaxed only gradually after around 2012.

Granger causality tests for quarterly changes in log real house price indices suggest that Greater London helps significantly in explaining UK ex. London, but

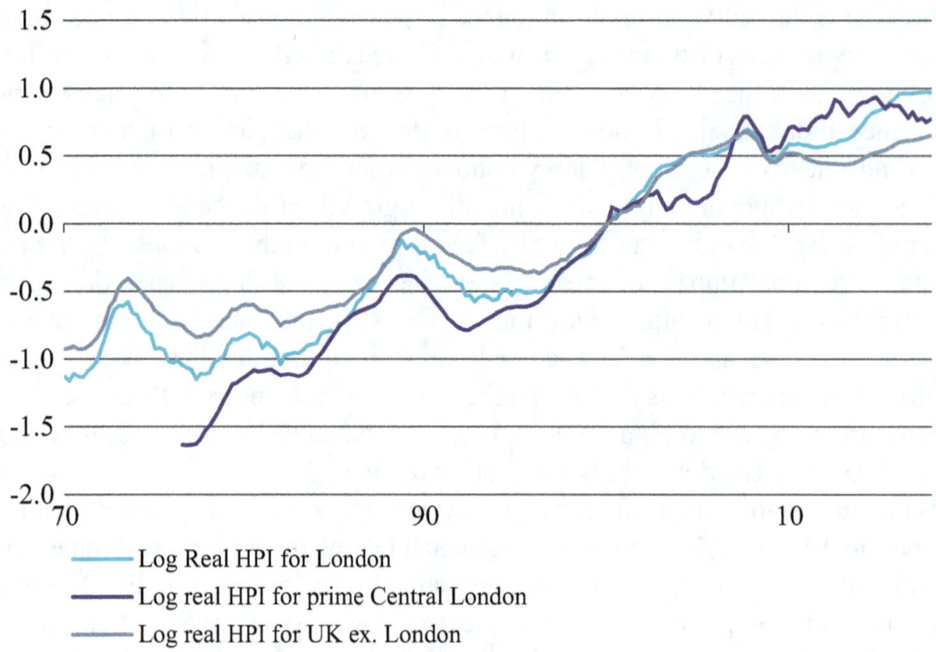

Sources: ONS (2018) HPI data base for UK and Greater London; prime Central London from 2000Q1, average of index for flats and houses from Property Vision, including data from Lonres (2018), spliced to the Knight-Frank (2018) index for prime central London for earlier years

Fig. 5.1 Log real house price indices for the UK excluding Greater London, for Greater London and for prime Central London

prime central London does not. In turn, *both* UK ex. London and prime central London help explain Greater London, but neither Greater London nor UK ex. help explain prime central London. Such tests have limited usefulness, but hint at substantial drivers of the prime central London market unconnected with macroeconomic conditions in the UK. The downturn in prime central London prices since 2015 is probably connected with sharp rises in Stamp Duty on property transfers and with attempts to clamp down on corporate vehicles previously used to evade such taxes. The latest data show the first annual decline in nominal house prices in greater London since 2009.

As far as risk factors for future house prices are concerned, higher interest rates are the most obvious, especially for London, which is more sensitive to interest rates than the rest of the country. The high levels of UK household debt relative to income and the negative feedbacks on consumer demand of lower house prices make the UK especially vulnerable, and is, of course, a reason for caution by the Bank of England in raising rates. It is also worth mentioning political economy as a risk factor. Unaffordable housing is a major part of the distributional conflict between those born after about 1980 and earlier cohorts. Higher student debt burdens, worse labour market prospects since 2007, higher levels of government debt and the burdens on government finances of an increasing aged population have added to the problems faced by post-1980 cohorts. Reforms of property taxes and property rights of landowners, which disproportionately favour landowners and wealthy older generations, are increasingly seen as desirable to restore some degree of generational justice; see Corlett and Gardiner (2018) and Muellbauer (2018b). These must diminish prospects for UK house prices.

3 The Case of Paris

Chauvin and Muellbauer (2018) estimate a model for house prices in France as part of a 6-equation system also including aggregate consumption, the stock of housing loans, liquid assets, consumer credit and permanent income. The data are quarterly spanning 1981–2016. The theory background for the aggregate house price equation is an inverse demand function, where real house prices, *rph*, are determined by household demand, conditional on the lagged housing stock:

$$\ln rph_t = h_{0t} + h_{1t} \ln nmr_t + h_{2t} \ln user_t + h_3 \left(\ln (y_t / hs_{t-1}) + h_{4t} E_t \ln \left(y_t^f / y_t \right) \right) \\ + h_5 demog_t + h_6 LA_{t-1}/y_t + h_7 IFA_{t-1}/y_t + h_8 spillover_{t-1} + h_9 trans_t \quad (5.3)$$

Here h_{0t} should increase with mortgage credit conditions, estimated as a latent variable common to consumption, housing loans and house price equations. The nominal mortgage rate is *nmr,* and user cost measuring interest rates minus expected appreciation is *user.* The parameter h_3 measures minus the inverse of the price elasticity of demand for housing, and is attached to the log ratio of income to the housing stock, which imposes the constraint that the income elasticity of demand for housing is one. The coefficient h_{4t} captures the relative effect of permanent to current income, analogously to a similar term in the consumption function. The remaining terms respectively represent the effects of demography, liquid and illiquid financial assets, spill-over effects from other countries' housing markets and transactions costs. Liquid and illiquid financial assets proved insignificant and international spill-overs are of modest quantitative importance. The remaining parameters are highly significant and h_3 is estimated to be close to 2, implying a price elasticity of demand for housing of about −0.5. Without mortgage credit conditions and demography, it is impossible to find stable and coherent parameter estimates for the 1981–2016 period.

Figure 5.2 shows the log real house price indices for Paris and France. The relative price for Paris fell in the 1970s, rose in the 1980s, fell in the first half of the 1990s, and rose since the financial crisis. The 6-equation model in Chauvin and Muellbauer (2018) was extended by including a seventh equation for log real house prices in Paris incorporating the common latent credit conditions measure. Given data limitations, income and housing stock data[3] for the region around Paris, Île-de-France, to which the capital is closely linked with an extensive rail network, were

[3]Even so, data before 1991 are sparse with regional GDP data used to extrapolate household income data back and dummies used to pick up possible deviations between the regional and national housing stocks.

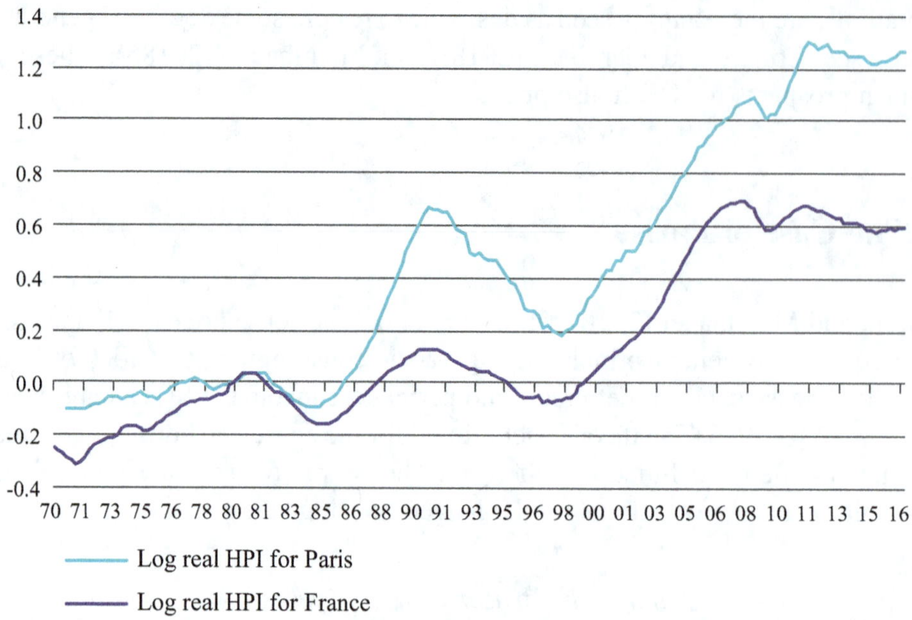

Source: OECD (2018) house price database for nominal house price index for France; INSEE (2018) for Paris price index for apartments, spliced in 1992 to Paris index from Friggit (2010). Both are deflated by the national accounts consumption deflator

Fig. 5.2 Log real house price indices for Paris and France

used for the Paris equation. The results can be summarised as follows: first, as for France, it is possible to accept the hypothesis of an income elasticity of one in the demand for housing, and liquid and illiquid assets are also insignificant. Second, regarding income per house, only that in Île-de-France matters in the long-run for Paris real house prices, with income per house in France being irrelevant. Third, nominal mortgage rates, mortgage credit conditions and a measure of risk all have substantially larger effects in Paris than they do for France. These results are consistent with higher levels of gearing needed to buy a house in Paris. Fourth, the coefficient on the lagged relative price of Paris to France is insignificant: as the discussion in Sect. 2 suggested, the sign is ambiguous since a substitution effect offsets a regional demand spill-over effect.

There are, however, major differences in short-term dynamics. The dynamic spill-over between Paris and France, measured by a weighted average of lagged 1 and 4 year rates of appreciation in Paris minus appreciation in France, is very significant. It captures a relative momentum or expectations effect: demand for Paris homes is higher if recent appreciation in Paris exceeds that in competing locations in France. An international spill-over goes in the opposite direction: it is measured as a weighted average of appreciation in the eight countries whose citizens are most represented in purchases of housing in France, minus appreciation in France. The interpretation is that citizens in those countries are able to invest some of their domestic housing gains in France, and Paris in particular. After monetary union, the size of this spill-over effect is higher.

To return to issues of financial stability, it is useful to consider the consumption estimates in Chauvin and Muellbauer (2018) for France during the house price boom between 1996 and 2008. These estimates suggest that the positive effects on consumption of higher housing wealth relative to income—a small but positive housing wealth effect—, and looser mortgage credit conditions, were largely offset by the negative effect of higher house prices and higher debt relative to income. France is therefore very different from the Anglo-Saxon economies where home equity loans produced large collateral effects of housing wealth on consumption. As a result, despite higher house prices, France did not experience an Anglo-Saxon-style consumption boom in which[4] the financial accelerator via home equity loans proved powerful and destabilising. Moreover, the induced increase in household debt will weigh negatively on future consumption.

The scale of extrapolative expectations in France is moderate. In Paris, it is also moderate, though there is also the momentum effect noted above by which recent appreciation in Paris relative to France feeds further appreciation. This can cause some overshooting of Paris prices and probably contributed to the subsequent greater decline in Paris home prices after 1991. In turn, this is likely to have been one factor in the rise in the proportion of non-performing bank loans in the mid-1990s, which is strongly correlated with mortgage credit conditions estimated by Chauvin and Muellbauer.

As is the case for France, the main potential downside risks in Paris come from higher interest rates, a renewed credit crunch and a downturn in real incomes given the background of a high level of French household debt relative to income. Of these, higher interest rates is the most relevant. If rates were to rise, and home prices fell, the rise in user cost would add to the downward pressure. The consumption equation for France, discussed in Chauvin and Muellbauer (2018), shows a substantial negative effect from real interest rates on housing and consumer loans, conditional on permanent and current income. Moreover, the estimated equation for permanent household income also shows a negative real interest rate effect, implying that aggregate demand in France is sensitive to higher real interest rates. Still, the absence of the amplifying feedback effect from house prices onto consumption, as found in the US and the UK, does limit the downside risks for France.

4 Conclusions

The evidence from the UK and France is that house prices in capital cities are more sensitive to interest rates and credit conditions. The upper ends of those capital city markets are also affected by international investment flows, which can create affordability problems for local residents and can divert residential construction

[4]As noted in Hendry and Muellbauer (2018), such effects were omitted in models, e.g. at the Bank of England and at the Federal Reserve.

away from homes for middle-income households. A decade of ultra-low interest rates has contributed to driving house prices in many OECD countries to levels exceeding the peaks reached before the global financial crisis. In many countries this has exacerbated generational divides, with the UK offering one of the most extreme examples. It seems probable that these divides have contributed to the rise of populism. After a period of deleveraging, household debt to income ratios have again risen strongly in many OECD countries. The road to 'normalisation' of interest rates remains a rocky one.

References

Abraham, J. M., & Hendershott, P. H. (1996). Bubbles in metropolitan housing markets. *Journal of Housing Research, 7*(2), 191–207.

Badarinza, C., & Ramadorai, T. (2018). Home away from home? Foreign demand and London house prices. *Journal of Financial Economics, 130*(3), 532–555.

Barros, C. P., Gil-Alana, L. A., & Payne, J. E. (2012). Comovements among U.S. state housing prices: Evidence from fractional cointegration. *Economic Modelling, 29*(3), 936–942.

Barten, A. P., & Bettendorf, L. J. (1989). Price formation of fish: An application of an inverse demand system. *European Economic Review, 33*, 1509–1525.

Cameron, G., & Muellbauer, J. (1998). The housing market and regional commuting and migration choices. *Scottish Journal of Political Economy, 54*, 420–446.

Cameron, G., Muellbauer, J., & Murphy, A. (2006a). *Housing market dynamics and regional migration in Britain* (discussion paper 5832). Centre for Economic Policy Research.

Cameron, G., Muellbauer, J., & Murphy, A. (2006b). *Was there a British house price bubble? Evidence from a regional panel* (discussion paper 5619). Centre for Economic Policy Research.

Capozza, D. R., Hendershott, P. H., & Mack, C. (2004). An anatomy of price dynamics in illiquid markets: Analysis and evidence from local housing markets. *Real Estate Economics, 32*(1), 1–32.

Cerutti, E., Dagher, J., & Dell'Ariccia, G. (2017). Housing finance and real estate booms: A cross-country perspective. *Journal of Housing Finance, 38*, 1–13.

Chauvin, V., & Muellbauer, J. (2018). Consumption, household portfolios, and the housing market in France. *Economie et Statistique/Economics and Statistics* (forthcoming).

Chiang, M.-C., & Tsai, I.-C. (2016). Ripple effect and contagious effect in the US regional housing markets. *Annals of Regional Science, 56*(1), 55–82.

Cook, S. (2003). The convergence of regional house prices in the UK. *Urban Studies, 40*(11), 2285–2294.

Cook, S. (2012). β-convergence and the cyclical dynamics of UK regional house prices. *Urban Studies, 49*(1), 203–218.

Cook, S., & Watson, D. (2015). A new perspective on the ripple effect in the UK housing market: Comovement, cyclical subsamples and alternative indices. *Urban Studies, 53*(14), 3048–3062.

Corlett, A., & Gardiner, L. (2018, March). *Home affairs: Options for reforming property taxation*. Resolution Foundation, Intergenerational Commission, pp. 1–66. https://www.resolutionfoundation.org/app/uploads/2018/03/Council-tax-IC.pdf

Deaton, A., & Muellbauer, J. (1980). *Economics and consumer behaviour*. Cambridge: Cambridge University Press.

Duca, J. V., Muellbauer, J., & Murphy, A. (2016). How mortgage finance reform could affect housing. *American Economic Review, 106*(5), 620–624.

Follain, J. R., & Velz, O. T. (1995). Incorporating the number of existing home sales into a structural model of the market for owner-occupied housing. *Journal of Housing Economics, 4*(2), 93–117.

Friggit, J. (2010). Le prix des logements sur le long terme, Conseil General de l'Environnement et du Développement Durable downloadable on http://www.cgedd.developpement-durable.gouv.fr/rubrique.php3?id_rubrique=138

Geanakoplos, J. (2009). The leverage cycle. In *NBER macroeconomics annual 2009* (Vol. 24, pp. 1–65). Chicago: University of Chicago Press.

Glaeser, E., Gyourko, J., & Saiz, A. (2008). Housing supply and housing bubbles. *Journal of Urban Economics, 64*(2), 198–217.

Green, R. K., Malpezzi, S., & Mayo, S. K. (2005). Metropolitan-specific estimates of the price elasticity of supply of housing, and their sources. *American Economic Review, 95*(2), 334–339.

Gupta, R., & Miller, S. M. (2010). 'Ripple Effects' and forecasting home prices in Los Angeles, Las Vegas, and phoenix. *Annals of Regional Science, 48*(3), 763–782.

Gupta, R., & Miller, S. M. (2012). The time series properties of house prices: A case study of the Southern California market. *Journal of Real Estate Finance and Economics, 44*(3), 339–361.

Hendry, D. F., & Muellbauer, J. N. J. (2018). The future of macroeconomic models: Macro theory and models at the Bank of England. *Oxford Review of Economic Policy, 34*(1/2), 287–328.

Holmes, M., Otero, J., & Panagiotidis, T. (2011). Investigating regional house price convergence in the United States: Evidence from a pair-wise approach. *Economic Modelling, 28*(6), 2369–2376.

Hwang, M., & Quigley, J. M. (2006). Economic fundamentals in local housing markets: Evidence from U.S. Metropolitan regions. *Journal of Regional Science, 46*(3), 425–453.

INSEE. (2018). *Price index of second-hand dwellings – Paris – Flats*. Accessed April 1, 2018, from https://www.insee.fr/en/statistiques/serie/010567012

Knight Frank. (2018). *Prime London sales index – March 2018*. Accessed April 1, 2018, from https://www.knightfrank.com/research/prime-central-london-sales-index-march-2018-5389.aspx

Lonres. Accessed April 1, 2018, from https://www.lonres.com/

Malpezzi, S. (1996). Housing prices, externalities, and regulation in U.S. Metropolitan areas. *Journal of Housing Research, 7*(2), 209–241.

Meen, G. (1999). Regional house prices and the ripple effect: A new interpretation. *Housing Studies, 14*(6), 733–753.

Muellbauer, J. (2012). When is a housing market overheated enough to threaten stability?, RBA Annual Conference Volume. In A. Heath, F. Packer, & C. Windsor (Eds.), *Property markets and financial stability*. Sydney: Reserve Bank of Australia.

Muellbauer, J. (2018a). The future of central banking: Festschrift in honour of Vítor Constâncio, May 2018. https://www.ecb.europa.eu/pub/pdf/other/ecb.futurecentralbankingcolloquium constancio201812.en.pdf

Muellbauer, J. (2018b, December). Housing, debt and the economy: A tale of two countries. *National Institute Economic Review, 245*, 20–33.

OECD. (2018). *Residential Property Price Indicators (RPPIs) – Headline Indicators*. Accessed April 1, 2018, from https://stats.oecd.org/Index.aspx?DataSetCode=HOUSE_PRICES

Office of National Statistics. (2018). *House price index*. Accessed April 1, 2018, from http://landregistry.data.gov.uk/app/ukhpi

Oikarinen, E. S., Bourassa, C., Hoesli, M., & Engblom, J. (2018). *U.S. Metropolitan house price dynamics*. https://www.aeaweb.org/conference/2018/preliminary/paper/kdr799FS

Teye, A. L., Knoppel, M., de Haan, J., & Elsinga, M. G. (2017). Amsterdam house price ripple effects in The Netherlands. *Journal of European Real Estate Research, 10*(3), 331–345.

Theil, H. (1976). *Theory and measurement of consumer demand* (Vol. II). Amsterdam: North-Holland Publishing Company.

Turner, A. (2009, March). The Turner review: A regulatory response to the global banking crisis. *Financial Services Authority.*

Chapter 6
Towards a Global Real Estate Market? Trends and Evidence

Laurent Clerc

1 Introduction

Several central banks and international institutions have recently ranked the risk of a snapback in interest rates at the top of their financial risk assessment. To some extent, the current situation presents some similarities with the period that preceded the global financial crisis of 2007–2008. In particular, it has been characterised in many countries by a sharp increase in residential house prices for almost 10 years, at a time when household debt levels are already high and certain countries have not yet completed the deleveraging process begun in the aftermath of the crisis. A sudden tightening of financial conditions could thus result in a strong decline in house prices and a significant increase in defaults in the household sector.

The dynamics of housing markets are a crucial determinant of financial stability as house price booms are generally closely related to credit and monetary developments and thus to financial firms' balance sheets. Historical evidence indeed shows that a significant number of banking crises were preceded by the bursting of house price bubbles (Reinhart and Rogoff 2008).

Over the past few years, there has been an increasing focus on the globalisation of financial markets, and more recently on housing markets. There is already compelling evidence that capital flows resulted in inflationary pressures and asset price booms in Latin America in the 1980s and 1990s, in emerging Asia in the late 1990s and, more recently, in the run-up to the financial crisis. Attention has now shifted to

The views expressed in this paper are those of the author and do not necessarily reflect the position of the ACPR, the Banque de France or the Eurosystem.

L. Clerc (✉)
Autorité de Controle prudentiel et de résolution, Direction d'étude et d'analyse des risques, Paris, France
e-mail: laurent.clerc2@acpr.banque-france.fr

R. Nijskens et al. (eds.), *Hot Property*, https://doi.org/10.1007/978-3-030-11674-3_6

the role of global financial conditions, and in particular of US monetary policy, in shaping asset price developments, and in particular house prices.

The idea that housing markets are exposed to the global economy is not completely new, but the evidence has mainly centred on "world" or "global" cities. These cities are hubs in a global network where global control functions are produced by global companies in core financial, business and economic activities.

In this paper, I analyse the extent to which the process of financial globalisation has become generalised and has been playing a role in the recent dynamics of housing markets. I find some evidence of increased synchronisation across housing markets for a sample of 18 OECD countries. The evidence is particularly clear for the period that preceded the financial crisis and points to a growing role of global financial conditions. However, national housing market characteristics tied to financial contracts, fiscal incentives and housing supply continue to play a significant role in shaping house price cycles, in particular their amplitude. As a result, national authorities still have significant leeway to insulate their housing markets from global fluctuations, in particular thanks to macroprudential policy.

The rest of the paper is organised as follows. Section 2 provides some evidence of the increasing role played by global factors in explaining the synchronicity of housing cycles across countries and large cities. Section 3 shows that the domestic structural features of housing markets remain important and explain some differences across countries, in particular regarding the dynamics and amplitude of housing cycles. Section 4 concludes by looking at the policy implications and the role of macroprudential policy in preventing systemic risks stemming from housing markets.

2 The Increasing Synchronicity in House Prices Across Countries

2.1 Towards a Global Real Estate Market...?

Figure 6.1 shows the developments and the trends in real house prices in 18 OECD countries since 1975. Several stylised facts emerge.

1. Real house prices have generally increased over the period 1975–2018. In most countries, prices have at least doubled if not tripled in real terms, with a couple of countries, such as the United Kingdom and Ireland, experiencing even sharper increases (five to six fold).[1]
2. Only four countries out of 18 have experienced declining trends over the period: Germany, where real house prices fell steadily in the aftermath of German

[1]In most cases, I estimated exponential trends and used polynomial trends for Spain, Sweden and Switzerland.

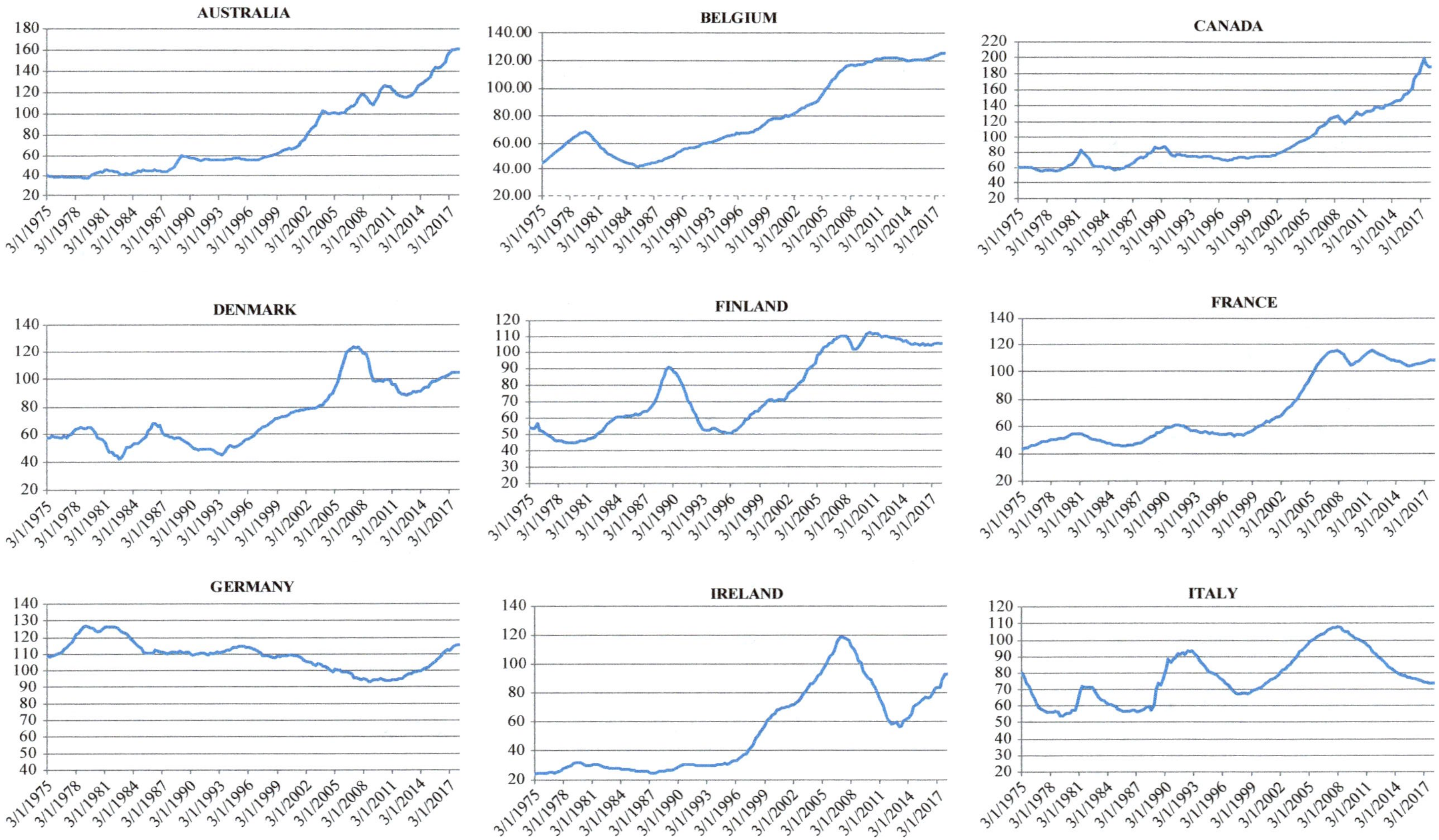

Fig. 6.1 Real house price indices and trends for a set of OECD countries

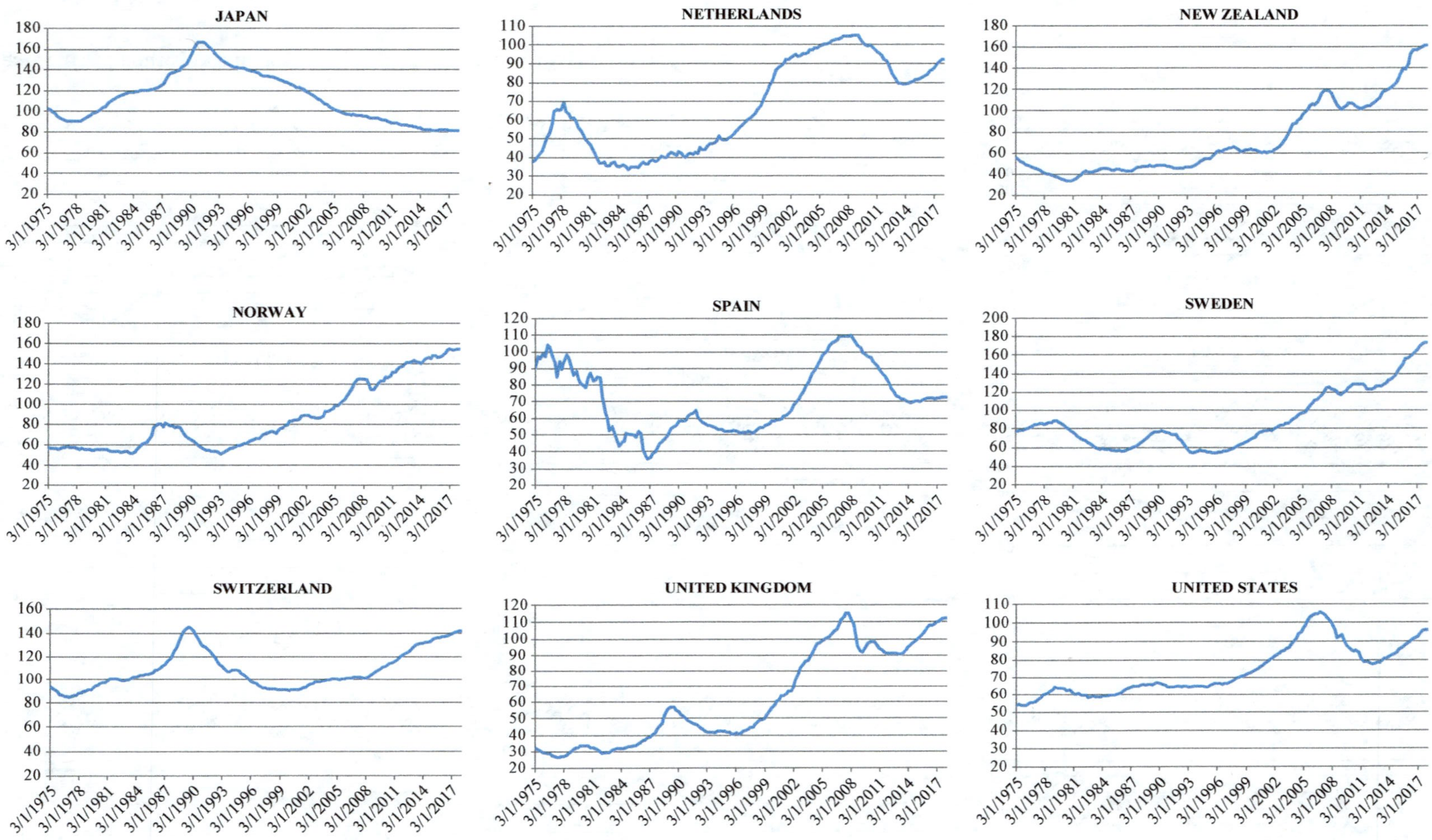

Source: Bank for International Settlements (2018a), Dallas Federal Reserve (2018) and Exponential or Polynomial trends in dotted lines (author's calculation)

Fig. 6.1 (continued)

reunification and have picked up significantly only recently; Japan, which experienced a massive housing bubble from 1977 to 1991, and has not yet recovered from the bursting of that bubble; Sweden and Spain, which began the period with a significant correction in real house prices, before experiencing sharp increases in the mid-1990s: the increase has held steady so far in Sweden, but proved unsustainable in Spain, which experienced a second dramatic price correction that is still ongoing.

3. Beyond these overall upward trends, several housing cycles can be observed, which differ in terms of frequency. The number of peaks is 3 for half of the countries over the sample period; 5 countries experienced more frequent cycles (Australia, New Zealand and Sweden have the highest frequencies, followed by France and Canada).
4. Some countries have seen only one or two housing cycles over the period, which have proved costly and destabilising for their economies, as in the case of Japan, Switzerland, Ireland and the Netherlands.
5. The amplitude of the housing cycles also differs across countries. Using the de-trended series to extract the cycle component, the amplitude measured by the standard deviation of this cycle component relative to the trend is huge for some countries: for instance, for Ireland and the Netherlands, it is greater than 25%, while for Spain and Japan it is higher than or close to 20%.
6. Despite this heterogeneity across countries, the boom episode starting in the mid-1990s is common to almost all countries, with the exception of Germany and Japan. It is also far more pronounced than previous booms, and significantly longer, ending almost everywhere with a sharp correction in real house prices, in around 2007 or 2008, that is to say almost 10–15 years after it started. This synchronicity both in the emergence of the bubble and its bursting provides initial evidence of the role played by global common factors in shaping house price dynamics.

To better characterise this synchronicity across countries, I compute diffusion indices (see Fig. 6.2). First, exploiting the persistence of house price developments, I compute indicator variables for each country, which take the value 1 if the quarterly increase in house prices is strictly positive and the value 0 otherwise. I then sum up these indicator variables across countries for each date to generate a time series. The corresponding index is presented in panel a) of Fig. 6.2. It shows the number of countries simultaneously experiencing a quarterly increase in real house prices at a given date.

Four real house price cycles show up in the data, a first one ending in 1981, a second ending in 1992, a third ending in 2008, and a last one which is still ongoing. These cycles are characterised by the following features:

First, housing booms tend to develop gradually and spread across countries, with almost all countries in the sample experiencing at some point similar periods of real price increases (up to 17 countries out of 18 at peaks). The current ongoing episode, which is tending to stabilise, seems less widespread than the two previous ones, but has already lasted for 10 years.

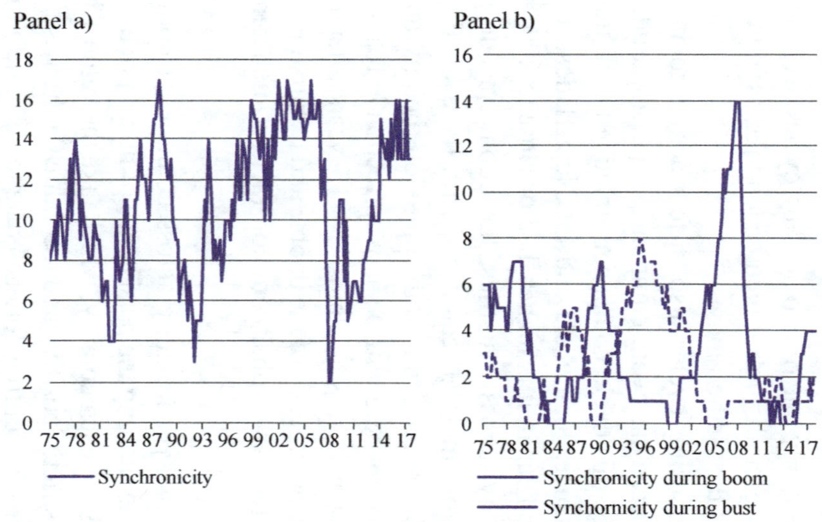

Source: Bank for International Settlements (2018a), Dallas Federal Reserve (2018) and Exponential or Polynomial trends in dotted lines (author's calculation)

Fig. 6.2 Synchronicity in real house price developments

Second, the length of the episodes tends to increase over the sample period, with the one preceding the global financial crisis proving particularly long.

Third, these cycles tend to be asymmetric, with the periods of price increases generally lasting significantly longer than the periods of decrease. The latter tend in addition to be abrupt and huge, as in 2008 where the fall in real house prices occurred almost simultaneously in all sample countries (except 2).

Panel b) of Fig. 6.2 provides additional information on the amplitude of housing cycles in particular in periods of booms and busts. I compute time diffusion indices for each country, which take the value 1 when de-trended real house prices exceed their historical trend by more than one standard deviation (characterising "boom periods") or are more than one standard deviation below trend ("bust periods"). I then sum up these variables across countries, disentangling "boom" and "bust" periods.

Starting with "booms", Fig. 6.2 panel b) highlights the singularity of the episode preceding the financial crisis. Whereas the two previous cycles as well as the current one tend to involve a relatively limited set of countries, the one starting in the mid-1990s affected almost all sample countries (14 out of the 18 experienced a simultaneous "boom" period). Using a more stringent definition of excessive real house prices (that is a gap of more than 2 times the standard deviation) roughly halves the number of countries simultaneously experiencing a boom (to around 3 or 4 countries, usually), but there were nonetheless 8 countries in that situation in the run-up to the financial crisis.

Turning to "bust" periods, a different picture emerges. Fig. 6.2 panel b) shows in particular that the immediate period following the bursting of a housing bubble is characterised by very different patterns across countries. Here again, the episode ending in 2008 stands out and illustrates the variety of policy responses and their impact on real price developments across countries.

2.2 ... *Or the Growing Importance of World Cities?*

Housing markets are notoriously heterogeneous at the national level, with prices generally proving higher in big cities due to a combination of lack of space and migration towards those areas where economic and financial activities are located. One question that arises is the extent to which house price developments at the country level reflect the role of big cities, in particular capitals, in shaping price dynamics. In addition, big cities are more likely to be influenced by global factors due to their global connections and their greater exposure to financial globalisation.

The influence and role of big cities are nothing new in history and geography. In Medieval Europe, for instance, large trade centres were already highly interconnected, as companies generally operated in foreign cities where they did business via trusted agents—usually family members (Taylor 2016). Those links were even further formalised through explicit commercial agreements as in the case of the Hanseatic cities up to 1648. Historians like Braudel (1984) and Wallerstein (1974) trace a first wave of globalisation during the 1450–1650 period, with the emergence of "world-empires" (see for instance Wallerstein 1974) and where the connections between cities stemmed from different forms of monopolistic control of production, trade and finance. A second wave of globalisation was triggered by the expansion of European countries that culminated at the end of the nineteenth century, a period known as "European imperialism". According to Taylor (2016), this globalisation process was accompanied by an unprecedented shift towards urbanisation, with big cities being "a crucial focus of the infrastructure enabling the new globalisation that included railways and telegraphs within countries and steam shipping and ocean cable networks between countries worldwide". A third wave of globalisation took place after World War II, with the expansion of multinational corporations mostly led by American firms.

Table 6.1 presents some selected statistics and rankings for capitals or big cities for a range of indicators illustrating economic or financial activity and quality of life.

For instance, the Global Financial Centres Index (GFCI) is a ranking of the competitiveness of financial centres based on over 29,000 financial centre assessments. The ranking is an aggregate of indices from five key areas: "Business environment", "Financial sector development", "Infrastructure factors", "Human capital", "Reputation and general factors". It is comparable to the ATKearney index, which ranks cities according to 5 areas: "Business activity", "Human capital", "Information and Exchange", "Cultural experience" and "Political engagement". An additional dimension is captured by the Mercer's Quality of Living ranking which establishes a ranking of the most liveable cities in the world, taking into account soft factors like the quality of leisure time or cultural diversity but also easy access to transportation, reliable electricity or drinkable water. This index is supposed to play an important role when multinationals decide where to establish locations abroad and send expatriate workers.

The table also includes Airbnb listings. Airbnb is the most popular supplier of home sharing on peer-to-peer markets. Empirical evidence suggests that an increase in listings is associated with an increase in both rents and house prices, the latter being in addition larger than the former (see for instance Barron et al. 2017). Home-sharing platforms would cause landlords to switch from supplying the market for long-term rentals to supplying the short-term market. Occupancy tax avoidance would be another reason for the development of home sharing platforms.

Finally, the table is completed with an index computed by the Gottlieb Duttweiller Institute (2017) which attempts to rank cities according to their connections in the digital world (based on the total number of connections on English Wikipedia, Twitter feeds and the World Wide Web as accessed by Google), while the last column provides a measure of capital flows or international investment for the top 10 cities in the world.

These indicators are compared to changes in real house prices during the period 2013 and 2017 (column 1) and to the UBS Global Real Estate Index which gauges the risk of a property bubble according to the pattern of indicators accounting for the

Table 6.1 Selected statistics and indicators on world cities

	Real house prices: Av. annual growth rate (2013–2017)	UBS real estate bubble index	GFCI ranks 2018	ATKearney global cities ranks 2017	Mercer index 2018	AirBnb listings	Twitter-Wikipedia-Web (rank)	International investment (number top 10 cities)
Auckland	10.8	–	–	–	3	208	–	–
Sydney	10.4	1.80[a]	9	17	10	29,935	19	121
London	8.5	1.77[a]	1	2	41	60,371	4	390
Oslo	8.5	–	55	–	25	641	–	–
Stockholm	7.7	2.01[a]	42	–	23	380	21	–
Copenhagen	7.3	–	58	–	9	7	20	–
Dublin	6.2	–	31	–	34	7209	16	132
Amsterdam	5.8	1.59[a]	50	22	12	16,691	52	124
Berlin	5.4	–	–	14	13	22,411	2	–
Tokyo	3.5	0.90	5	4	50	1577	8	112
Toronto	3.1	2.12[a]	7	16	16	13,456	10	114
Zurich	3.0	1.08	16	–	2	341	68	–
Brussels	2.3	–	62	11	27	6882	9	–
New York	1.9	0.20	2	1	45	49,747	5	156
Madrid	1.5	–	41	13	49	14,766	7	–
Helsinki	−0.8	–	85		32	157	–	–
Paris	−1.2	1.31	24	3	39	62,607	1	338
Rome	−4.2	–	65		57	18,251	38	–
Correlation with HP increases (col.1)	–	−0.36	−0.29	0.35	−0.60	−0.13	−0.05	−0.12
Correlation with UBS index (col. 2)	–	–	0.87	0.76	−0.36	−0.15	0.25	0.65

Sources: ATKearney (2017), BIS (2018a), Dallas Fed (2018), UBS (2017), IMF (2018), Mercer (2018), Global Financial Centres Index (2018), Gottlieb Duttweiller Institute (2017) and AirBnB

[a]Indicates that a bubble risk exists according to UBS (index >1.5); (author's calculation)

decoupling of local prices from local incomes and rents, or indications of excessive lending and construction activity.

While the ranking of cities is not necessarily fully consistent across the board, the table first reveals that the big cities in our sample countries almost all belong to the top world cities according to various criteria, with a significant number featuring in the top 20. Second, these rankings are usually not related to the size of the city. The different indicators make it clear that capitals or big cities belong to a network of highly interconnected cities.

The link between these different indicators and the average real house price growth rate over the period 2013–2017 is not clear and the correlation coefficients are not fully consistent across the board. By contrast, all of these indicators are highly and positively correlated with the UBS bubble index, but the Mercer index, which is expected as excessive house prices may deteriorate the quality of live in a specific city. Finally, we do not find evidence of a positive correlation between Airbnb listings and price developments or the UBS bubble index in our sample.

Figure 6.3 provides additional information by comparing real house price developments in these big cities to the developments taking place in their respective countries. The figure shows that real house prices at the city level tend to evolve in line with real prices observed at the country level, with a tendency to overshoot, sometimes significantly, national developments, as in Amsterdam, where house prices overshoot the average price increase in the Netherlands by a factor of 15.

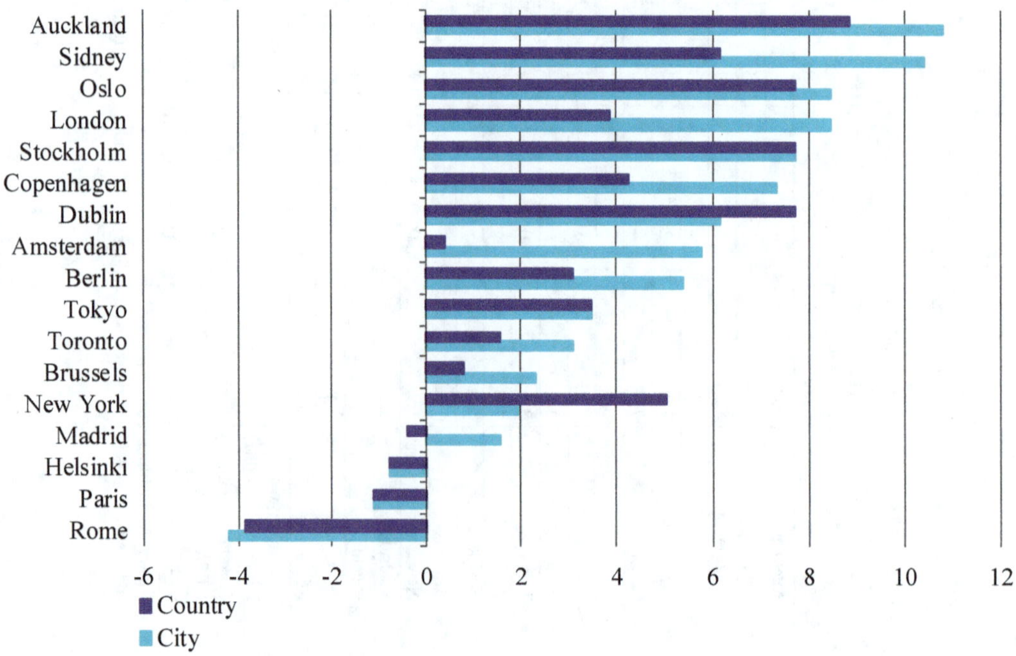

Source: International Monetary Fund (2018)

Fig. 6.3 Average annual real house price growth in top cities and their respective countries

3 House Price Determinants

3.1 Synchronicity: The Role of Global Factors

In a previous paper with Borgy et al. (2014), I explored the ability of a system of early indicators to detect ex-ante the build-up of financial imbalances, in particular in housing markets, for a similar set of OECD countries. The three most robust and powerful early warning indicators to detect costly[2] real house price booms are real interest rates (both short and long) and real stock prices. These indicators can be combined into financial conditions indices. These variables, in particular long-term rates and stock prices are particularly influenced by global factors.

The increasing synchronisation of global financial cycles has received a lot of attention over the past 3 years. In a seminal contribution, Miranda-Agrippino and Rey (2015) demonstrated the existence of a common movement in global asset prices in international equity and bond markets.

Rey (2015) highlights in particular the central role played by US monetary policy which tends to spread through the financial system by impacting on the balance sheets of global banks, which in turn affects credit conditions and developments in credit supply.

Extending this approach to housing markets, Luo and Ma (2017) find that, for an average country, the implied global housing market risk premium is the most important determinant of housing market volatility, especially in the period preceding the financial crisis in 2007–2008. This global premium appears to be strongly influenced by US monetary policy, both through the risk-taking and the credit channels.

This evidence is shared by the recent IMF *Global Financial Stability Report* (2018), which devotes its Chap. 3 to house price synchronisation and finds that global financial conditions provide a convincing explanation for the synchronicity of housing markets, both at the city and country levels.

Figure 6.4 shows the evolution of the financial conditions indices provided by the IMF since 1991 for most sample countries. As can be seen, while financial conditions may vary across countries, their pattern is very similar and closely mirrors that of the US financial conditions index. Comparing Figs. 6.2 and 6.4 also makes it clear that favourable or accommodative financial conditions tend to be associated with periods of house price increases and booms, while the tightening of these financial conditions is concomitant with house price decreases or even busts, as can be seen in particular around 2007 and 2008.

Figure 6.4 also shows that the volatility of financial conditions indices differs significantly across countries. The first panel, which displays the highest volatility across countries, consists mostly of Anglo-Saxon countries.

---

[2]Costly booms refer to booms in real estate prices which are followed by severe recessions, that is periods of at least 3 years in which overall real GDP growth was at least 3% points lower than potential output growth.

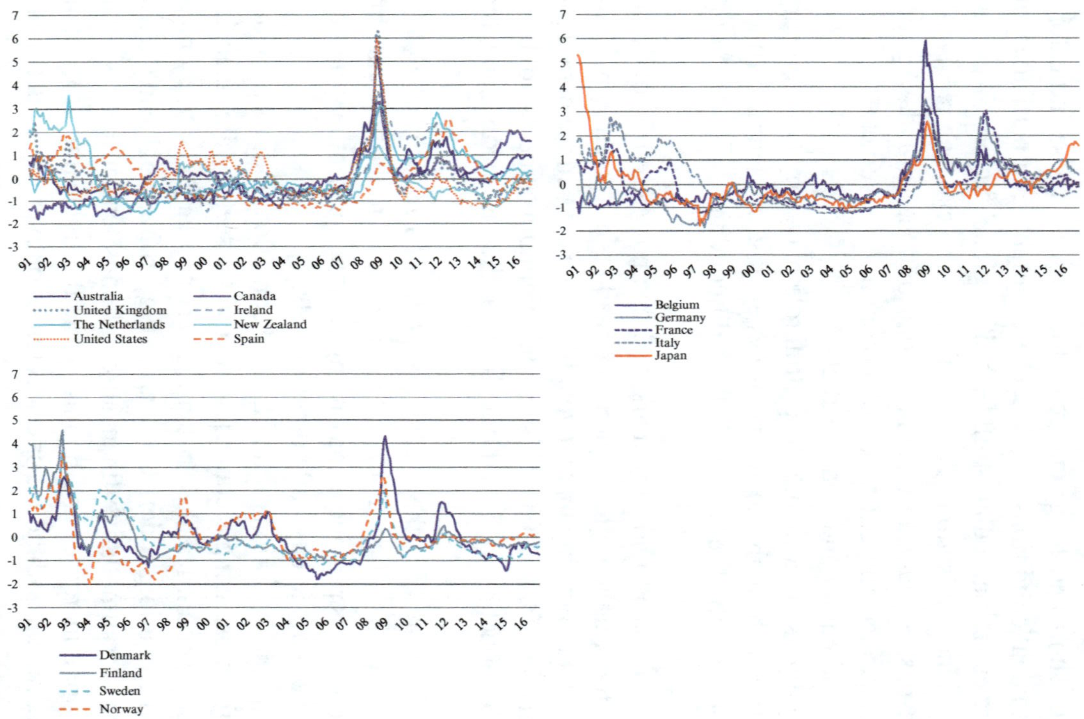

Source: International Monetary Fund (2017)

Fig. 6.4 Financial conditions indices in OECD countries

The housing markets in these countries share similar features, in particular the ability of households to cash in their mortgage equity, which can alleviate their credit constraints. The top-right panel, which groups together continental Europe and Japan, is characterised by an absence of mortgage equity withdrawals and in general the dominance of fixed mortgage rates. The variation is lower than in the previous set of Anglo-Saxon countries. Finally, the bottom left panel groups together certain Nordic countries which all experienced a severe housing market correction at the beginning of the 1990s, and which tend to behave similarly over the sample period, again with less variation across countries than in the first group.

These differences in developments tend to emphasise the role of domestic features as amplifiers of house price dynamics.

3.2 *Local Amplifiers*

National features, related to the nature of financial contracts, fiscal incentives and housing supply, play a very important role in determining the functioning of housing markets. Table 6.2 presents selected national market characteristics.

A first important feature differentiating countries is the existence of mortgage equity withdrawals (MEW) that is the possibility for households to cash in their

Table 6.2 Selected national housing market characteristics

	SDEV house price cycle	MEW	Refinancing (fee free repayment)	Prevailing type of interest rate	Max LTV	Typical term to maturity
Australia	10.5	Yes	Limited	Variable	100	25
Belgium	16.6	No	No	Fixed	100	20
Canada	14.3	Yes	No	Mixed	95	25
Denmark	18.0	Yes	Yes	Mixed	80	30
Finland	15.6	Yes	No	Variable	80	20
France	14.2	No	No	Fixed	100	20
Germany	5.7	No	No	Fixed	80	15
Ireland	29.1	Limited	No	Mixed	100	40
Italy	15.2	No	No	Variable	80	22
Japan	19.5	No	No	Mixed	80	30
Netherlands	25.4	Yes	Yes	Fixed	125 to 100	30
New Zealand	17.4	Yes	–	Variable	85	30
Norway	15.0	Yes	No	Variable	85	20
Spain	24.0	Limited	No	Variable	100	20
Sweden	11.4	Yes	Yes	Variable	95	45
Switzerland	13.9	Yes	–	Fixed	80	20
UK	16.6	Yes	Limited	Variable	110	25
US	9.4	Yes	Yes	Mixed	100	30

Source: Cerutti et al. (2017) and ESRB (2015)

mortgage equity. This is an important mechanism through which the financial accelerator mechanisms, highlighted by Bernanke et al. (1999) or Kiyotaki and Moore (1997), can be activated and feed boom-bust dynamics.

With such a mechanism in place, households can relax their borrowing constraints and increase their consumption spending, in particular to improve their house's value, in periods of house price booms. Using the value of their house as collateral, they can borrow more and further relax their borrowing constraints. Such a mechanism is absent in countries where the value of the house is based on historical costs in debt contracts.

In the sample, for countries where MEW is possible, the amplitude of the cycle is on average 3% points greater than in countries where it is not implemented.

The third column shows whether or not it is possible to refinance housing debt in each particular country without incurring a fee. This facility in not widespread and tends to play a limited role. However, the low level of interest rates that has resulted from very accommodative monetary policies across the world, coupled with fierce competition amongst lenders, have dramatically reduced these fees, allowing households to massively renegotiate the terms of their mortgage contracts in the recent period, at little or no cost.

Column 4 shows the prevailing type of interest rate in mortgage debt contracts. It links mortgage rates to key short-term interest rates in economies where these mortgage rates are adjustable, and to long-term interest rates where they are fixed. Some countries propose mixed mortgage rates where the mortgage rate is fixed for the first few years and adjustable for the rest of the term. In recent years, the very low level of interest rates has generally led households to lock into fixed interest rate debt contracts. In our sample countries, adjustable rates remain dominant in countries with MEW.

Maximum observed LTV, in column 5, refers to the country-specific upper LTV limit (in general legal limits). They can serve as a proxy for borrowing constraints (especially for new borrowers). Most countries are in the 70–80 and 90–100 LTV buckets. High LTV limits tend to be associated with deeper mortgage markets but may also result in increased risks, in particular when they are associated with excessively rapid house-price and credit growth in boom periods.

Finally, the term to maturity (column 6) is on average around 25 years in our sample, although in some countries, such as Ireland and Sweden, it is over 40 years. Such high terms may reflect differences in home affordability.

The interaction between these various structural and local features should lead to very different economic patterns in both the borrowing capacity of households and the resilience of housing markets.

Regarding household debt, Fig. 6.5 clearly shows a significant difference between, on the one hand, countries where households can cash in their mortgage equity, where interest rates are mostly adjustable and LTV ratios are high (Anglo-Saxon and Nordic countries), and on the other continental European countries where debt levels are significantly lower. The difference is particularly striking in the

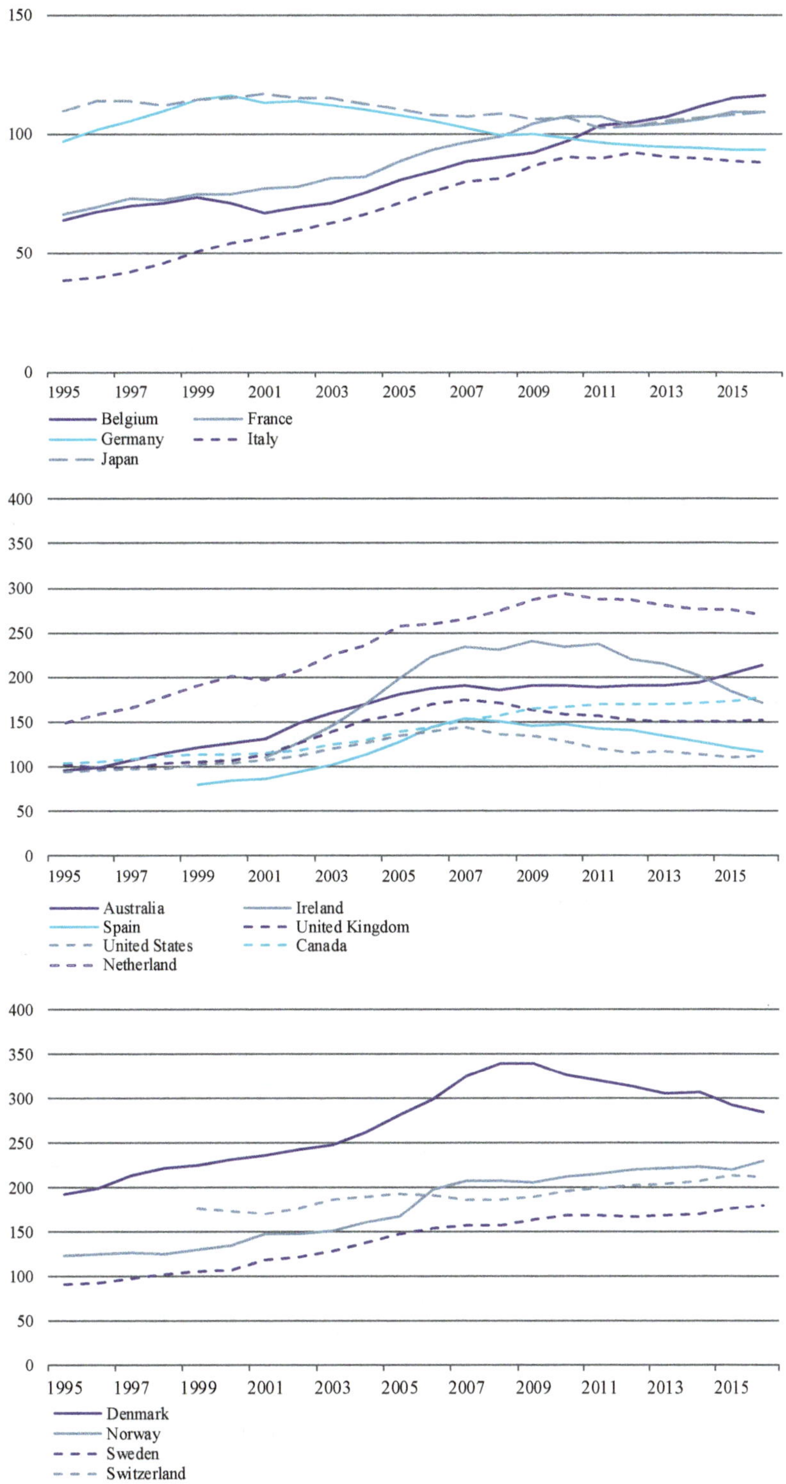

Source: OECD (2018a)

Fig. 6.5 Household debt as a percentage of net disposable income

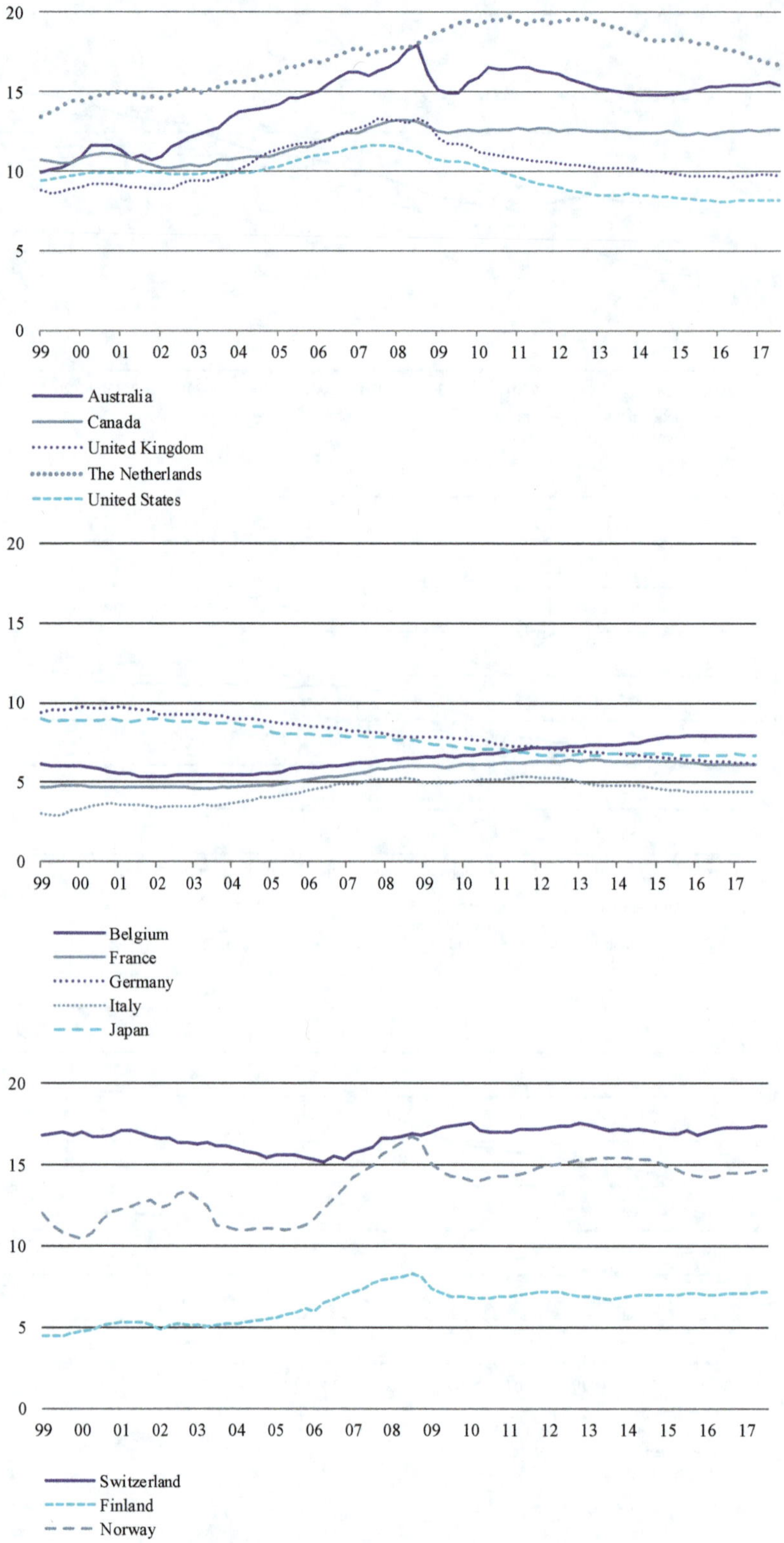

Source: Bank for International Settlements (2018b)

Fig. 6.6 Debt service ratios for the household sector

run-up to the crisis, less so afterwards, due to the deleveraging process that took place in many countries in the first group.

Similar conclusions can be drawn from the developments in debt service ratios presented in Fig. 6.6, both in terms of debt-service levels and dynamics. Continental European countries are characterised by significantly lower debt service ratios. Here again, the predominance of fixed mortgage rates, which are generally associated with lower LTV limits and a limited ability for households to relax their borrowing constraints, has certainly contained the house price boom while at the same time maintaining the resilience of the household sector. However, the incentives to deleverage have certainly been reduced and have led to a continuous increase in the debt level of households in countries such as France or Belgium, which could lead at some point to concerns regarding their sustainability.

4 Policy Implications

The low level of interest rates and the very favourable financial conditions have renewed financial stability concerns. In several countries, a decoupling can clearly be seen between house prices on the one hand and rents and income on the other.

Figures 6.7 and 6.8 respectively show changes in price-to-rent and price-to-income ratios over time and across countries. While the general trend is that of an increase in the price-to-rent ratio and a decrease in the price-to-income ratio, several countries are experiencing a sharp increase in both ratios, notably Australia, Canada, New Zealand, Norway and Sweden.

Real house prices in these countries are well above historical levels, and are also currently growing much faster than their long-term trend. In addition, house prices in their big cities are overshooting national developments. In all of these countries, household debt, which was already fairly high, has been increasing steadily and the pace of growth has even accelerated in Australia.

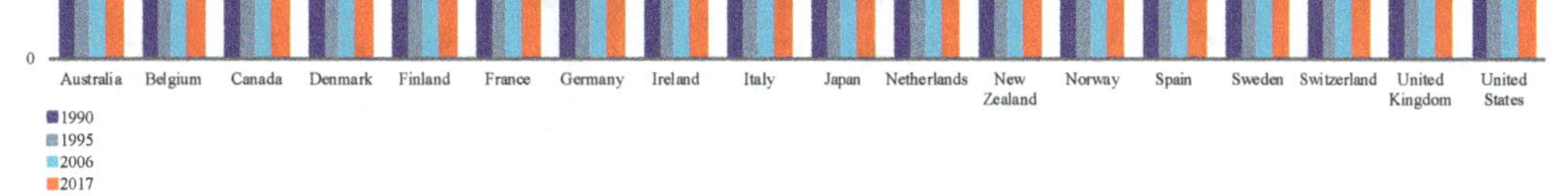

Source: OECD (2018b)

Fig. 6.7 Price-to-rent ratios in selected OECD countries

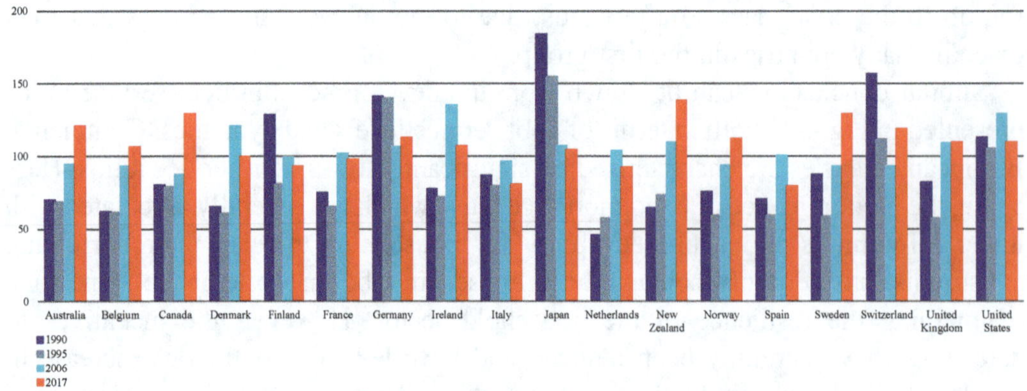

Source: OECD (2018b)

Fig. 6.8 Price-to-income ratios in selected OECD countries

Despite the increasing synchronicity in housing cycles at the global level, the fact that domestic structural features continue to play a significant role in shaping house price dynamics and explain the differences observed in the amplitude of housing cycles is reassuring for national authorities.

It means that they still have some leeway both to counteract cyclical developments in their housing markets and to insulate their economies from global financial shocks by resorting to active macroprudential policies. Sweden and Norway have already activated their countercyclical buffers, while other countries have tightened their LTV limits (Finland, Ireland, Netherlands and Norway) or their loan-to-income limits, as in the UK. Alternatively, Canada started to increase its key policy rates last year without resorting, as yet, to macroprudential policy to contain credit expansion.

This last example points to the fact that macroprudential policy can be used in coordination with other policies: monetary policy, which can affect domestic financial conditions and curb credit growth; and fiscal policies, with the removal of fiscal incentives associated with mortgage debt or the adoption of fiscal policies to encourage housing supply. The value added of macroprudential policy in this context is not only that it can be used to "lean against the wind" but also that it can increase the resilience of financial institutions by raising their loss absorption capacity or reducing their exposure to risky borrowers. It also allows for a more targeted policy.

References

Airbnb. Accessed April 1, 2018, from https://www.airbnb.com/

ATKearney. (2017). *Global cities 2017: Leaders in a world of disruptive innovations*.

Bank for International Settlements. (2018a). *Residential property prices*. Accessed April 1, 2018, from https://www.bis.org/statistics/pp_selected.htm?m=6%7C288%7C596

Bank for International Settlements. (2018b). *Debt service ratios for the private non-financial sector*. Accessed April 1, 2018, from https://www.bis.org/statistics/dsr.htm

Barron, K., Kung, E., & Proserpio, D. (2017, October 20). *The sharing economy and housing affordability: Evidence from Airbnb* (NBER working paper).

Bernanke, B., Gertler, M., & Gilchrist, S. (1999). The financial accelerator in a quantitative business cycle framework. In J. B. Taylor & M. Woodford (Eds.), *Handbook of macroeconomics* (Vol. 1, pp. 1341–1393). Amsterdam: Elsevier.

Borgy, V., Clerc, L., & Renne, J.-P. (2014). Measuring aggregate risk: Can we robustly identify asset-price boom-bust cycles? *Journal of Banking and Finance, 46*, 132–150.

Braudel, F. (1984). *The perspective of the world*. London: Collins.

Cerutti, E., Dagher, J., & Dell'Ariccia, G. (2017). Housing finance and real-estate booms: A cross-country perspective. *Journal of Housing Economics, 38*, 1–13.

Dallas Federal Reserve. (2018). Accessed April 1, 2018, from https://fred.stlouisfed.org/release?rid=171

European Systemic Risk Board. (2015, December). *Report on residential real estate and financial stability in the EU.*

Global Financial Centres Index. (2018). *The global financial centres index 23*. London: Long Finance.

Gottlieb Duttweiller Institute. (2017). *Global city index 2017: The most connected cities.*

International Monetary Fund. (2017, April). Are countries losing control of domestic financial conditions? *Global Financial Stability Report*, Chapter 3, Annex 3.1.

International Monetary Fund. (2018, April). House price synchronization: What role for financial factors? *Global Financial Stability Report*, Chapter 3.

Kiyotaki, N., & Moore, J. (1997). Credit cycles. *Journal of Political Economy, 105*(2), 211–248.

Luo, S., & Ma, J. (2017). *Global housing markets and monetary policy spillovers: Evidence from OECD countries* (Working Paper).

Mercer. (2018). *Quality of living rankings 2017*. Accessed April 1, 2018, from https://mobilityexchange.mercer.com/Insights/quality-of-living-rankings

Miranda-Agrippino, S., & Rey, H. (2015). *World asset markets and the global financial cycle*. NBER Working Paper N° 21722.

OECD. (2018a). *Household debt*. Accessed April 1, 2018, from https://data.oecd.org/hha/household-debt.htm

OECD. (2018b). *House price indicators*. Accessed April 1, 2018, from https://stats.oecd.org/Index.aspx?DataSetCode=HOUSE_PRICES

Reinhart, C., & Rogoff, K. S. (2008, December). *Banking crises: An equal opportunity menace*. NBER Working Paper N° 14587.

Rey, H. (2015). Dilemma not trilemma: The global financial cycle and monetary policy independence. *IMF Review, 64*(1), 6–35.

Taylor, P. J. (2016). Geohistory of globalisation. *Protosociology, 33*, 131–148.

UBS. (2017). *UBS global real estate bubble index.*

Wallerstein, I. (1974). *The modern world system*. New York: Academic Press.

Chapter 7
Managing House Price Booms: Evolution of IMF Surveillance and Policy Advice

Hites Ahir and Prakash Loungani

1 Introduction

In April 2008, the IMF's flagship publication *World Economic Outlook* provided estimates of overvaluation in house prices for a group of advanced economies. Though house prices had fallen in the United States in the preceding years, they had continued to rise in many other countries. The IMF's analysis suggested that, with only a few exceptions, house prices were overvalued by between 10% and 30%, as shown by the bars in Fig. 7.1. The dots show the decline in house prices that occurred over the subsequent 4 years. In many countries where the IMF had assessed house prices to be overvalued, house prices did indeed fall quite significantly—these cases include Denmark, Ireland, the Netherlands and the United Kingdom.

Fast forward to the present: The IMF's Global House Price Index—a simple average of real house prices for 57 countries—is now back to its level before the global financial crisis (GFC). The index has been inching up since 2012, making the duration of the run-up comparable to one in 2001–06 that ended in house price collapses in many countries. Is it time to worry again about overvaluation?

This chapter describes the evolution of IMF monitoring—"surveillance" in the IMF's jargon—of housing markets from 2008 to the present. Section 2 describes

---

The views expressed are those of the authors and should not be attributed to the IMF or the Independent Evaluation Office (IEO). This chapter builds on work largely carried out when the second author was in the IMF's Research Department and should not be considered as an IEO evaluation of IMF activities.

H. Ahir
IMF Research Department, Washington, DC, USA
e-mail: hahir@imf.org

P. Loungani (✉)
IMF Independent Evaluation Office, Washington, DC, USA
e-mail: ploungani@imf.org

R. Nijskens et al. (eds.), *Hot Property*, https://doi.org/10.1007/978-3-030-11674-3_7

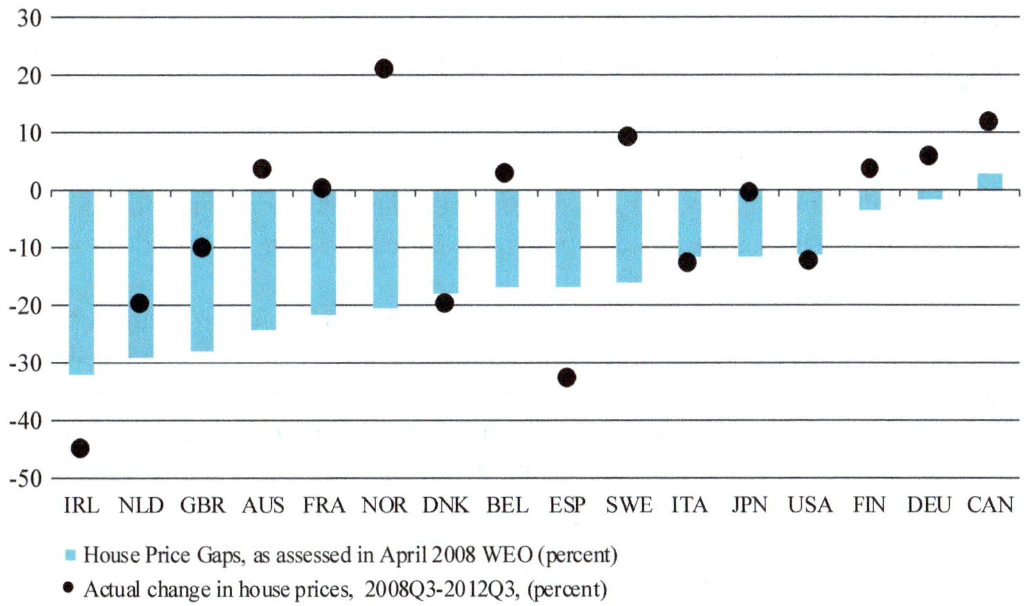

Sources: House price gaps: April 2008 World Economic Outlook (WEO). Change in house prices: IMF Global Housing Watch.
Labels: AUS = Australia, BEL = Belgium, CAN=Canada, DEU = Germany DNK = Denmark, ESP=Spain, FIN=Finland, FRA = France, GBR = Great Britain, IRL = Ireland, ITA = Italy, JPN = Japan, NLD = the Netherlands, NOR = Norway, SWE = Sweden, and USA = United States

Fig. 7.1 Estimated overvaluation and subsequent house price changes

how the IMF has assessed overvaluation in housing markets and the advice it offered on the policy tools needed to manage house price booms. It lays out the IMF's 'corporate view' or 'house view' that macroprudential policies must be the first line of defense to deal with house price booms. Section 3 takes up the issue of whether the run-up in house prices over the past few years should be a source of worry. Section 4 describes how IMF surveillance has adapted as housing markets have become more 'glocalized' and developments at the sub-national level gain greater prominence.[1] Section 5 has some concluding observations.

2 The Changing Lines of Defense

2.1 Explaining Booms

A common approach to explaining house price growth is to see to what extent it can be explained by fundamental drivers such as growth in real GDP and working age

[1]Encyclopedia Britannica defines glocalization as "a hybrid of globalization and localization: the importance of global [factors] occurring together with the increasing salience of local and regional [factors]".

population. The underlying assumption is that these factors impart a demand-side momentum which, unless supply of housing is extremely elastic, translates into a short-term boost to housing prices.

Interest rates are another fundamental driver of house price growth. Often, some covariates, such as credit growth and equity price growth, are included to control for other difficult to measure factors that could be driving house price growth. An error-correction term, such as the lagged house price-to-income ratio, is included to allow reversion of house prices to historical norms.

Illustrative panel regressions of this kind are shown in Table 7.1, using quarterly data for a large number of countries since 1970. The coefficients of the independent variables all have the expected signs and are statistically significant. Real GDP growth, working age population growth and the short-term interest rate, along with an error- correction term (the lagged house price-to-income ratio), explain about 30% of the variation in house price growth. One can get similar explanatory power by replacing real GDP growth with growth in equity prices. Including all variables raises the explanatory power to about 40% and all variables stay statistically significant, except for equity prices.

The assessments of overvaluation shown in Fig. 7.1 were based on regressions of this kind, estimated country-by-country. Specifically, house price growth was modeled as a function of growth in disposable income per capita, short-term interest rates, long-term interest rates, credit growth, changes in equity prices and changes in working-age population. The "unexplained increase" in house prices could reflect omitted variables "but could also be interpreted as a measure of overvaluation and, therefore, used to identify which countries may be particularly prone to a correction in house prices" (IMF 2008).

Table 7.1 Drivers and covariates of real house price growth

Independent variables	(1)	(2)	(3)
Real GDP (growth)	0.3		0.2
Working age population (growth)	0.1	0.1	0.1
Short-term interest rate	−0.4	−0.5	−0.6
House price-to-income ratio (lagged)	−0.1	−0.1	−0.3
Credit (growth)		0.1	0.1
Equity prices (growth)		0.06	*0.00*
Fiscal balance (change)			−0.1
Constant	1.1	2.3	1.5
R-square	0.28	0.30	0.39
Number of observations	3519	3148	2291

Note: Numbers shown are coefficient estimates; all are significant at conventional levels (except the one shown in italics)

2.2 Managing Booms

What policies, if any, should be used to address such overvaluations in house prices? In the April 2008 *WEO*, the IMF took a heterodox view. It noted that "central bank orthodoxy" was that monetary policymakers should not target a particular level of house (or other asset) prices and should respond to changes in house prices only if they affected output and inflation outcomes and expectations. However, the counter-argument was that a pre-emptive monetary policy response "could diminish the risk that a bigger crash would occur later on, with serious consequences for the real economy and inflation."

The IMF balanced these considerations by suggesting that monetary policy should take a "risk management" approach. Under such an approach, "house prices would seem relevant for calculating the risks to the outlook for overall economic activity, particularly during periods of rapid change in house prices and when house prices seem to be moving out of line with historical norms," due to "speculative forces". It concluded, however, that monetary policy "should not bear the full weight of responding to asset price bubbles" and other policies could also have a critical role.

A year later, as the global financial crisis intensified, the IMF's policy message started to change. The IMF became a strong advocate of the use of unconventional monetary policies to close output gaps and raise inflation to target levels. It recognized that these policies could have the side-effect of triggering house price booms and it advocated that these risks should be managed largely by using macro-prudential (and microprudential) policies. Such policies were the "first lines of defense in safeguarding financial stability," according to Vinals (2010), the IMF's Financial Counsellor.

As in the April 2008 *WEO*, the IMF did not advocate a clean break between monetary policy and considerations of financial stability. While monetary policy should not adopt financial stability as a goal, Viñals argued that "financial stability concerns should be integrated much more systematically into monetary policy decision making." The models and analysis needed to do this would take time, so "in the meantime," Viñals advocated "practical behavioral rules in order to ensure that financial stability considerations are sufficiently taken into account in the pursuit of price stability. I believe that monetary policy should lean—in a non-mechanistic way—against the buildup of financial imbalances during an upswing in the cycle (as exemplified in excessive credit growth or asset prices). More "leaning" in this stage will hopefully lead to the need for less "cleaning" in the downturn thus rendering monetary policy more symmetric over the business cycle." Over time, the IMF has become less of an advocate of 'leaning against the wind', thus leaving macroprudential policies to play an even greater role in safeguarding financial stability. An IMF Policy Paper in 2015 took a fairly clear line:

> In principle, monetary policy should deviate from its traditional response only if costs are smaller than benefits (the principle of doing no harm on net). Costs arise in the short term, from lower output and inflation. Benefits materialize mainly in the medium term, as financial risks are mitigated, though effects are more uncertain. Based on current knowledge, the case for leaning against the wind is limited, as in most circumstances costs outweigh benefits.

Views seem to have evolved in similar fashion in many central banks and international institutions. Having elevated the importance of macroprudential policies, researchers at the IMF and elsewhere have devoted increased attention to studying the effectiveness of such policies in managing house price booms (IMF 2013, 2014). Cerutti et al. (2017) study the effects of several macroprudential policies for 119 countries over the 2000–13 period. They find that tightening these measures does significantly lower household credit growth; the impact on house price growth is also negative but not statistically significant. They argue that since "house price booms associated with increased leverage are the most destructive," macroprudential policies can play a useful role by "dampening household indebtedness." Over the same period but using a different data set of policy measures, Zhang and Zoli (2016) compare the impact in Asia, where the "economies appear to have made greater use of macroprudential tools, especially housing-related tools," with that in other regions. They find that housing-related policy measures have curbed real credit growth in Asia and other regions; in Asia these measures have lowered real house price growth as well but in other regions the impact on prices is not significant (Vandenbussche et al. 2015).[2]

In sum, while there is some evidence on effectiveness of macroprudential policies, it is mixed and it is difficult to be confident of medium-run effects given the short span of data that is available to researchers. Therefore, country-by-country assessments and detailed case studies of the use and effectiveness of macroprudential measures are useful.

3 Time to Worry Again?

As mentioned in the introduction, the IMF's Global House Price Index has inched back up to its pre-GFC level (Fig. 7.2). Does this reflect overvaluations in many countries, and if so, what policy actions are needed? The IMF has not provided recent updates of the overvaluation estimations reported in Fig. 7.1.[3] We make the case here, admittedly based on very casual empiricism, that there are a couple of important differences between the pre-GFC and post-GFC periods.

First, there is lower synchronization in house price growth across countries in the latter period than in the former; moreover, growth in quantities remains subdued. Second, countries are much more active in using macroprudential policies to manage house price booms—"the era of benign neglect of house price booms is over" (Zhu 2014)—and, as discussed in the previous section, there is some evidence that the policies are effective. On these two grounds, we argue that it is time for vigilance, not panic.

[2]Vandenbussche et al. (2015) find evidence of the effectiveness of some macroprudential policy measures on house price inflation in Central, Eastern, and South-Eastern Europe (2015).

[3]Some individual IMF country teams have provided estimates—see for example Geng (2018).

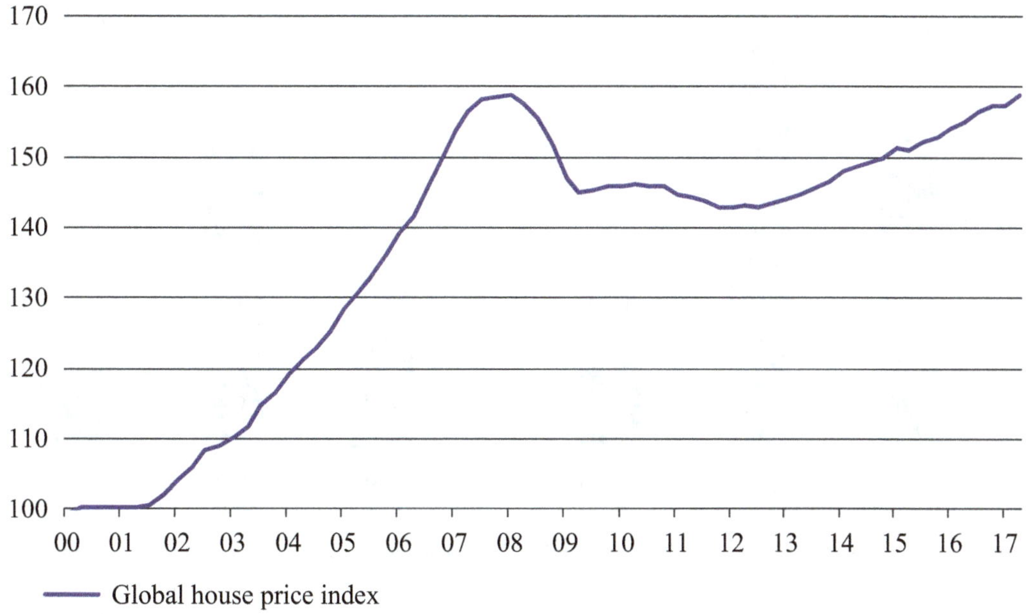

Source: IMF Global Housing Watch (2018)
(Based on data from BIS, ECB, FRB Dallas, Savills, and national sources)

Fig. 7.2 Global house price index

To illustrate the differences in synchronicity, it is useful to segment the countries included in the global index into three clusters. The first cluster—*gloom*—consists of 14 economies in which house prices fell substantially at the onset of the Great Recession, and have remained on a downward path.[4] The second cluster—*bust and boom*—consists of 19 economies in which housing prices fell sharp during 2007–12 but have since rebounded.[5] The third cluster—*boom*—comprises 24 economies where the drop in house prices in 2007–12 was quite modest and followed by a quick rebound.[6]

Countries in the third cluster had a lower incidence of financial crisis and smaller output losses over the 2007–12 period (Fig. 7.3). House prices in these countries have, on average, resumed their pre-GFC trend rate of growth. In the second cluster, house prices are growing at a slower pace than before the crisis (Fig. 7.4). In contrast, the pre-GFC period was marked by synchronous behavior in house prices across all three groups. The behavior of residential permits—is also different across the two periods (Fig. 7.5). Pre-GFC, the 'bust and boom' cluster had a very rapid growth in permits; post-GFC the rate of increase for this group has been far more subdued.

[4]Brazil, Croatia, Cyprus, Finland, France, Greece, Italy, Macedonia, Morocco, Russia, Singapore, Slovenia, South Africa, and Ukraine.

[5]Bulgaria, Denmark, Estonia, Germany, Hungary, Iceland, Indonesia, Ireland, Japan, Latvia, Lithuania, Netherlands, New Zealand, Portugal, Serbia, Spain, Thailand, United Kingdom, and United States.

[6]Australia, Austria, Belgium, Canada, Chile, China, Colombia, Czech Republic, Hong Kong SAR, India, Israel, Kazakhstan, Korea, Malaysia, Malta, Mexico, Norway, Peru, Philippines, Poland, Slovak Republic, Sweden, Switzerland, and Taiwan POC.

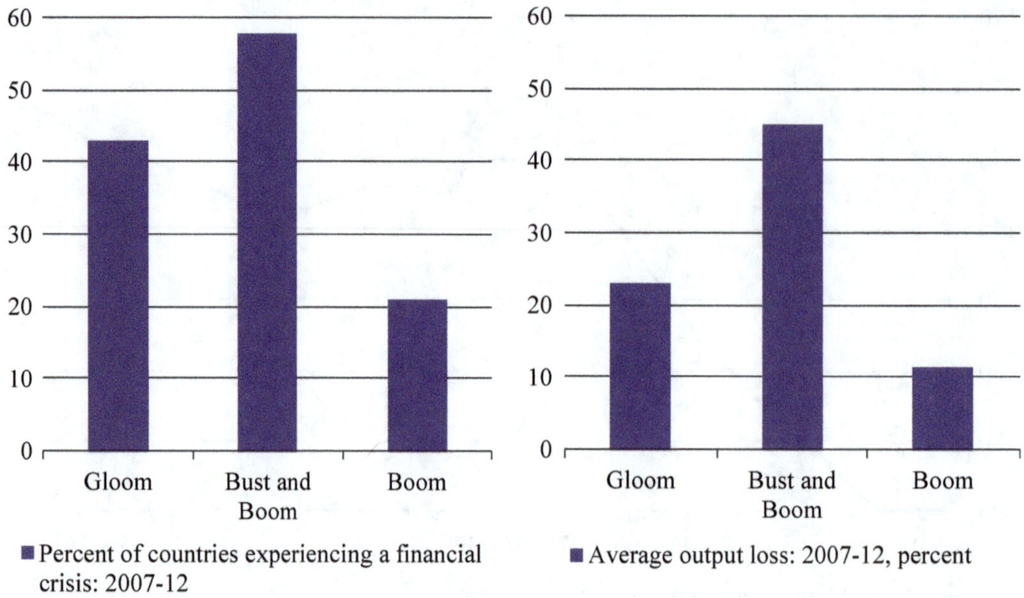

Source: Based on data from "Systemic banking crises database: An update" by Valencia and Laeven (2012)

Fig. 7.3 Country clusters: incidence of financial crisis

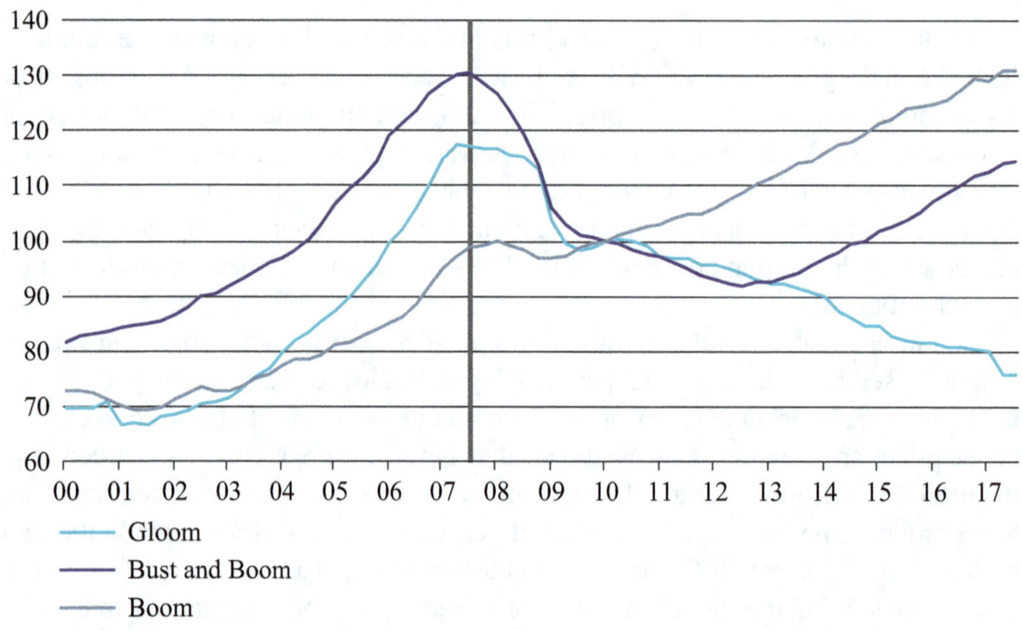

Source: IMF Global Housing Watch (2018)

Fig. 7.4 Country clusters: average house price indices

The extensive use of macroprudential policies to tame housing booms since the crisis is shown in Fig. 7.6. The main policies used are limits on loan-to-value (LTV) ratios, limits on debt-service-to-income (DSTI) ratios and sectoral capital requirements.

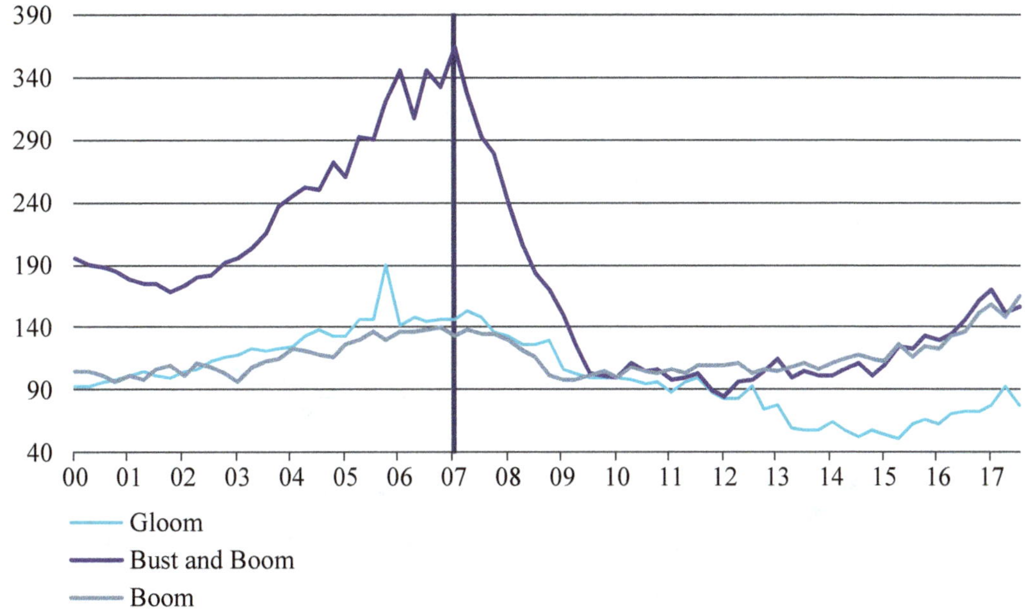

Source: Eurostat (2018), Haver Analytics, and OECD (2018)

Fig. 7.5 Housing permits in each cluster

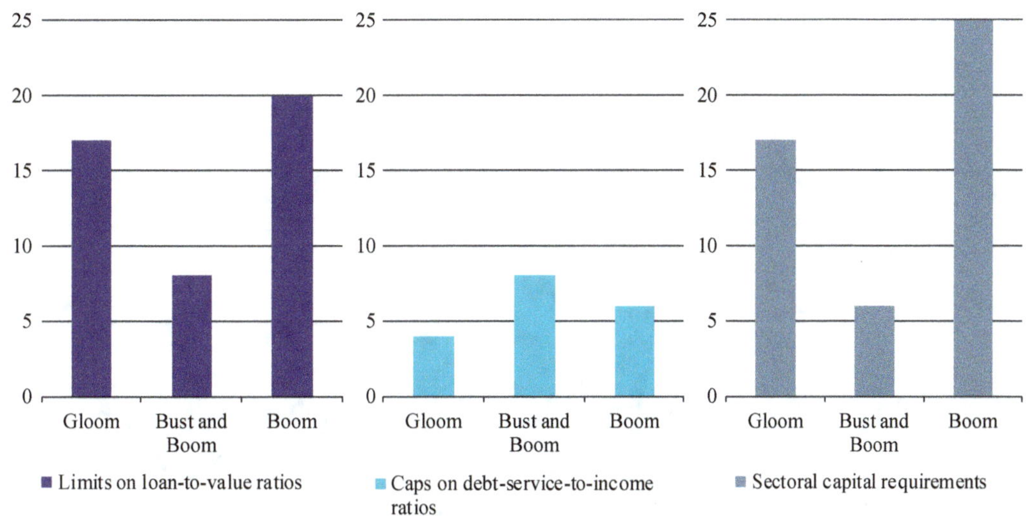

Source: International Monetary Fund (2018b)

Fig. 7.6 Use of macroprudential policies

4 Dealing with Glocalization

4.1 Explaining Local Booms

In recent years, there is some evidence that house prices in major cities are diverging from the national average and that booms are often restricted to one or a few cities. Some examples of local booms are Vienna, Vancouver, Amsterdam and London, where house prices are rising far more than the national average (Fig. 7.7).

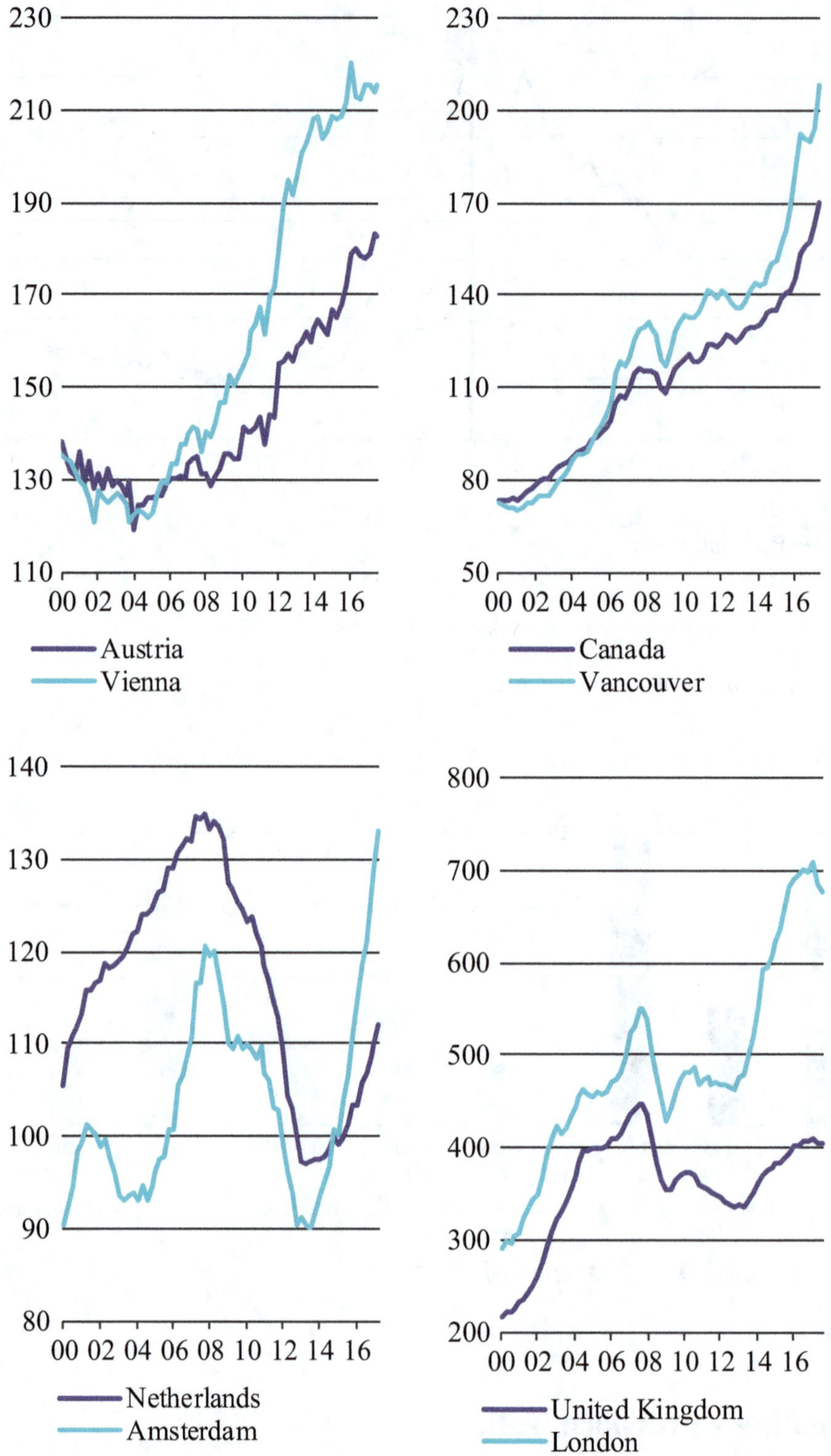

Source: Haver Analytics

Fig. 7.7 City-level booms

In all these cases we again see a difference between the pre-GFC and post-GFC periods: prices in these cities moved much more in tandem with national prices in the former period.

Consequently, surveillance of housing markets by both national and international agencies is also turning to more granular data and seeking out explanations for the divergence between national-level and local developments. Along with other agencies, the IMF is being drawn into assessing whether there are house prices 'bubbles' in major cities. For example, in the case of Austria, the IMF's latest assessment was that there was an overvaluation of property prices of about 22% for Vienna, while prices in the rest of the country were broadly in line with fundamentals. In Japan, the IMF judged condominium prices appear to be moderately overvalued in Tokyo, Osaka, and several outer regions.

While assessments of housing price overvaluation at the national level are difficult, assessments of city-level overvaluation are likely even more so. City-level house prices reflect the confluence of local factors (supply constraints, regulations and zoning) and global trends (role of foreign investors; impact of migration; development of internet-based markets such as Airbnb)—the phenomenon of 'glocalization'.

The role of housing supply constraints in driving local house prices has been a staple in academic work**.** Glaeser et al. (2005) famously argued that it is "the interaction of strong latent demand for markets such as Manhattan combined with restrictive or inelastic supply that largely accounts for relatively high house prices in those places. Strong demand itself is not enough. Dallas has very strong demand, as population has grown substantially over many decades; yet, its constant quality house prices have not risen much at all in real terms. What is different about Dallas is plentiful building whenever prices rise enough for developers to supply new homes and make a normal profit. In Manhattan, local authorities are able to impose sufficiently high costs on new development (or simply limit it outright), so that higher demand results in higher prices without much increase in the number of housing units."

As it turns to more granular analysis of housing markets, the impact of supply constraints has been increasingly emphasized by the IMF in the case of many of cities with house price booms. In Copenhagen, the increase in the housing stock has not kept up with population growth, feeding some of the price increase that is observed there. Booms in Stockholm and Malmo have also been attributed in part to growth in the number of dwellings not keeping up with the population growth. In recent years, the IMF has also flagged the role of supply constraints in Australia and Canada, as well as in many European countries—France, Germany, Ireland, Netherlands, Norway and the United Kingdom.

Housing supply constraints have also been exacerbated by the global factors mentioned earlier—the growing role of international investors and internet-driven tourist booms. The IMF's April 2018a *Global Financial Stability Report* documents that institutional investors, private equity firms, and Real Estate Investment Trusts have been increasingly active in major cities such as Amsterdam, Sydney, and Vancouver as they seek out higher returns. In cities in Norway, the IMF flagged the impact of a large influx of asylum seekers. In Iceland, the IMF noted that the increase in housing prices of almost 10% in 2016, centered on Reykjavík, appeared driven by the crowding out of homebuilding by hotel construction and of rentals by residents to tourists.

4.2 Managing Local Booms

In keeping with its advice to rely on macroprudential policies to manage housing booms, the IMF has been active in suggesting specific and targeted macroprudential policies to manage local booms. A few examples may suffice to give a flavor of the policy advice. In China, the IMF agreed that city-specific macroprudential policies were appropriate given the diversity in housing conditions, and should continue to be deployed to ensure a smooth adjustment in housing markets. In Macao, the IMF suggested that if the impact of speculative demand on real estate prices is a material concern, policymakers could consider more targeted macroprudential measures such as tighter loan-to-value ratios on second-home purchases. In Malaysia as well, the advice was that if rapid house price growth resumes, LTV caps on second and first mortgages could be considered.

However, along with local macroprudential policies, the IMF has also increasingly recommended policies to ease housing supply constraints. Again, a few examples may be illustrative of the nature of the policy advice. In Germany, the IMF suggested that encouragement for local authorities to relax zoning and height restrictions in areas under pressure and lowering the effective transaction tax rate on new construction. In Israel, the advice was to improve municipal incentives for development, ensure adequate land privatization and urban renewal, shorten approval times, and reduce construction costs.

5 Concluding Remarks

This chapter has traced the evolution in IMF surveillance of housing markets and its policy advice to countries on how to manage house price booms. Despite our focus on the IMF, the discussion should be of more general interest as other national and international agencies involved in monitoring and regulating housing markets have undergone a similar evolution. By now, there appears to be a broad consensus on the use of macroprudential policies to tame housing booms and some evidence that such policies are proving to be effective. However, the increasing shift in the action to the city-level raises a number of issues that will require increasing attention from policymakers.

First, several local and national authorities have taken measures to deter foreign real estate investors. The authorities view these as macroprudential measures needed for financial stability, whereas institutions like the IMF seem to consider some of

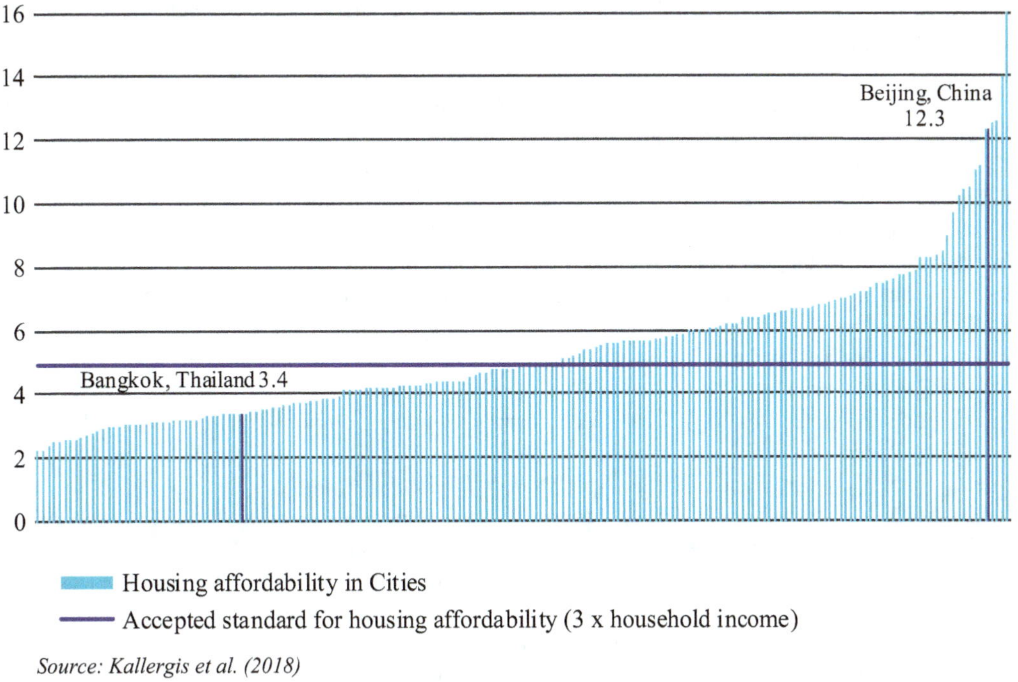

Fig. 7.8 Housing affordability in cities

them as capital flow management measures ('capital controls'). This is emerging as a point of contention.

Second, issues of housing affordability that often get lost when looking at national-level averages are much more salient at the city level. The UN's Land and Housing Survey of 170 cities shows that the median house-price-to-income ratio was 4.8 and the median rent-to-income ratio was 30% (Fig. 7.8), above what is considered affordable (house-price-to-annual household income ratio of 3.0, and rent-to-monthly household income ratio of under 25%).

Third, the focus on city-level developments has also brought to the fore the need to view housing markets through a broader lens of growth and economic development. As argued by Ed Glaeser (2011), cities are essential for growth, which makes policy actions to manage city level housing booms much more than just a matter of financial stability. Affordability is becoming an issue in advanced countries, but the situation is worse in emerging markets and low-income countries, which are much more populous and where the need for sensible urban policies for development is much more pressing (Jedwab et al. 2018).

References

Cerutti, E., Claessens, S., & Laeven, L. (2017). The use and effectiveness of macroprudential policies: New evidence. *Journal of Financial Stability., 28*, 203–224.

Eurostat. (2018). *Building permits – quarterly data.* Accessed July 1, 2018, from http://appsso.eurostat.ec.europa.eu/nui/show.do?dataset=sts_cobp_q&lang=en

Geng, N. (2018). *Fundamental drivers of house prices in advanced economies* (IMF Working Paper) (forthcoming).

Glaeser, E. (2011). *Triumph of the city: How our greatest invention makes us richer, smarter, greener, healthier, and happier*. New York: Penguin Books.

Glaeser, E. L., Gyourko, J., & Saks, R. E. (2005). Why is Manhattan so expensive? Regulation and the rise in housing prices. *The Journal of Law and Economics, 48*, 331–369.

IMF, Global Housing Watch. (2018). Accessed July 1, 2018, from https://www.imf.org/external/research/housing/

International Monetary Fund. (2008, April). *World Economic Outlook.*

International Monetary Fund. (2013, June). *Key aspects of macroprudential policy* (IMF Policy Paper).

International Monetary Fund. (2014, December). *Staff guidance note on macroprudential policy* (IMF Policy Paper).

International Monetary Fund. (2015, December). *Monetary policy and financial stability* (IMF Policy Paper).

International Monetary Fund. (2018a, April). *Global financial stability report.*

International Monetary Fund. (2018b). *Macroprudential policy survey database*. Accessed July 1, 2018, from https://www.elibrary-areaer.imf.org/Macroprudential/Pages/Home.aspx

Jedwab, R., Loungani, P., & Yezer, T. (2018). *New urban giants in low-income countries: Stylized facts about land areas, building heights, and interior density*. Draft.

Kallergis, A., Angel, S., Liu, Y., Blei, A., Sanchez, N., & Lamson-Hall, P. (2018, November). *Housing affordability in a global perspective*. Cambridge, MA: Lincoln Institute of Land Policy.

OECD. (2018). *Permits issued for dwellings sa, Index.* Accessed July 1, 2018, from https://stats.oecd.org/Index.aspx?querytype=view&queryname=92

Valencia, F., & Laeven, L. (2012). *Systemic banking crises database: An update*. IMF Working Paper 12, no. 163: 1.

Vandenbussche, J., Vogel, U., & Detragiache, E. (2015). Macroprudential policies and housing prices: A new database and empirical evidence for Central, Eastern and Southeastern Europe. *Journal of Money, Credit and Banking, 47*(S1), 343–377.

Vinals, J. (2010, November 10). *Towards a safer global financial system.*

Zhang, L., & Zoli, E. (2016). Leaning against the wind: Macroprudential policy in Asia. *Journal of Asian Economics, 42*, 33–52.

Zhu, M. (2014). *Era of benign neglect of house price booms is over*. IMFBlog. https://blogs.imf.org/2014/06/11/era-of-benign-neglect-of-house-price-booms-is-over/

Part III
Housing Supply in Urban Areas

Chapter 8
The Macroeconomic Implications of Housing Supply Restrictions

Edward L. Glaeser

1 Introduction

A large literature now documents that housing supply restrictions can increase housing prices, decrease construction and even distort national productivity (Katz and Rosen 1987; Glaeser et al. 2005; Hsieh and Moretti 2017). Almost all of the policy analysis of these restrictions, which are even more prevalent in Europe than in the U.S., focuses on static microeconomic issues, such as the negative externalities from new construction (Glaeser et al. 2005; Glaeser and Ward 2009). Yet there are also dynamic implications of restricting housing supply, and these dynamic implications matter both for counter-recessionary policy and for reforming land-use policies.

Real estate is a major asset class, and real estate busts are often associated with the onset of larger banking crises, such as the Asian financial crisis of 1997 and the global financial crisis that began in 2007. Looking forward, the great Chinese housing boom may also end up having consequences for the global economy. The elasticity of housing supply helps determine whether a real estate boom ends in a financial crisis or an employment crisis, or both.

When real estate booms are modest, then the intuition of supply and demand holds. Elastic areas, like the American south, will see larger fluctuations in the amount of building, and hence the amount of construction employment. Inelastic areas, including much of urban Europe, will see larger fluctuations in prices, and

I am grateful for financial support to the Taubman Center for State and Local Government. I received helpful comments from seminar participants at the Netherlands Bank.

E. L. Glaeser (✉)
Department of Economics, Harvard University, Cambridge, MA, USA

NBER, Cambridge, MA, USA
e-mail: eglaeser@harvard.edu

R. Nijskens et al. (eds.), *Hot Property*, https://doi.org/10.1007/978-3-030-11674-3_8

smaller construction fluctuations, which is more likely to generate major shifts in the balance sheets of financial organizations that are long in real estate. When real estate booms are so large that construction disappears in the ensuing bust, then more elastic supply may be associated with larger busts in both price and employment, which is what was observed in Phoenix and Las Vegas after 2007.

In highly elastic areas, credit market interventions will generally shift the level of construction rather than price, and hence this will boost employment but do less to help underwater buyers and their creditors. In inelastic areas or elastic areas with excessive overbuilding, credit market interventions will impact price, rather than employment, directly. In boom periods, such price increases would normally increase consumption (Case et al. 2005), but during busts underwater borrowers are often unable to borrow against their housing value and so the consumption effects will be muted (Ganong and Noel 2017). If, during a boom, the level of excess supply reaches the point that construction is likely to disappear entirely during the bust, then the central bank must expect that its counter-recessionary tools will be quite limited.

One message of this paper is that financial market interventions, like monetary easing, that impact the willingness-to-pay for housing, are mediated by the physical limitations on housing markets. Credit-related interventions that are meant to make housing more affordable, such as raising loan-to-income limits, will have little impact on housing consumption unless building restrictions are also eased. The second message is that housing-market reform must consider the implications for cycles. If European countries were to adopt a more permissive construction policy, then they would presumably be exchanging an environment with more price volatility for an environment with more employment volatility. That shift might require less bank oversight and better unemployment insurance in the construction industry. If it is less dangerous for the larger economy to relax building restrictions during a boom, then given the slow pace of reform it may be necessary to start planning those reforms years in advance, even during a bust.

2 Hot Property Markets and the Microeconomics of Construction Constraints

If you had asked the residents of Amsterdam or New York City in 1978 what their city's largest problems 40 years in the future would be, few would have said the high cost of housing. Many might have mentioned crime or urban unemployment or the loss of manufacturing jobs. Indeed, those who bought homes and apartments in those years were seen as gigantic risk-takers, buying themselves a seat on an urban Lusitania.

Four decades later, Amsterdam and New York are rich and safe. Both found post-industrial future in information-intensive industries, such as finance, which recall the erstwhile prominence of the Dutch West Indies Company in both places. The loss of the industrial base can even seem like an asset, since pollution fled along with the factories. Indeed, almost none of the front-page problems from the 1970s remained on a primary concern. Moreover, both Amsterdam and New York manage to succeed as centers of consumption, as well as production, as shown by the ability of both cities to attract tourists and reverse commuters.

But economic revitalization and declining crime rates meant an increase in demand for real estate. This revitalized demand was met in both places by quiescent supply. In both cities, height restriction and historic preservation limit the ability of private new construction to satiate demand. In the decades after World War II, the Netherlands built a great deal of social housing and New York City built massive public housing structures. While the Dutch social housing system is far more successful than its public housing counterpart within the U.S., both cities reduced their new supplies of public housing in recent decades. As rising demand hit fixed supply, prices rose dramatically.

The scarcity of urban space is one cause of the social unrest that is linked to urban inequality and gentrification. The demand of the rich for urban space would not be so harmful to the poor if living space was elastically supplied. When houses are in short supply and real estate becomes a zero-sum game, then a boost in demand from the rich raises prices for the poor.

Progressive leaders now see the costs of the limited housing supply, but instead of deregulating, they promote new regulations, such as inclusionary zoning, meant to supply a modest number of "affordable units." These units are then allocated to lucky lottery winners. Under Mayor Bloomberg, developers could choose to include affordable units and would be rewarded with the ability to build up. Under Mayor DeBlasio, inclusionary zoning has become mandatory. Conventional microeconomics suggests that mandatory inclusionary zoning represents a tax on the construction of market-rate units to subsidize non-market rate units.

Microeconomic analysis tries to measure the negative externalities from construction, and then finds that those externalities, at least in New York and Massachusetts, are far smaller than the implicit tax of building that is created by zoning (Glaeser et al. 2005; Glaeser and Ward 2009). De Groot et al. (2015) present the closest similar analysis for the Netherlands. The case for restricting new construction is certainly stronger in central Amsterdam, which is truly part of the cultural patrimony of the world, than it is in most of New York.

The public debate about high housing prices, macroeconomic evidence suggesting that restrictions can distort the entire economy (Hsieh and Moretti 2017) and concern about real estate as a vast asset class have increasingly lead macroeconomists to take an interest into hot property markets. That interest is most welcome, especially since macroeconomically oriented entities, like central banks, typically enjoy a privileged place in policy debates. Yet as macroeconomists turn their minds to housing supply, they should also consider the implications that housing supply restrictions have for the business cycle.

3 Housing Bubbles, Credit Conditions and Extrapolative Beliefs

Housing markets are typically volatile, moved both by changing economic fundamentals and by shifts in beliefs that seem closer to animal spirits. In the U.S., there is strong momentum in housing-price changes over 1-year frequencies, and strong mean reversion over 5 year frequencies. Both facts are compatible with a model in which semi-rational buyers extrapolate underlying trends from recent growth in housing prices (Glaeser and Nathanson 2017).

The most popular rational explanations for wide swings in housing prices is that they are being driven by credit conditions, either borrowing rates or approval rates. Glaeser et al. (2012) present theory and data suggesting that swings in interest rates were far too small to explain much of the price boom and bust between 2000 and 2010 within the U.S., at least if we assume buyer rationality. If buyers are not rational, then interest rates could play a role in generating price swings perhaps by generating small price movements that then lead to extrapolative bubbles.

In this section, we take the existence and macroeconomic importance of housing bubbles as given, and ask what impact housing-supply restrictions will have on the housing cycle and on macroeconomic responses to that cycle. I present a simple model of housing volatility that is based on Glaeser et al. (2008). I first (and primarily) treat the case where housing volatility is generated by an irrationally overoptimistic belief in high future housing prices. I then speculate briefly on the impacts of housing supply when bubbly beliefs become more endogenous.

The flow utility from owning a house is a function of an exogenous demand shift (A_t) and the overall number of households (N_t) and so equals $A_t - \gamma N_t$. The temporal indifference condition is that $P_t = A_t - \gamma N_t + \beta\delta E(P_{t+1})$, so that the price equals the flow utility plus the discounted expected value of the price tomorrow, where β is the discount factor and $1 - \delta$ represents the depreciation of the housing stock. The cost of supplying housing is a function of the flow of new housing construction, denoted I_t, and this must equal the expected price next period so that $C_t + c_1 I_t = E(P_{t+1})$. Finally, the flow of motion for the housing stock is that $N_{t+1} = \delta N_t + I_t$, where δ represents the share of housing that remains after each period.

If the exogenous parameters are fixed so that $C_t = C$ and $A_t = A$, then the steady state values for population and price (N and P) equal $\tilde{N} = \frac{A-C(1-\beta\delta)}{c_1(1-\beta\delta)(1-\delta)+\gamma}$ and $\tilde{P} = \frac{c_1(1-\delta)A+\gamma C}{c_1(1-\beta\delta)(1-\delta)+\gamma}$. With fully rational actors, then given any starting value N_t (as long as $\frac{(1-\theta)}{(\delta-\theta)}\tilde{N} > N_t$ which implies that P_{t+1} is greater than C), $N_{t+j} = \tilde{N} + \theta^j\left(N_t - \tilde{N}\right)$, $I_{t+j} = (1-\delta)\tilde{N} + \theta^{j-1}(\theta-\delta)\left(N_t - \tilde{N}\right)$ and $P_{t+j} = \frac{c_1(1-\delta)A+\gamma C}{c_1(1-\beta\delta)(1-\delta)+\gamma} + c_1\theta^{j-1}(\theta-\delta)\left(N_t - \tilde{N}\right)$, where $\theta = \frac{\left(\left(1+\beta\delta^2\right)c_1+\gamma\right)-\sqrt{\left(\left(1+\beta\delta^2\right)c_1+\gamma\right)^2-4\beta\delta^2c_1^2}}{2\beta\delta c_1} < \delta$.

If $\frac{(1-\theta)}{(\delta-\theta)}\tilde{N} < N_t$, then we have reached the vertical part of the supply curve, and $I_{t+j} = 0$, until $\frac{(1-\theta)}{(\delta-\theta)}\tilde{N} > N_{t+j}$. If t + k denotes the time period in which building begins again, then $\frac{N_{t+k}}{1-\delta} > \frac{(1-\theta)}{(\delta-\theta)}\tilde{N} > N_{t+k}$. At time t + k, $P_{t+k} = C + c_1(1-\delta)\tilde{N} + c_1\theta^{j-1}(\theta-\delta)((1-\delta)^k N_t - \tilde{N})$. Iterating, the prices during earlier periods satisfy $P_{t+j} = \frac{1-(\beta\delta)^{k-j}}{1-\beta\delta}A - \frac{1-(\beta\delta(1-\delta))^{k-j}}{1-\beta\delta(1-\delta)}\gamma(1-\delta)^j N_t + (\beta\delta)^{k-j}P_{t+k}$.

We can interpret bubbles in this model as errors about future values of A (or C). For example, assume that in time t, the city is in steady state, and builder (and buyers) believe that next period the new value of A will equal $\varphi + A$, with $\varphi > 0$. This belief implies that the new steady-state population will be $\frac{A+\varphi-C(1-\beta\delta)}{c_1(1-\beta\delta)(1-\delta)+\gamma}$. Consequently, while the bubble lasts, $I_t = \frac{(1-\delta)(A-C(1-\beta\delta))+(1-\theta)\varphi}{c_1(1-\beta\delta)(1-\delta)+\gamma}$ and $P_t = C + c_1\frac{(1-\delta)(A-C(1-\beta\delta))+(1-\theta)\varphi}{c_1(1-\beta\delta)(1-\delta)+\gamma}$, which means that price has increased by $\frac{c_1(1-\theta)\varphi}{c_1(1-\beta\delta)(1-\delta)+\gamma}$ (relative to the steady state) due to the belief bubble and quantity has increased by $\frac{(1-\theta)\varphi}{c_1(1-\beta\delta)(1-\delta)+\gamma}$.

If the bubble lasts exactly one period (I am being consciously vague about the length of a period), then buyers and builders recognize that there has been an error and that there has been too much building. If $\frac{(1-\delta)(A-C(1-\beta\delta))}{(\delta-\theta)(1-\theta)} > \varphi$ so that $\frac{(1-\theta)}{(\delta-\theta)}\tilde{N} > N_t$, then there is building even after the bubble. In that case, the post-bubble level of housing construction will equal $I_t = \frac{(1-\delta)(A-C(1-\beta\delta))-(\delta-\theta)(1-\theta)\varphi}{c_1(1-\beta\delta)(1-\delta)+\gamma}$, which represents a fall of $\frac{(\delta-\theta)(1-\theta)\varphi}{c_1(1-\beta\delta)(1-\delta)+\gamma}$ relative to pre-bubble levels, and $\frac{(1+\delta-\theta)(1-\theta)\varphi}{c_1(1-\beta\delta)(1-\delta)+\gamma}$ relative to the level during the bubble $C + c_1(1-\delta)\tilde{N} + c_1\theta^{j-1}(\theta-\delta)(N_t - \tilde{N})$.

The price in the first period of the bust will equal $\frac{c_1(1-\delta)A+\gamma C-c_1(\delta-\theta)(1-\theta)\varphi}{c_1(1-\beta\delta)(1-\delta)+\gamma}$, which is a decline of $\frac{c_1(\delta-\theta)(1-\theta)\varphi}{c_1(1-\beta\delta)(1-\delta)+\gamma}$, relative to prices before the bubble, and of $\frac{c_1(1+\delta-\theta)(1-\theta)\varphi}{c_1(1-\beta\delta)(1-\delta)+\gamma}$ relative to the bubble's peak. Booms will have smaller effects on construction and larger effects on prices in places with inelastic housing supply. This result is an unsurprising application of the basic logic of introductory economics, but it fails if the boom is sufficiently large.

If $(1-\delta)(A-C(1-\beta\delta)) < (\delta-\theta)(1-\theta)\varphi$, then the boom generates so much an oversupply of housing that there will be no construction during the immediate recovery. In that case, construction will fall by $\frac{(1-\delta)(A-C(1-\beta\delta))+(1-\theta)\varphi}{c_1(1-\beta\delta)(1-\delta)+\gamma}$ relative to the bubble and $\frac{(1-\delta)(A-C(1-\beta\delta))}{c_1(1-\beta\delta)(1-\delta)+\gamma}$ relative to the pre-bubble period. More elastic areas will have the largest drops in construction, and presumably employment as well. These areas had the most employment to lose, and the elastic regions overbuilt by the larger amount.

The price during the bust will equal $\frac{1-(\beta\delta)^k}{1-\beta\delta}A - \frac{1-(\beta\delta(1-\delta))^k}{1-\beta\delta(1-\delta)}\gamma\frac{(1-\delta)(A-C(1-\beta\delta))+(1-\theta)\varphi}{c_1(1-\beta\delta)(1-\delta)+\gamma} + (\beta\delta)^k P_{t+k}$. When there is no construction during the bust, more elastic supply will lead to a larger price drop because there was so much overbuilding. This result may capture the experience of places like Las Vegas and Phoenix, where supply was enormous during the boom, and the crash was also enormous. The puzzle about these cities is that buyers during the boom seemed oblivious to the fact that these areas were elastically supplied with housing.

This discussion treated the size of the erroneous belief as given, but it also seems quite plausible that overoptimism is easier to sustain in markets where supply is constrained. Homes along the Keizersgracht are in fixed supply. The view is lovely and urbane and we can easily believe that a greater fool will show up shortly who is willing to by the home at an even higher price. It is almost impossible for economists to know whether a rare and intrinsically attractive product in fixed supply is overpriced or underpriced. Conversely, economics has a clear prediction about the equilibrium price of products that are generated flexibly with a simple constant-returns-to-scale production technology, which is true of housing in many markets, such as Houston. If bubbles are more likely to occur in supply-constrained settings, then the extra volatility of price bubbles generates another reason why macroeconomists should be interested in housing supply.

3.1 Housing Supply Elasticity and Counter-Recessionary Policy

After the bust, the monetary authority may try to boost the demand for housing, with low interest rates and other credit market interventions. Any sort of full analysis of interest rates is beyond the scope of this paper. I treat an interest rate intervention as an increase in the value of the discount factor, β. As long as the bubble was modest, a reduction in the interest rate will increase the value of housing and boost the amount of construction. Moreover, the impact of lower interest rates on prices will be higher in places where housing supply is more inelastic. The impact of lower interest rates on construction employment will be higher in places where housing supply is more elastic.

If the ultimate goal of monetary policy is to increase labor demand, then low interest rates should do this directly through the construction sector in places that have inelastic supply for housing. In places where the supply of housing is inelastic, then the impact of lower interest rates on the economy must either come from outside the housing sector, or through wealth effects. While Case et al. (2005) find significant effects of housing wealth on consumption, Ganong and Noel (2017) find that these effects are muted during the Great Recession, possibly because people cannot borrow against their houses during the downturn.

This logic suggests that in unconstrained areas, like Texas, macroeconomic policy should worry primarily about layoffs associated with a downturn in the housing market. Robust unemployment insurance may be a natural means of protecting against the job loss. In constrained areas, housing fluctuations will appear mostly in changing housing prices. Larger price changes may require more financial regulation that anticipates housing price volatility. Specifically, it may be sensible for regulators to consider any historic tendency towards mean reversion of housing prices when imposing balance-sheet requirements on lenders.

If the bubble is big enough so that there is no ex post construction, then marginal changes in the interest rate will certainly not induce any change in construction levels or in construction employment. The price effects of changes in the interest rate can be significant. Yet again, those price effects may not translate into consumption and employment if people are unable to borrow against their housing wealth. Consequently, housing and real estate cycles have the potential to end up in recessions where standard monetary policy tools have little ability to impact the economy through the housing sector.

The relative impotence of monetary policy during a bust suggests the stronger need for macro-prudential policies during a boom. This analysis suggests that big housing booms are not just larger versions of small housing booms, but they lead to a categorically more difficult situation ex post. Consequently, it may be sensible to lean aggressively against big building booms, even if smaller building booms can be safely ignored.

4 The Complementarities Between Housing and Macroeconomic Policy

I now turn to the topic of housing market reform, particularly in the Netherlands. I first discuss some microeconomic considerations, and the turn to housing reform and the business cycle. I end this section by discussing the timing of land reform over the course of the business cycle.

The basic microeconomic case for building reform in the Netherlands, and much of Europe and coastal America, is that prices are far higher than construction costs. This fact does not imply that there should be more building everywhere. The distinctive beauty and character of Amsterdam could easily be destroyed by massive rebuilding in the city center. Yet, I suspect that there are places in the Netherlands where the difference between the willingness to pay and the marginal cost of construction are higher than any plausible negative externality from new building.

Even though the Netherlands is small geographically, the space needs of the Netherlands are likely to be limited, at least by U.S. standards. If the country needed to build one million more housing units, that might require about 100 million square meters of built space. The number of square kilometers required to deliver this space is 100 divided by the maximum Floor Area Ration (FAR), the average height at which building is possible.

At an average FAR of 10 (which is extremely high), one million homes require only 10 km^2, which is a circle with a radius of 1.8 km. At an average FAR of 5, one million homes require only a circle of land with a radius of 2.5 km. Large housing-supply growth is compatible with very modest loss of land, and little disturbance of historic city centers, as long as heights can be high enough.

Naturally enough, there would have to be sufficient demand for these higher-rise dwellings to justify their construction, which generates a link between the land use deregulation and transit access. For new construction to generate the most value, it needs to be in areas that are within easy commuting distance of the economic centers of the Netherlands, which include Amsterdam, Rotterdam and Brabant.

These then are the key ingredients in the microeconomic considerations around housing space. How much land to decontrol? How much density to allow in that land? How close will the land be to central cities? How much transportation access will there be? It is not the place of this essay to resolve these issues, but rather to stress that as macroeconomists enter into these debates, they must also consider other questions.

A more elastic supply of space in the long run, which means easier new building and easier rebuilding, seems likely to lead to more housing consumption and lower prices. More consumption means more construction employment and more volatile construction employment. Construction employment also means more immigration and more volatile immigration.

Macroeconomists should recognize that added employment volatility may be a downside of allowing more building, but that downside should be offset by decreasing housing-price volatility. As loan defaults are far rarer in the Netherlands than in the U.S. because of full recourse mortgages, this reduction in price volatility may be less important than it would be in the U.S. context. If Dutch consumers also spent their housing wealth, then increased price stability would lead to less consumption volatility.

Yet even if there was more elastic supply on the urban edge, some areas of the Netherlands would still be quite constrained. Owners within those areas could still experience large changes in housing wealth, even if prices on the urban edge were more fixed. Consequently, it is possible that increasingly elastic housing supply could boost employment volatility while still maintaining large amounts of price volatility among the most valuable Dutch homes.

I suspect it is unlikely that the Netherlands could ever experience a massive housing overbuild of the form seen in Las Vegas, Phoenix and possibly Spain in 2006. Still, if deregulation were massively successful, macroeconomically oriented entities would still need to display some prudential care against the possibility of such events.

A final issue is the relation between the business cycle and the timing of land reform. Typically, interest in land-market reforms heats up when prices are rising during a boom. This process occurred in Massachusetts between 2003 and 2006. A similar interest in land-use control reform is going on now in coastal California. Yet interest in such reform then disappears during a bust for understandable reasons.

Voters are far less interested in reducing housing prices during a recession. Cyclical concerns also suggest that hammering a down market further may be counter-productive. Surely, it would be far easier and economically healthier for housing market deregulation to coincide with the upswing in a market. Yet achieving this happy coincidence will not be easy, given the long delays in generating anything as contentious as land deregulation.

If deregulation is going to coincide with an upswing, then almost surely there needs to be enabling legislation passed during a downswing that will make progress relatively quick once prices start to move again. A similar argument also suggests that any desired reductions in public support for housing market entities like Fannie Mae and Freddie Mac should be set in motion during a downturn, but then implemented during an upturn.

5 Conclusion

Housing is typically analyzed through a static, or at least non-cyclical perspective. Yet housing markets frequently display enormous booms and busts that move larger financial markets along with them. The increasingly inelastic supply of housing in cities like Amsterdam seems likely to make housing-price fluctuations more severe, which increases the need for sound macro-prudential polices that protect against price drops. Conversely, there is less need to worry about large drops in construction employment.

Generally, we need worry less about price fluctuations in areas where housing supply is elastic, such as Texas, except when bubbles become so extreme that construction completely disappears during a bust. In those cases, elastic supply can be associated with extreme shifts in both price and quantity. Ex-post attempts to boost housing prices in these areas may have little impact on either employment or consumption if borrowers are largely underwater. In China, today, there are many third- and fourth-tier cities where construction has been enormous and there is at least the possibility of large price drops.

Going forward, macroeconomic policy should take the microeconomics of housing markets more seriously. Housing policy should consider more seriously the macroeconomic implications of any changes that would impact the elasticity of housing supply. The need to bring together the financial and the real sides of the housing markets is one of the clearest implications of the housing bust of 2007 and the Great Recession that followed it.

References

Case, K. E., Quigley, J. M., & Shiller, R. J. (2005, May). Comparing wealth effects: The stock market versus the housing market. *The B.E. Journal of Macroeconomics* (De Gruyter), *5*(1), 1–34.

De Groot, H. L. F., Marlet, G., Teulings, C., & Vermeulen, W. (2015). *Cities and the urban land premium*. Cheltenham: Edward Elgar Publishing.

Ganong, P., & Noel, P. (2017). *The effect of debt on default and consumption: Evidence from housing policy in the great recession* (Unpublished Working Paper).

Glaeser, E. L., & Nathanson, C. G. (2017). An extrapolative model of house price dynamics. *Journal of Financial Economics, 126*(1), 147–170.

Glaeser, E. L., & Ward, B. A. (2009). The causes and consequences of land use regulation: Evidence from greater Boston. *Journal of Urban Economics, 65*(3), 265–278.

Glaeser, E. L., Gyourko, J., & Saks, R. (2005). Why is Manhattan so expensive? Regulation and the rise in housing prices. *The Journal of Law and Economics, 48*(2), 331–369.

Glaeser, E. L., Gyourko, J., & Saiz, A. (2008). Housing supply and housing bubbles. *Journal of Urban Economics, 64*, 198–217.

Glaeser, E. L., Gottlieb, J. D., & Gyourko, J. (2012). Can cheap credit explain the housing boom? In *Housing and the financial crisis* (pp. 301–359). Chicago: University of Chicago Press.

Hsieh, C.-T., & Moretti, E. (2017). *Housing constraints and spatial misallocation* (NBER Working Paper # 21154).

Katz, L., & Rosen, K. T. (1987). The interjurisdictional effects of growth controls on housing prices. *The Journal of Law and Economics, 30*(1), 149–160.

Chapter 9
Some Brief Thoughts on Housing Supply and Policy

Albert Saiz

1 Introduction

Housing markets have come to occupy a central position in the contemporaneous policy discourse of developed countries. In the past two decades, many of our cities experienced episodes of rapid home value appreciation, oftentimes accompanied by a subsequent correction. In many of the largest and most popular European cities—usually political or commercial capitals—these cyclical fluctuations cannot disguise a discernable longer run trend of substantial housing price inflation.

Raising housing prices—which may or may not imply higher user costs and lower affordability—are coming to garner substantial interest from policymakers and the public. Housing is first-order necessity, and as such commands the attention of us all.

The reasons for affordability issues in key European cities can be summarized in four major separate themes. First, increased income inequality and economic stagnation in some countries signify that the purchasing power of low-income households and the middle-class is growing slowly. This is an economic growth problem beyond and above the dynamics of housing markets (Glaeser and Gyourko 2018). Second, the productivity of the construction sector typically lags that of the economy at large. The costs of building only rise slightly faster than inflation, but are clearly growing *relative* to other consumer goods. Given the lackluster rates of income growth in many EU countries, this signifies that the share of household expenditures on housing for wide sections of the population may be growing (Albouy et al. 2016). Third, some of the most increasingly popular cities display relatively inelastic housing supplies and *not-in-my-backyard* (NIMBY) anti real estate development attitudes. Finally, a fourth set of factors relates to capital markets and an environment

A. Saiz (✉)
Department of Urban Studies and Planning, Massachusetts Institute of Technology, Cambridge, MA, USA
e-mail: saiz@mit.edu

R. Nijskens et al. (eds.), *Hot Property*, https://doi.org/10.1007/978-3-030-11674-3_9

of low interest rates pushing up real estate valuations. This may not represent a problem for households with access to cheap credit—which may after all be enjoying low mortgage costs. However, it may create an insurmountable barrier for an increasing share of the population after the 2008 crisis who are unable to access credit or do not posses the substantial down payments that are now required to buy a home. In addition, a few key cities are experiencing direct foreign investment into housing, thereby further heating their markets.

In parallel to the realization that price levels are becoming unaffordable for some, there has been increasing recognition of the role of the housing market on economic fluctuations. Indeed, prominent economists have argued that "housing is the business cycle" (Leamer 2015). Consequently, housing issues have now become critical for monetary policy, as much as they are for urban planning and for national policies focusing on social welfare and cohesion.

In this short piece, I will make several considerations about the impact of housing supply on housing prices, affordability, and macroeconomic aggregates. I am focused on elucidating the key interactions between supply and demand that generate macroeconomic problems and lack of affordability. I put some emphasis on the distinction between short run and long run housing supply. My main conclusions are not new: policymakers should be aware of the Tinbergen rule. We should use multiple tools to address the multiple problems arising from housing markets. By solely focusing on one dimension we may miss big on all objectives. I will also argue that countercyclical supply-side policies are particularly damaging. I will further advocate for better data-driven mortgage underwriting models that go beyond mark-to-market and try to forecast future equilibrium prices. Finally, I will make an argument for a return to ambitious master-planned city building endeavors in our most expensive cities.

2 User Cost, Demand for Dwellings, and Housing Prices

A good starting point to understand equilibrium housing values is the simplified version of the equation in Poterba's (1984) capital asset pricing model:

$$v_t P_t = \Delta P_t + R_t \tag{9.1}$$

Here P_t stands for housing prices at time t, R_t for rents in the same period, and v_t for the gross *user cost rate* of capital, excluding capital gains. The rate v captures all monetary and opportunity carry costs of owning a home, expressed as a percentage of its value. This parameter includes—most saliently—mortgage costs, home maintenance expenses, tax deductions, and other more technical terms such as a factor capturing the relative cash-flow risks of owning versus renting (Sinai and Souleles 2005). The left-hand side can be interpreted as the full annual homeownership cost of carry. At any point in time, the arbitrage condition requires that the cost of ownership equals its benefits. Assuming zero mobility costs, households should try to ensure that they obtain housing in the cheapest way possible by either renting or owning, thereby enforcing the equality. The benefits of owning—on the right hand side—equal net real capital appreciation (ΔP_t) and savings from eschewing rental payments to a landlord (R_t). In turn, long term equilibrium rental prices should be driven by the fundamental drivers of demand for the city, interacted by the long term housing supply therein.

If the temporal path of rents were known and user costs were constant, then the path of housing price growth should be fully determined in advance. It is worth restating this once again: in the absence of bubbles, all changes in housing prices should be due to either future rental growth or changes in the cost of capital. Expectations about *future* changes in prices should also be derived from either expected changes in rental growth or to the cost of capital. Note that Eq. (9.1) implies convexity: in environments with low initial percent user costs, the same percentage point decrease in mortgage rates is expected to increase housing demand and prices by more.

Note further that this simple model abstracts from housing quality; $v_t P_t$ here is the annuitized cost of home ownership. Cheaper capital implies lower annuitized user costs and higher housing asset demand. However, as annuitized housing ownership costs go down, it is likely for some consumers to derive part of their increased purchasing power into acquiring better housing *quality*. Therefore, the income effect of a low interest rate environment can manifest itself through relatively more demand—and pricing pressures—in prime neighborhoods.

3 Capital Markets and Housing

I have no doubt that part of the story explaining growing housing valuations in many countries was the availability of cheaper capital, as would be expected from the asset pricing formula. An abundance of global capital and low yields in the last 15 years have therefore made their way into the mortgage and real estate investment markets. The reasons for the—probably misnamed—savings glut are many and controversial, and may include: loose monetary policies; global capital market consolidation; and the phenomenal growth of large economies with trade surpluses. Simultaneously, increasing global product competition from emerging markets has kept inflationary pressures on manufactured goods and wages at bay.

In my view, ad hoc national stories are just representations of the same global phenomenon: capital inflows or easy monetary policy allowing for low user costs and yield compression. Of course, the actors in this play are different in the different countries. It is sometimes tempting to blame the specific characters in one's own national cast of institutions for skyrocketing housing prices. For instance, in the United States some observers blamed the housing bubble of the 2000s on the ease at which subprime lenders were able to unload their toxic assets onto the securitized MBS market, under conditions of strong asymmetric information.

While local institutions matter, I think that we can liken this situation to that of a number of different homes, all with leaky roofs. If the storm is big enough, as water (capital) comes down the roof it will eventually find its way to the basement (housing markets), but using different channels in each home; be it through the stairs, piping, siding, or down the chimney.

Capital and money abundance found a way to housing markets through securitization in the USA. In Spain, the bank channel, was the most important: the Maastricht treaty and accession to the Euro generated swift prime interest rate converge, as Spanish banks could get easy credit in safe currency from the European interbank market. Mortgage rate convergence to the core countries was abrupt. In prime markets, such as the UK and Scandinavian countries, we have seen a tightening of real estate yields and risk premia, especially after the financial crisis: capital investors—some of them local—have found it less appealing to invest in more exotic destinations. In other countries—such as Mongolia, Kazakhstan, and Azerbaijan—the housing boom and bust cycle was associated with a Dutch disease phenomenon: the increasing prices of export staples before the global crisis implied large inflows of foreign currency and growing prices of non-tradeables. In China, housing price inflation is partially driven by domestic small investors; a large share of national capital there is non-investable, controlled by state-owned enterprises. The large savings of the populace are finding their way into the housing market via direct investments in second homes. In a few global cities—London, Dubai, New York, Vancouver, Sidney, Auckland—abundant global capital has similarly found its way into the local housing market via direct purchases from foreign investors.

Nevertheless, it is important to remember that demand pressures are necessary but not sufficient conditions for price growth. Their interaction with supply is what matters in the long run (Saks 2008; Saiz 2010). A housing market with no significant barriers to entry cannot sustain continued housing price growth.

It is in this context that we sometimes confuse the problem of long-term housing unaffordability with that of bubbles or irrational exuberance. The former arises from demand fundamentals interacted with inelastic housing supply. The latter can happen even with regards to real estate assets that can be easily replicated at replacement costs, and whose value should not deviate much from such.

Incidentally, irrationalities in economic markets abound. The issue for macroeconomists is whether institutional factors negate such behavioral biases in the aggregate. For instance, irrational bubbles are less likely in markets where all information is available, salient, and common; where assets are easily tradable; short-selling is possible; with attentive participants or sophisticated arbitrageurs; small transaction or moving costs; frequent transactions for buyers and sellers to acquire experience; or mostly driven by professional investors (as opposed to retail buyers). Many of these features are missing in the housing market. Arguably, we came out of the rational expectations revolution too focused on individual rationality as opposed to the more relevant question: when and where do behavioral biases matter?

4 Housing Supply, Affordability, and Overheating

I want next to hypothesize on how differences between short-term versus long-term housing supply may exacerbate the information problems that feed into behavioral mispricing and oversupply in housing markets. Consider Fig. 9.1 below. Largescale housing production requires of a long-lagged production process, entailing among others: land entitlement, zoning, planning, permitting, financing, pre-sales, infrastructure, building construction, interior finishes, utility servicing, marketing, and sales. This means that the short-run supply of housing with regards to unexpected or sudden shocks to demand is very inelastic (purple segment), because we can only rush or repurpose a few units quickly into production. As demand pressures surpass previous expectations (from D1 to D2) they may translate mostly into higher prices for some time (P_{boom}). Of course, no rational buyer should pay substantially more than the long run equilibrium price as justified by fundamentals (P*) for such durable good. Nevertheless real consumers seem to be doing just that. Especially when using other people's money to do so. More vexingly, financial systems seem to underwrite long-term collateral at such short-term prices, which are not based on long run fundamentals.

Naturally, at P_{boom} developers want to be producing and selling as many units as financially profitable, at Q_{LR}. The issue of whether developers believe that boom-times pricing is sustainable is only relevant to account for the speed at which they will want to unload their newly-produced stock. Globally, some of the areas that experienced the worst boom-bust cycles were those with rapid demographic growth. It is certainly possible that homebuyers and speculators there had a harder time extracting signals about how much of the parallel booms in pricing (P_{boom}) and new

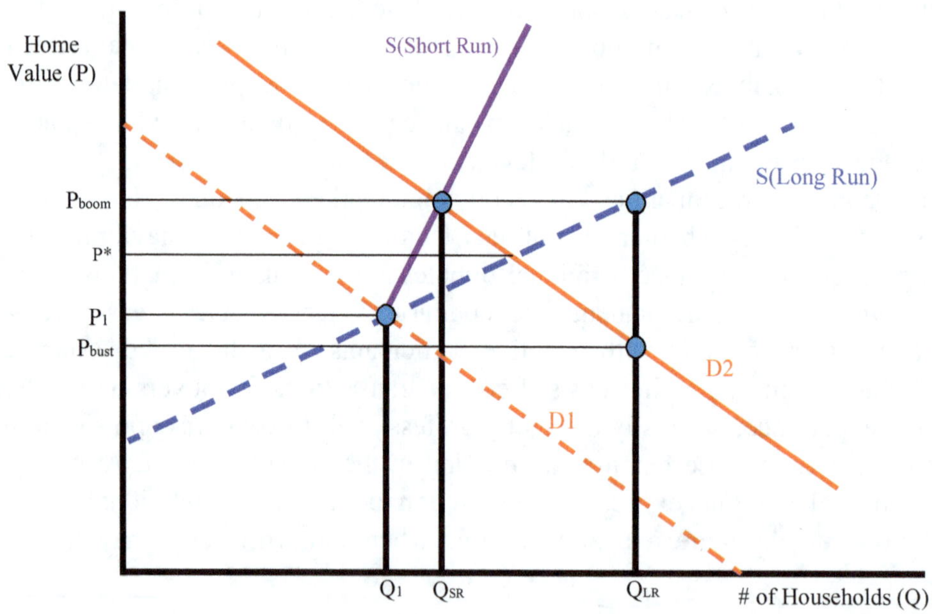

Fig. 9.1 Housing supply and demand with elastic supply

development construction (Q_{LR}-Q_1) were due to fundamental growth versus exuberance.

Conversely, in areas with secularly limited household growth, it was the potential large development boom (Q_{LR}-Q_1) that may have seemed exuberantly unlikely to investors, thereby dampening lending and investments in new construction.

Expectations must catch up with reality eventually. At P_{boom} developers may have supplied up to Q_{LR}. And the new housing stock is extremely durable. Hence, the new equilibrium—back to demand expectations based on fundamentals (the ability of households to carry housing costs under reasonable appreciation paths)—should take us all the way down to P_{bust}. Remember that housing is totally inelastic on the way down (Glaeser and Gyourko 2005).

The differences in the slope of the short term and long run housing supply could thus be behind over-construction cycles during periods with large demand shifts, like the ones prompted by decreasing user costs of housing capital.

Local observers are often astute in pointing to over-supply issues at the peak of housing boom-busts cycles. I have, unfortunately, heard arguments advocating for constraining real estate development and construction in order to avoid overbuilding cycles. In the minds of people who make such arguments, boom and bust cycles are due to the excessive "liberalization" of the housing market. In my view, this concern is misplaced. In fact, I would argue that housing supply constraints are already too tight in many large European cities. The temptation to restrict supply in order to prevent overbuilding will exacerbate long-term affordability problems in the most successful cities.

Consider Fig. 9.2 below, applying to city with a much more inelastic housing supply. Here, because the long run supply schedule is already very steep, the

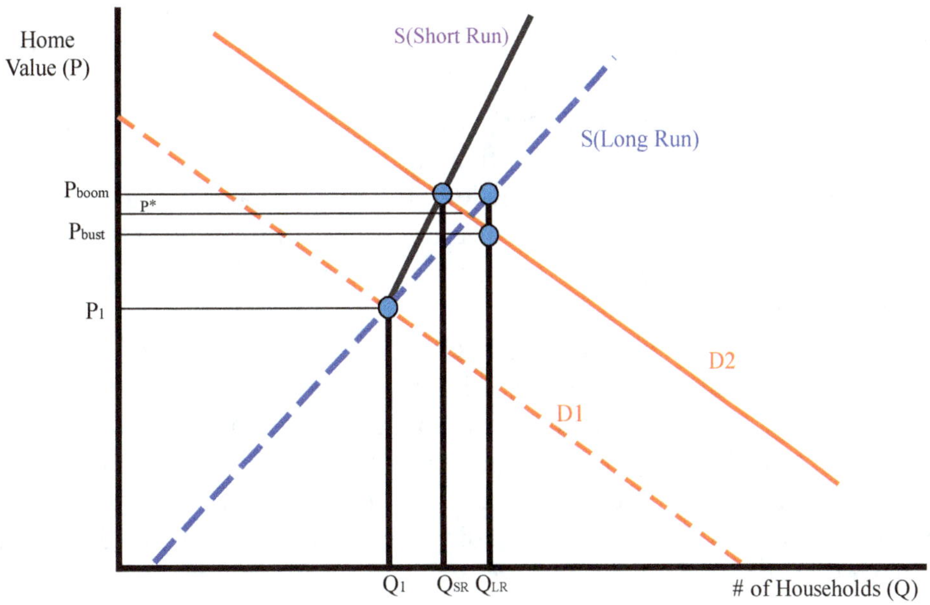

Fig. 9.2 Housing supply and demand with inelastic supply

differences between short term and long term supply are not as large. There is less over-construction and the boom-bust price difference is small. Anti-supply policies can indeed retard development and reduce the gap between long term and short-term construction. However, this would be a pyrrhic victory: the housing market has now become very unaffordable, a much worse problem for most citizens.

The main problem with using constraining supply-side policies countercyclically is that regulators do not know the nature of the shocks that are hitting the housing market, and may therefore confuse irrational overbuilding with fundamental demand pressures.

Policymakers have more than one objective with regards to housing markets. They should therefore heed Tinbergen's rule, and use a different policy instrument to attain each objective. It is problematic to use the same policy instrument—e.g. constraints on credit expansion—to combat both housing unaffordability and irrational market overheating or overbuilding.

For two potential problems we need at least two separate policy instruments. It is probably best to use demand-side instruments to fight against market overheating. The set of existing tools here typically revolves around setting more conservative underwriting standards—lower Loan-To-Value (LTV) ratios, more stringent household income validation, higher mortgage rates. These instruments have been somewhat effective in the past. However, we should hope for better ones in the future.

5 Mortgage Underwriting Using Fundamental Housing Valuation Forecasts (FHVF)

A potential idea is for banks to underwrite mortgages using forecasted expected equilibrium prices, rather than current mark-to-market valuations. Going back to Fig. 9.1, it is really strange to see financial institutions underwriting long-term credit at P_{boom}, even in markets where the supply elasticity is very high and a new building can be eventually begotten at construction cost plus a modest land outlay. Underwriting based on current market transaction prices is mandatory in many countries, so laws and banking regulations will need to change. More stringent capital ratios should be applied to any mortgage lending that goes above and beyond a maximum percentage of FHVFs.

Imagine—hypothetically and going back to seventeenth Century Netherlands—that the authorities had required banks and wealthy merchants to extend credit for up to 90% of the market value of tulip bulb contracts to anyone buying them. Such policy would have *likely* exacerbated the tulip mania of 1636–1637. But regardless of the extent of its general equilibrium impact on prices, the policy would have *certainly* forced the collapse of more lending institutions. Inducing creditors to lend at collateral valuations that are potentially determined by a bubble does not make much sense. But many housing finance policies and institutions around the world are doing just that!

I propose that financial institutions or central banks use data from past urban growth and housing values in each city, plus other urban characteristics—extent of restrictive planning, green belts, geographic constraints, urban structure, rental gradients within cities—in order to estimate local housing supply elasticity schedules. One could then come up with estimates of housing demand shocks—e.g. the impact of changes in user costs on demand, or demographic growth—in order to forecast long run equilibrium prices. To reiterate, it makes sense for institutions that have a long-term stake on an asset to estimate alternative valuation scenarios at 5, 10, 15 year maturities, and so on. Nowadays, professional assessments or automated valuation models (AVM) simply estimate what people are paying *right now* for similar properties. Even simple FHVF time series models with mean reversion to an equilibrium price are likely to do better than AVMs to assess long-term credit risk.

Publically traded futures or over-the-counter forward contracts based on metropolitan price indexes—which could attract sophisticated analytical players—have achieved so far limited reach. Therefore, central banks may be well positioned to offer FHVF models for several of the largest metropolitan areas at different future maturities, as a public good to the banking system.

Allowing for underwriting standards that mark to FHVFs would feature positive automatic stabilizer qualities. Consider a thought experiment with two cities: A and B. Housing supply in A is very inelastic, whereas it is very elastic in B. Both cities feature the same demand shock, perhaps due to lower mortgage rates. However, both cities have experienced similar rapid housing price appreciation, with home values doubling. It is possible—though uncertain—that city A's housing market is overheated. But it is very clear that housing prices in B should have grown much less than in A. With good estimates of the elasticities of demand and local supply, the central bank can come up with a forecast that predicts lower long-term equilibrium prices at B. Banks therefore underwrite their 30-year mortgage credit using lower long-run valuations there. Mark-to-market LTVs at B automatically decrease, making it hard for people to pay exuberant prices. In equilibrium, this dampens demand pressures until prices at B moderate to, approximately, their fundamental values.

Note that applying FHVF underwriting standards is not tantamount to the banks setting housing prices themselves. Consumers can always decide to pledge more funds toward paying for any market price they want to buy at, however farfetched. FHVF underwriting just prevents them from using other people's money to do so.

Without a doubt, it is very difficult for politicians to pass measures that seem to restrict access to credit, even if banks are now underwriting rationally and countercyclically. As the boom frenzy feeds the housing market in city B above—and until credit constraints dampen prices—some households may be unable to afford the required down payments. They will typically be young and less well off.

Nevertheless, politicians should be aware of the general equilibrium implications of letting credit standards blindly follow after housing price growth. By providing powerful weapons—credit—to all customers, they are effectively putting them in a circular firing squad: it may be precisely the generalized availability of credit that reinforces the problem of over-pricing, fueling the bubble and exacerbating unaffordability. With a substantial share of credit-constrained households—in theory—mortgage underwriting that marks to long-term fundamental valuations should impede for bubbles to arise in the first place.

6 Make Supply Elastic Again

Going back to the Tinbergen rule, long-term affordability issues need separate policy tools than those applied to overheating. Supply side interventions are the optimal candidates here. Generally speaking, policymakers may want to make both long and short term housing supply as elastic as possible.

There remain substantial barriers to construction and densification in many of the more attractive European cities. These areas are experiencing growing demand due to the consumer city phenomenon (Glaeser and Gyourko 2018; Carlino and Saiz 2008). European countries may have been expected to experience lackluster housing demand expansion. Most countries do not display strong demographic growth; the process of reduction in household sizes seems to have reached a limit (remember that: total number of homes demanded = population × [homes/person]); the positive income elasticity of space could perhaps be decreasing due to cultural changes that emphasize compact-city, green living. However, the competition between cities to attract talent and provide an improved lifestyle has unambiguously grown. Excepting for immigrant arrivals, the main driver of real estate development in European cities is therefore the redistribution of national demand towards the most attractive cities.

Of course, this implies symmetrical negative pressures on second and third tier cities and markets, which may experience decline. This phenomenon may translate into political pressures for national governments to enact anti-development regulations or to discriminate against the most successful cities. These turn to be counterproductive, rendering successful cities even more expensive and pricing out their working classes, without avoiding the exodus of entrepreneurs and the highly skilled from lower-tier areas. More strategically, anti large city policies may be really missing the point: do Europeans want to have global cities that are able to hold their own in the worldwide competition for talent and employers, or not?

I have discussed innovative supply-based strategies to provide affordable housing elsewhere (Saiz and Salazar 2017). Some of the ideas include: adaptive reuse; residential development in post-industrial cities; inclusionary upzoning; densification; infill; suburban master-planned communities; micro-units; accessory units; co-living; sweat equity in construction; building cooperatives; mixed for/non-profit developments; negotiations with unions; use of prefab materials and technology in construction; and the development of flexible rental market institutions.

Notwithstanding any potential innovations, NIMBY opposition to real estate development will keep on being a major issue in Europe, as it is in the United States.

But, in fairness, many isolated housing development projects do not provide much to current homeowners in terms of aesthetics, urbanistic externalities, amenities and services, or civic virtue. As Saiz and Salazar (2017) write:

> Reducing NIMBY pressures in the suburbs requires building coalitions and garnering some support from local communities. This can be done by offering a positive holistic vision for development. In some cases this underscores the need for large master-planned neighborhoods that offer plenty of amenities to be enjoyed by all in town. The execution of suburban development master plans can add value to existing residents' lives by delivering mixed-use, walkable town centers that provide amenities such as parks, promenades, playgrounds, and restaurants. These large-scale, multi-period developments can also anchor civic activities—festivals, farmers' markets—or integrate and centralize public buildings—senior centers, libraries—in a convenient and enjoyable location. Existing residents may be even more likely to support such plans if they bring permanent local jobs, have well-designed positive impacts on local education systems, and replace previously developed sites that were eyesores.

I would like to exhort European civic leaders to think big again, and create templates for massive, new, mixed-used developments within our most expensive metropolitan areas. These should include plans for tens of thousands of market-supplied new residential units. By frontloading most the planning and approvals processes within these special zoning areas, developers can flexibly phase in or out construction: stopping when markets slow down; quickly responding to increasing demand. Our leaders should inspire the public to get deeply involved in improving the *quality* of new development, eschewing counterproductive obsessions about its quantity. The scale of the new megacities cities now arising in the developing world—China, Saudi Arabia, Korea—is unlikely to be suitable to the European situation. Yet citizens in super-expensive metros do need inspiring projects that pass market muster, are self-financing, have net positive environmental impact, help resolve affordability problems, and allow them to dream big. It is incumbent among our political leaders to thus drive the renewal of our collective ambitions into such economically productive endeavors.

References

Albouy, D., Ehrlich, G., & Liu, Y. (2016). *Housing demand, cost-of-living inequality, and the affordability crisis* (National Bureau of Economic Research Working Paper No. w22816).

Carlino, G. A., & Saiz, A. (2008). *Beautiful city: Leisure amenities and urban growth* (FRB of Philadelphia Working Paper No. 08-22).

Glaeser, E. L., & Gyourko, J. (2005). Urban decline and durable housing. *Journal of Political Economy, 113*(2), 345–375.

Glaeser, E., & Gyourko, J. (2018). The economic implications of housing supply. *Journal of Economic Perspectives, 32*(1), 3–30.

Leamer, E. (2015). Housing really is the business cycle: What survives the lessons of 2008–2009? *Journal of Money, Credit and Banking, 47*(S1), 43–50.

Poterba, J. M. (1984). Tax subsidies to owner-occupied housing: An asset-market approach. *The Quarterly Journal of Economics, 99*(4), 729–752.

Saiz, A. (2010). The geographic determinants of housing supply. *The Quarterly Journal of Economics, 125*(3), 1253–1296.

Saiz, A., & Salazar, A. (2017). *Real trends: The future of real estate in the united states* (SSRN Working Paper 3100934).

Saks, R. E. (2008). Job creation and housing construction: Constraints on metropolitan area employment growth. *Journal of Urban Economics, 64*(1), 178–195.

Sinai, T., & Souleles, N. S. (2005). Owner-occupied housing as a hedge against rent risk. *The Quarterly Journal of Economics, 120*(2), 763–789.

Chapter 10
The Smouldering Issue

Laurens Ivens

'Hot Property' is what De Nederlandsche Bank has called this conference proceedings and the seminar held on the 24th and 25th of May 2018. The Amsterdam housing market has indeed become overheated. As Alderman for Housing, I am the fire brigade, with the task of limiting the human risks, keeping adjacent parcels wet and preventing the fire from spreading.

1 Shifting Towards the Market for Two Decades

The Amsterdam housing market has changed enormously in the last quarter century. In the 90s, almost 90% of the supply of housing consisted of rental homes, largely in the affordable segment. Many of these rental homes were owned by housing associations. Until that time, the associations were an extension of the government, until they were privatized in the mid-nineties because the national government wanted to economize and believed that the building of homes should be left to the market sector. The owner-occupied sector was almost completely absent in Amsterdam. At the same time, the Municipality of Amsterdam had just started to provide a countervoice to the years of outflow of higher-income households to other parts of Noord-Holland and the new cities of Flevoland. The Municipality entered into competition with this suburbanization by building new districts on the edge of the city and on released port and factory sites. Mostly larger homes were built in the more expensive rental and owner-occupied segment, intended for households with a need for space (families) and higher incomes. The construction of owner-occupied homes was the means of keeping these households in Amsterdam. Such construction

L. Ivens (✉)
Amsterdam, The Netherlands
e-mail: l.ivens@amsterdam.nl

R. Nijskens et al. (eds.), *Hot Property*, https://doi.org/10.1007/978-3-030-11674-3_10

of owner-occupied homes has seen to it that over thirty per cent of the Amsterdam housing supply consists of owner-occupied homes. From a Dutch point of view, this is still a negligible share, but in terms of Amsterdam it meant a considerable change to the composition of the housing market. The sale of rental homes also contributed to this. In the nineties, many private rental homes were converted to owner-occupied homes. Housing association homes were already being converted into privately owned homes before the turn of the century (a few hundred each year), but as from 2003 the number of homes being converted increased to thousands of homes per year. In addition, substantial urban renewal had been taking place for years in the post-war residential areas of the city, during which many housing association homes were demolished, rebuilt in part, but also replaced by privately owned homes.

Reduction of the social rental sector and stimulation of the market sector, both privately owned and more expensive rental, had gained the upper hand for several decades. The municipal authorities carefully monitored whether this trend was still in line with the households and income composition of the Amsterdam population. The survey Living in Amsterdam (*Wonen in Amsterdam*), which the Municipality conducts every two years together with the housing associations, provides a measurement for this. Before the economic crisis from 2008 to 2014, which had a substantial effect on the housing market in Amsterdam as well, it was already clear that the argument for reducing the social rental sector was starting to lose strength. The social rental sector was actually shrinking more quickly than the number of low-income households was decreasing, and the difference between the two started becoming smaller. During the crisis the number of low-income households appeared to increase again. Therefore the shrinking of the social rental sector is now being examined more critically in Amsterdam.

Characteristics of the Amsterdam Housing Market

In early 2017, Amsterdam had almost 428,000 homes: privately owned 33%, housing associations 43%, private rental 24%. Of these homes 29% are in the expensive segment (with purchase prices over €250,000 and rents over €971 per month), 16% in the moderately priced segment (with purchase prices between €156,000 and €250,000 and rents of €711 and €971 per month) and 55% in the cheap segment (with purchase prices below €156,000 and rents below €711 per month).

After the crisis, from 2014 an average of 6600 new homes were built per year. The average price of a privately owned home rose by 50% in de period 2014–2017 (the Netherlands: 10%) and is now €359,000 (the Netherlands: €244,000). The largest price rises were observed in the central city zone defined by the A10 Ring Road and the Northern IJ shore. The pressure on the Amsterdam housing market will continue unabated in the next few years. The number of residents of Amsterdam has increased in the last few years by about 10,000 people per year. Half of the growth is due to natural accretion

(continued)

(births minus deaths) and half is due to a positive migration balance. On 1 January 2018 Amsterdam had 856,000 residents. The demographic forecasts for 2030 vary from 922,000 to 1,019,000 residents.

Looking back two decades, in 1997 Amsterdam had 715,000 residents, 359,500 homes, of which 15% were privately owned, 57% owned by housing associations and 29% private rental.

2 Agreements with Housing Associations are at the Forefront

In the meantime, several things have changed, owing to which the Municipality of Amsterdam has no longer been able to take charge of the development of the affordable part of the housing supply as well as before. Until 2013, the sale of homes owned by housing associations and transfer of controlled rental homes to the profit rental market was a matter of sensible consultations with the housing associations, but since that year the Landlord Levy imposed by the national government on housing associations has influenced the policy of the housing associations. We found this for example in the high number of housing association homes sold in 2014 and 2015 (more than 5000 in these 2 years together). Housing associations felt compelled to earn money by selling in order to pay the Landlord Levy. The other change is the amendment of the House Pricing System.[1] Because of this the WOZ value counts to a substantial degree in the number of quality points and therefore determines the potential amount of the rent. This is mainly significant for the tens of thousands of rental homes of private landlords who because of this change are easily able to transfer them from the rent-controlled segment to profit rental market. And this is where the link is found to the overheating of the market. The WOZ value of homes has risen enormously in the last few years. During the housing market crisis the prices on the market of privately owned homes in Amsterdam experienced a fall, but now that the crisis is over, the selling prices are breaking records. The price development on the privately owned market also has an effect on the value of rental homes.

The financial situation of housing associations has meanwhile calmed down somewhat. The possibility to ask higher rents has provided enough money to enable

[1]Since 1 October 2015 the national system has been changed by which it is determined whether a rental home belongs to the rent-controlled segment (<€711) or to profit rental market. The determining factor is whether the number of quality points of a home is below or above a certain number. Until 1 October 2015 quality characteristics such as the surface area of the home were strongly determinative of the number of points. After this date the location has also counted to a significant extent. The location variable is derived from the WOZ value (value for the purposes of the Valuation of Immovable Property Act), and this is relatively high in Amsterdam.

them to abandon a large number of sales, and housing associations have now become more careful with their possessions. In the last cooperative agreements between the Municipality, housing associations and tenants (2014) the number of homes to be sold has meanwhile been reduced to a maximum of 2000 per year and the number of homes to be converted to the profit rental sector to 1000 per year. But the housing associations are striving for considerably lower numbers. In addition, it has been agreed with the housing associations not to allow the number of housing association homes with a monthly rent up to €711 to fall below 162,000, with the aim of staying far away from that lower limit. Housing associations are being forced more and more by government policy to limit themselves to the management and rental of rent-controlled homes, i.e. homes with a maximum rent of up to €711 per month and primarily intended for low-income households.

3 Overheating of the Amsterdam Housing Market

Privately owned and rental homes are rapidly becoming more expensive in Amsterdam at present. Since 2014 the average WOZ values of homes have risen by about 50% and the prices are already far above the level of before the crisis on the housing market (2007). This is making the homes increasingly more unaffordable for low and middle income households. This is no problem for households that already live in Amsterdam as long as they do not wish to move house. But it is difficult for families with children to find an affordable larger home. Consequently they remove more and more often to a regional municipality. And it is difficult for starters to capture a spot on the Amsterdam housing market. Young people seek refuge in shared homes or, for those who can afford it, small studios.

The demand for profit rental homes has surged in the past few years. This is the result of the labour market becoming flexible, stricter mortgage requirements and internationalization. Temporary employment contracts are making it increasingly difficult to obtain a mortgage. In addition, the mortgage requirements have been toughened since the economic crisis, owing to which starters on the housing market may borrow less and have to repay more than households that already have a privately owned home and may take their existing type of mortgage along to a new home. Moreover, Amsterdam is growing to an increasing extent through the influx of international students and more highly educated foreign starters. This group mainly seeks homes in the profit rental segment because they are often quickly available and provide the flexibility this group needs. This rapidly growing demand has caused the prices of rental homes to rise more quickly in many parts of Amsterdam than those of privately owned homes. In the profit market segment of the private rental sector the average rent in 2017 was €1248 per month, according to the survey Living in Amsterdam 2017, whereas this was €1185 on average per month in 2015. The rents on the profit rental market are therefore reaching values that are no longer feasible for middle-income households.

Another consequence of the demand for expensive rental homes, combined with the low interest rates which make buying attractive, is that (smaller) private investors are buying homes to let, so called buy-to-let. Exact numbers of these homes are not available, but the impression exists that this phenomenon will gain ground quickly in Amsterdam.

4 Exerting Counterpressure on the Market

Overheating has seen to it that more and more groups that previously had easy access to the Amsterdam housing market are now excluded from it. This is putting pressure on the old ideal of the undivided city in which rich and poor live amongst one another. Amsterdam politicians therefore decided in 2017 to exert counterpressure on the market developments. The Housing Agenda 2025 has been adopted, in which it is stipulated that the target for new construction is 40% controlled rent (rents up to €711 per month), 40% moderately priced rent or purchase and 20% market-value homes. It was agreed as well that the share of social rentals in the different parts of the city may not end up below 35%. The main means of management of the Municipality of Amsterdam is new construction; for the existing supply of housing, the Municipality is dependent on national legislation. The Municipality of Amsterdam owns approximately 80% of the land in the Municipality and issues it under long-term leases. This gives the Municipality private law instruments in addition to public law instruments to manage the development of property in the city. The land is also issued under long-term ground leases in the event of new construction. This working method makes it possible by applying private law to include requirements for designated use (for example rental in a specific segment) in the long-term lease.

Together with the Housing Agenda, new policy was developed in 2017 for the construction of moderately priced rental homes. The basis of this policy is the possibility to set requirements by way of the issue of land under a long-term lease. The starting points of the policy are as follows:

- Construction of at least 1500 moderately priced rental homes per year by way of new construction or transformation (in case of transformation of buildings on leasehold land the Municipality can also set out agreements for the new designated use in the long lease because in case of transformation it will be necessary to amend the long lease);
- 25-year rental in the moderately priced rental sector (rents of €711–€971 per month, price level 2017);
- Inflation-related rent increases;
- No required purchase of a parking space;
- No more than 50% of homes assigned to persons moving on from the social sector;

- Other homes are assigned to households with an income up to 1.5 times the average income;
- The possibility exists, contrary to the market, to construct larger moderately priced rental homes.

The first four sites where moderately priced rental homes have been planned under these conditions have now been put on the market by way of tenders. There is much interest from the market in tendering for them.

In 2017 the Municipal Council also asked to have research done on the possibilities to manage the market for privately owned homes. This study was conducted[2] and shows that in a booming economy, a choice can best be made of measures that increase the supply of moderately priced privately owned homes. According to the study, the measures with the best chance of success are the additional construction of privately owned homes on market terms, entering into discussion with housing associations about offering privately owned homes under conditions (*KoopGarant*), introducing an obligation to occupy and experimenting with purchaser's cooperatives. In addition, the researchers advise entering into discussion with the national government about national legislation concerning the purchase market. One can think of raising the limit of the National Mortgage Guarantee in Amsterdam and making it possible to assign homes in the privately owned sector.

Further to these outcomes, the Municipality is now going to examine in what way the obligation to occupy in combination with an anti-speculation clause can be established for newly constructed homes. The Municipal Council has also asked if it is possible to establish an obligation to occupy for existing privately owned homes. The study of the feasibility of this is still in progress at present.

5 Limits on the Management Possibilities of Municipalities

As stated, taking charge of new construction is one of the Municipality's main management instruments. We can eventually use it to make an important contribution to keeping the housing market accessible. For the construction of homes, however, the Municipality is also dependent on market players: the Municipality provides development sites and indicates on which schedule they can be constructed; the market builds. Present price developments have caused the new homes to be increasingly smaller, in the social sector as well as in the moderately priced and expensive segments. This has made increasingly less room for families and there is a risk that these small homes will lead to a shorter duration of occupation and

[2]This study, commissioned by the Municipality of Amsterdam, was conducted by the research agency Rebel Strategy and Development BV in collaboration with the Research Institute OTB of the TU Delft.

negligible social cohesion. These market developments can only be adjusted to a limited extent.

A great impact will have to be made in the short term by measures for the existing housing supply, which is many times larger in size than the annual construction carried out. In the Netherlands, the municipalities are responsible for housing policy, but not for the legislation and the funds, and that is pressing. For instance, rental policy is the same for all locations in the Netherlands, whereas the high market pressure in Amsterdam requires a customized local approach. One can think of raising the profit market threshold, which will cause more homes to end up in the rent-controlled segment. Amsterdam also argues in favour of allowing housing associations to invest in the moderately priced segment again. In conclusion, Amsterdam will benefit from measures that prevent excesses such as conversion into houses in multiple occupation, holiday rental and buy-to-let.

Chapter 11
Housing Markets in Scandinavia: Supply, Demand and Regulation

Kjersti Næss Torstensen and Kasper Roszbach

This chapter discusses the recent developments in the housing markets of Scandinavian capital cities and some of the policy challenges these developments are bringing about.[1] First, we will briefly review some demographic trends, both over the past 10 years and looking ahead. Next, we will show some statistics on the build-up of housing supply shortages and what has happened to the price of housing. Then, drawing on a few recent housing market studies, we will go over the observed and likely consequences of housing shortages and house prices rises. Finally, we will discuss the geographical mortgage policy that was implemented in Norway, with a particular focus on restricting mortgage lending in Oslo a year ago. We conclude with a few takeaways.

This text is based on a presentation Kasper Roszbach gave at the seminar on "Hot Property: the housing market in major cities" held at De Nederlandsche Bank on May 24–25, 2018. The views expressed in this chapter are those of the authors and do not necessarily reflect those of Norges Bank or the Executive Board of Sveriges Riksbank.

[1]Because it is hard to get uniform statistics across all dimensions of housing markets in Scandinavia, we will discuss data for single countries and generalize these to other Scandinavian cities, while being aware of the limitations of the data. We will, very selectively and in a non-random way, draw on a number of reports and sources that have investigated the housing market in mostly Norway, Sweden and Iceland.

K. N. Torstensen
Norges Bank, Oslo, Norway

K. Roszbach (✉)
Norges Bank, Oslo, Norway

University of Groningen, Groningen, Netherlands
e-mail: Kasper.Roszbach@Norges-Bank.no

R. Nijskens et al. (eds.), *Hot Property*, https://doi.org/10.1007/978-3-030-11674-3_11

1 Background

Over the past 10 years, several Scandinavian capital regions have experienced a period of rapid growth. Stockholm's population grew by about 16% while Oslo grew at an even faster rate of close to 19%. Although neither of these cities belongs to the group of European cities that have grown most in absolute terms, like Paris, Madrid and Rome, the rapid growth *rate* of these metropolitan areas and the intensity of the resulting frictions in housing markets pose particular challenges, that we believe provide generally useful insights into the challenges that cities are confronted with in the face of rapid expansion.

Metropolitan area population growth in Scandinavia is projected by the European Commission to continue being robust. Eurostat projections, plotted in Fig. 11.1, suggest that the Stockholm metropolitan area will grow by close to 50% in the next 30 years, while Oslo will grow by more than 55%. At the same time some other metropolitan areas in southern and eastern Europe are projected to shrink, while for example Amsterdam finds itself in an intermediate position. While projections do not account for substantial changes that may take place in confounding living conditions, like reduced affordability due to housing scarcity or severely lagging infrastructure, they do provide an indication of the challenges these cities may come to face.

Since 2005, the metropolitan area of Stockholm has built up a substantial housing deficit as the net annual migration rate has been hovering between 10,000 and 20,000 households while construction of new houses and apartments has been ranging from 7000 to 14,000 units (see Katinic (2018) and Fig. 11.2). The migration to Stockholm has several drivers. Among other things, there is a tendency to migrate domestically, away from rural areas. At the national level, Scandinavia and in particular Sweden, has experienced a large inflow of refugees. Net immigration in Sweden was over 100,000 in 2016, about 1% of the ten million population. Oslo's

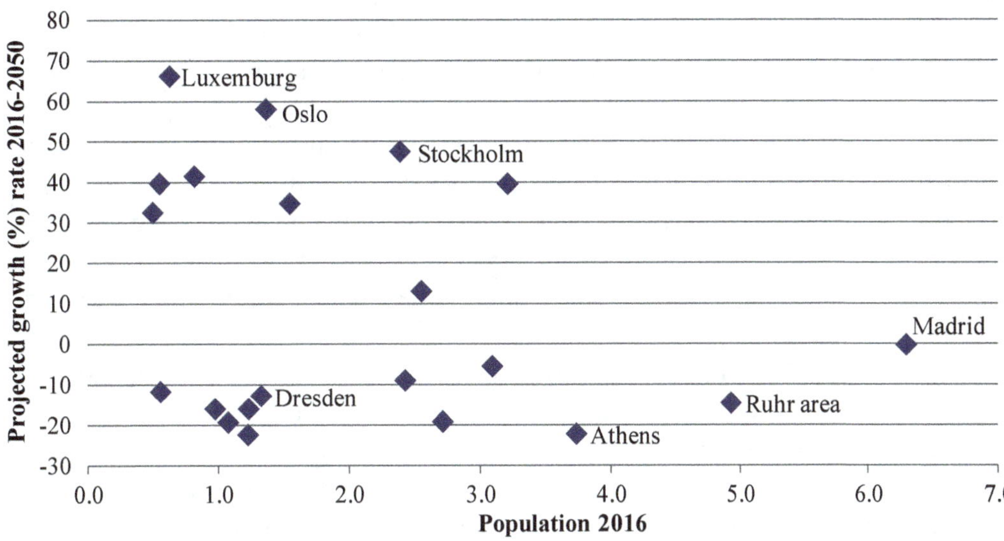

Source: European Commission (2015)

Fig. 11.1 Projected population growth rates metropolitan areas 2016–2050

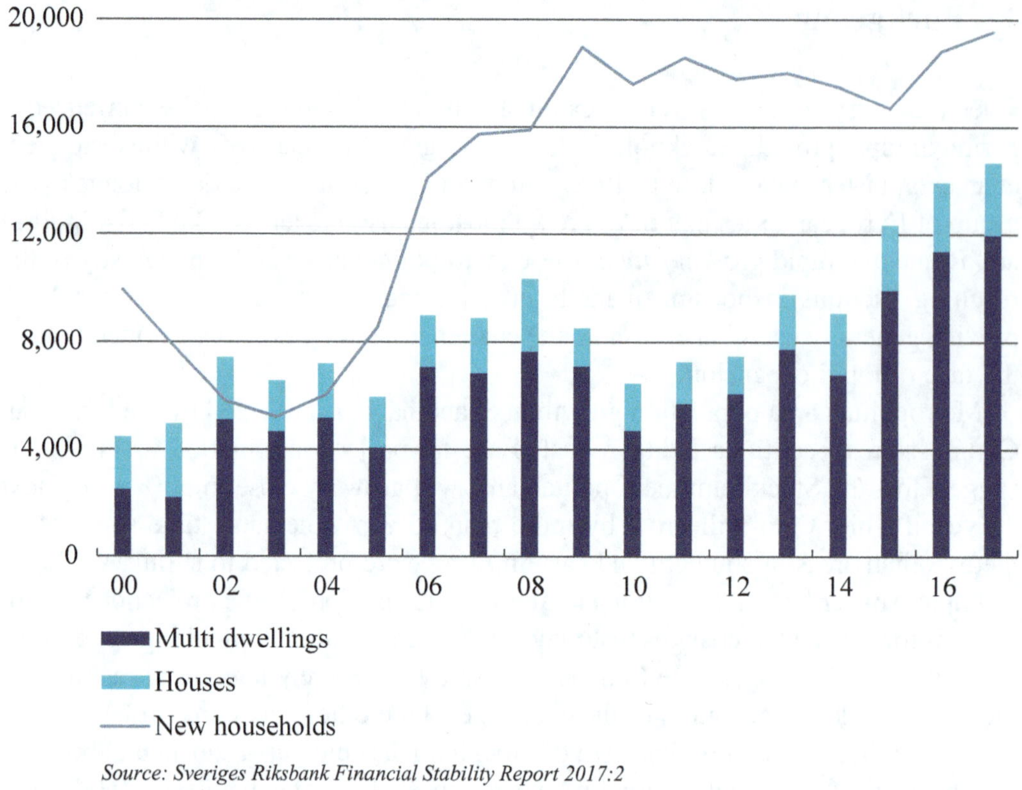

Fig. 11.2 Housing construction versus population growth in Stockholm

metropolitan area has also experienced a housing construction deficit in the period 2006–2016, although not as dramatic as Stockholm. There are some intuitively appealing explanations for this difference, which we will discuss in the next section.

The shortage of new housing has had its effect on house prices. Although Oslo and Stockholm recently experienced moderate drops in house prices, both cities saw house prices more than double in 12 years. Over the same period inner city Stockholm apartments almost tripled in price and rose by approximately 50% more than the country average (including Stockholm itself). Generally, price developments in metropolitan areas, with predominantly multifamily dwellings, can differ substantially from more rural areas with mostly single-family houses. Differences in subletting regulations, as in Sweden where single family house subletting essentially is unregulated while apartment subletting is highly restricted, have kept up the supply of single-family houses. This has exerted a dampening effect on price developments outside metropolitan areas.

In Oslo the corresponding rise in house prices has been a little more muted with a 150% increase and a slightly smaller differential vis-à-vis the rest of the country. The latter can partially be explained by the fact that oil is an important driver of the economy and thereby house prices on the west coast of Norway. Figure 11.3 illustrates how west-coast Stavanger experienced a drop in house prices when oil prices sharply fell in 2015 and 2016, while the rest of the country and was much less affected. In the past year, with oil prices recovering, house prices in Stavanger have started to recover.

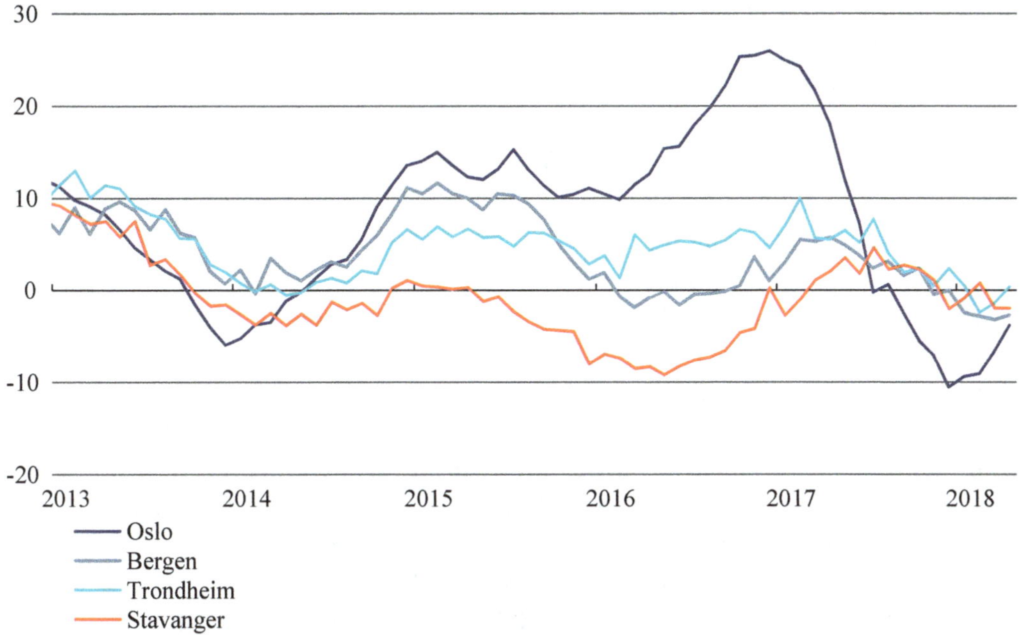

Sources: Norges Bank Financial Stability Report 2017, updated using data from Eiendomsverdi AS, www.finn.no and Real Estate Norway

Fig. 11.3 House price changes in metropolitan areas in Norway

To what extent and how rapidly the supply of housing responds to price fluctuations will among other things depend on the financial incentives produced by local housing regulations. Norway, for example, effectively has had no rent control since 2000 and experienced that new housing starts closely tracked house prices changes with a lag of up to a year.[2]

2 Explanations for the Shortage and Rise in Prices of Housing

There are a number of plausible explanations for the combination of sharply rising demand and a lagging supply of new houses in Oslo and Stockholm. In particular Stockholm has faced a shortage of land for housing construction, despite the ample availability land in the proximity of Stockholm.

[2]The Norwegian Tenancy Act of 1999 makes it possible for landlords, every third year, to mark up the rent to an existing rent level of comparable objects—to a "fair" rent. The last part of the old rent control was removed in 2010, affecting a small number of pre-World-War-II blocks of apartments in Oslo and Trondheim. The act restricts price increases in ongoing tenancy agreements. Rent increases on a yearly basis cannot exceed the increase in the Consumer Price Index (CPI). See Nygaard (2013) for details.

In Sweden, a recent Official Government Report (2015), the "Long-Term Survey of the Swedish Economy", identifies rigid planning processes, building restrictions, for example noise standards that place certain locations off limits for housing construction, and building permit appeal procedures as important hurdles for more rapid house construction. Another friction negatively affecting housing construction is the mismatch between the budgetary and political responsibility for major infrastructure investments (central government and provinces) and the planning authority for housing construction (municipalities).

Rental regulations are also keeping rents on rent controlled apartments low, which is severely restricting the turnover of apartments because the subsidies disincentivize people to move to self-owned homes. The same government report observed that while it is common in many countries for people living in rental apartments or rental homes to be more flexible on the labor market, Swedes in self-owned dwellings are actually more mobile than those living in rentals.

On the demand side, a few non-negligible policy changes have spurred housing demand: In 2007 the wealth tax was abolished while the real estate tax was capped at approximately 600 euro per year in 2008. Instead, the capital gains taxes were raised from 20 to 22%. The real estate tax had become a highly unpopular tax after several elderly people had been forced to leave their houses when they couldn't generate the cashflow to pay the annual tax, although they had substantial assets. The first two tax reforms freed up assets for housing purchases while the wealth tax abolishment also made it easier for family members to support each other in entering the housing market. The increase in the capital gains tax, in an environment with steep increases in house prices, has likely made people less inclined to move, in particular after the introduction of the LTV requirement which made cash at hand more valuable.

Simultaneously several other, secondary, factors are likely to have been at work in Scandinavia. Tourism to Scandinavia grew briskly over a 10-year period from 2007. In Stockholm overnight stays grew by 50%, in Oslo they increased by 55% while Iceland had a true tourist boom with a growth rate of 290%.

Part of the growth in tourism has been accompanied by the rise of Airbnb. There is some research indicating that the activity level of Airbnb can have a significant effect on house and rental prices. Elíasson and Ragnarsson (2018) estimate that Airbnb rental activity in Reykjavik has led to an additional annual house price increase of 2%, or 6 in total, over the period 2014–2017. Of all new apartment construction in Reykjavik in 2016, 50–70% is estimated to be undertaken to replace houses that have been put up for rent on Airbnb and taken out of the long-term rental market.

The idea put forward in Elíasson and Ragnarsson is supported by qualitatively similar findings for other countries. Barron et al. (2018) estimate for the U.S. that in zip code areas with the median owner-occupancy rate (72%), a 1% growth of Airbnb listings leads to a 0.018% rise in the rental rate and a 0.026% increase in house prices.[3] A study for The Netherlands (ING Bank 2016) estimated that house prices in Amsterdam may have increased permanently by 2–4% because the rental income home owners collect can be used to obtain larger mortgages.

Other factors that may have contributed to an already upward trend in Scandinavia are a safe haven effect after the sovereign debt crisis, the low interest rates and a shift in credit standards. Sweden, for example, gradually moved from a system with unregulated but "conventional" downpayments and regular amortizations into a system without or with very low downpayments or amortizations.[4]

A sharp rise in house prices, possibly followed by a steep downturn, can lead to generational differences in wealth effects and can produce random winners and losers in housing markets. This eventually can have other unforeseen and undesirable side effects. A recent paper by Haughwout et al. (2018) shows how temporary shifts in lending standards are likely to be the driving force behind the fall in home ownerships among the young in the US since the financial crisis. Because of the recent rise in house prices, this has also led to young households missing out on wealth accumulation and future collateral for lending.

3 Policy Options

To address both the structural frictions in housing markets as well as the consequences of rapidly rising house prices, economic policymakers have several options available to them.

With respect to structural policies, Bergendahl et al. (2015) suggest that making large infrastructural investments conditional on beneficiary municipalities committing to local housing construction can mitigate the misalignment of incentives between different layers of government. Building permit processes, which are often slow and prone to lengthy appeals, can also be made more efficient. More flexibility can be introduced into the regulated rental market and the market for subletting, for example by allowing for longer periods of subletting or by incentivizing renters to move to the non-regulated sector when their income situation improves.

Structural policies are most likely to provide long-term solutions to structural changes, such as a change in housing demand. They can, however, also take years from decision to actual delivery and are therefore unlikely to alleviate frictions in the short or medium run. Fiscal and credit market policies can then complement structural policies by providing quicker relief to credit and housing markets.

[3] They also find that the effect of Airbnb listings on rental rates and house prices is decreasing in the owner-occupancy rate.

[4] Recently, an amortization policy was introduced that implies mandatory amortization for borrowers with a high LTV.

On the fiscal side, tax incentives for households to assume debt can be lessened by limiting interest rate deductibility, while lock-in effects of capital gains taxes can be mitigated by allowing for a deferral of tax payments. Reducing interest rate deductibility does not, however, necessarily reduce the fragility of households or the affordability of housing, while it does lead to a complicated wealth transfer from older to younger generations. The prime advantage of a change in the fiscal treatment of mortgage debt is therefore likely to be that alternative investment forms receive a more equal treatment.

Credit market policies can be employed to protect consumers and financial institutions against excessive leverage and risk stemming from concentrated exposure to mortgage lending and housing collateral. Borrowing constraints, such as a debt-to-income ratio, and mandatory amortization can reduce indebtedness and the risk of a mortgage default. Loan-to-value (LTV) ratios can be used to limit the risk to banks if a default occurs. Typically, LTV's are less effective in restricting mortgage lending, unless they are allowed to vary over the cycle. Agarwal et al. (2014) show that counseling consumers about mortgage risks and alternatives can sometimes be an effective tool to mitigate mortgage risk and show evidence from a US policy experiment that led lower risk mortgage applicants to choose safer mortgage contracts.

4 An Example of a Macroprudential Policy Measure

Finally, we will provide some more details on a recently adopted macroprudential policy in Norway that generally restricted mortgage lending and imposed additional restrictions on lending in Oslo.

In 2015, as house prices in Oslo were rising at a rate of more than 10% per year, the Norwegian government imposed an 85% LTV requirement (see Table 11.1). The LTV was accompanied by a 5% interest rate stress test requirement, implying that borrowers should be able to repay their loans if the interest rate rises by 5%. A mandatory annual amortization of 2.5% for mortgages with an LTV over 70% was introduced as well.[5] Each bank was allowed an exemption quota which permits a bank to grant loans that breach one or more of the policy requirements for up to 10% of its quarterly mortgage volume.

In January 2017 these requirements were tightened and complemented with a debt-to-income requirement (DTI) of five times gross income while amortization was made mandatory for mortgages with an LTV exceeding 60%. For second dwellings in Oslo, which in principle are buy-to-let, the new policy set a stricter LTV of 60%. For new mortgages with collateral in Oslo, the exemption quota was tightened to 8%.

[5] In December 2011 the same rules were introduced as "Guidelines to prudent mortgage lending" by the Financial Supervisory Authority of Norway.

Table 11.1 Mortgage restrictions in Norway 2015–2018

Requirement	June 2015	Jan 2017—June 2018	July 2018—Dec 2019
Max. loan-to-value (LTV)	85%	85%	85%
Debt servicing possible with interest rate increase of	5 p.p.	5 p.p.	5 p.p.
Maximum debt-to-income (DTI)		5x pre-tax earnings	5% pre-tax earnings
Compulsory principal payment	For LTVs above 70%	For LTVs above 60%	For LTVs above 60%
Regional requirements		Max. LTV 60% for secondary dwellings in Oslo	Max. LTV 60% for secondary dwellings in Oslo
Exemption quota		10% 8% in Oslo	10% 8% in Oslo
Other exemptions			Broader income and wealth definitions, certain exemptions on amortization and debt-to-income requirements for retirees

Time periods refer to the start and end period of policies. Source: Borchgrevink and Næss Torstensen (2018)

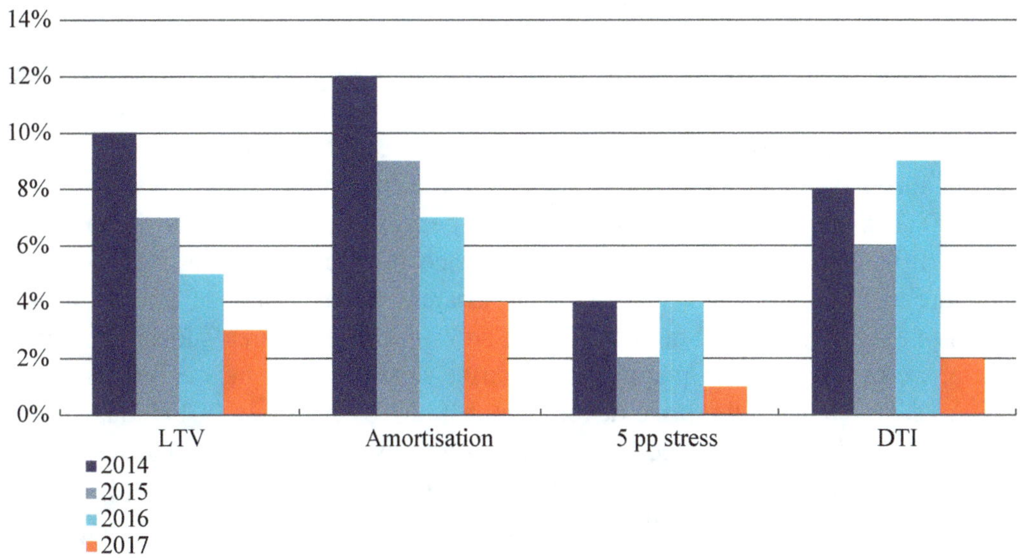

Source: Borchgrevink and Næss Torstensen (2018)

Fig. 11.4 Mortgage policy breaches in Norway 2015–2018. For 2014–2016 we assume the 2017 mortgage policy already applied and calculate what share of all loans would have been in excess of each criterion

Figure 11.4 shows that the policy has had a substantial impact on the share of loans that exceed the DTI, fail the stress test requirement or do not amortize at the prescribed rate. The share of loans with a DTI in excess of five fell from 9% in 2016 to less than 2% in 2017, less than 1% of mortgages failed the stress test in 2017

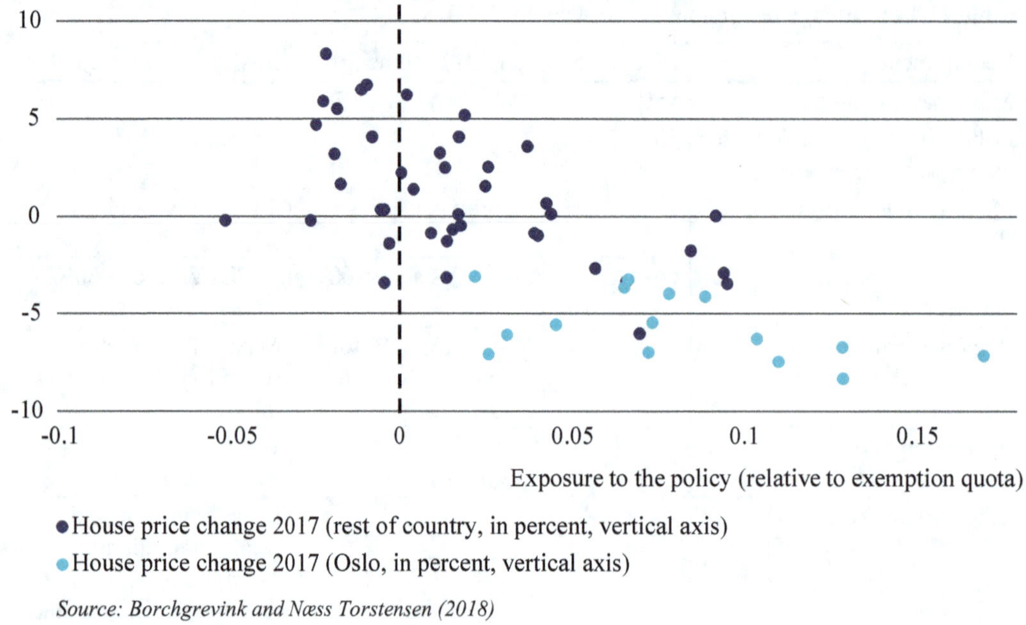

Fig. 11.5 House price changes and "exposure" to the DTI lending restriction. Exposure is measured as the percentage of households "with a DTI greater than five" that exceeds the exemption quota ("speed limit"). Blue dots are residential areas in greater Oslo, black dots are residential areas in the rest of the country

(2016: 4%) and less than 4% of mortgages with an LTV over 60% amortized at a rate of below 2.5% (2016: 7%).[6] A more granular breakdown of the data shows that these effects have been strongest among younger borrowers.

Because the 2017 policy change appears to have been most binding with respect to the DTI, we have taken a closer look at how geographical variation in the exposure to the DTI constraint has affected house price development (Borchgrevink and Torstensen 2018). When we sort residential areas by the share of loans that was given in excess of the DTI policy in 2014, and subtract each area's local exemption quota, we see in Fig. 11.5 that a clear negative relation exists between the share of "high" DTI loans and the price development in 2016–2017.[7] In 2017 house prices rose by 4.7% less in "exposed" areas than in non-exposed areas. When we control for "fundamental" differences between regions (unemployment, the supply of new houses et cetera), the size of the effects falls to 2.3%. If we exclude municipalities in the Oslo area (the white dots), the effect falls to 1.7% but remains statistically significant.

At the same time house sales have not been affected in any greater way, except for people in the age range 20–24 as well as in Oslo, where the share of borrowers with a

[6]For 2016 we assume "hypothetical" breaches of the requirements, i.e., we assume the policy already applied, and calculated what share of all loans was in excess of these criteria in one or more dimensions.

[7]We classify an area as exposed if the share of loans with a DTI greater than five exceeded the exemption quota of that region (10%, but 8% in Oslo).

DTI greater than 5 had been high. We are also observing that the negative relation between the regional share of mortgages with a DTI above five and mortgage debt increases in 2017 has been particularly large for households in the age range 20–40.

These preliminary data show that the Norwegian mortgage policy likely dampened house price development and mortgage debt growth in regions with initially high debt levels and with more borrowers impacted by the policy. This could be indicative of a reduction in both riskier second house purchases and riskier lending/borrowing.

On June 18, 2018, the government decided to extend the mortgage policy by another year and a half, until December 31, 2019.[8]

5 Conclusions

Scandinavian capitals have grown fast and are projected to be among the fastest growing cities in Europe in the next decades. Rising house demand has not been matched by construction over a longer time period. Taxes, regulation and lack/mismatch of incentives to build have been identified as the main frictions. Growth in tourism, low interest rates, a safe haven effect and credit "innovation" have likely contributed to house price rises. In markets with fewer frictions, leveraged investments have taken place in secondary housing for rent.

The mismatch between housing supply and demand can have several negative side effects, including unintended wealth transfers between generations. Structural policies are first best solutions to address mostly structural frictions. Macroprudential policies, such as a mortgage policy, can mitigate some of these side effects.

A more tempered growth rate of house prices can be beneficial to housing market entrants. Macroprudential policies can therefore complement structural policies. A preliminary assessment of a policy to restrict the demand for housing credit in Oslo displays signs of success.

Acknowledgements We would like to thank Paulina Tedesco and Marius Hagen (Norges Bank) as well as Kerstin Hallsten, Goran Katinic and Peter van Santen (Sveriges Riksbank) for their kind assistance.

[8]The government made a few adjustments to the mortgage regulations, by allowing banks to include documented and stable tax-free income, such as child allowance, in the calculation of the DTI and funds in a "tax deduction for young people's housing savings" (BSU) account as equity in calculating the LTV.

References

Agarwal, S., Amromin, G., Ben-David, Z., Itzhak, S. C., & Evanoff, D. (2014). *The effectiveness of mandatory mortgage counseling: Can one dissuade borrowers from choosing risky mortgages?* www.ssrn.com/abstract=1285603

Barron, K., Kung, E., & Proserpio, D. (2018). *The sharing economy and housing affordability: Evidence from Airbnb*. https://ssrn.com/abstract=3006832

Bergendahl, P.-A., Löfmark, M. H., & Lind, H. (2015). *Bostadsmarknaden och den ekonomiska utvecklingen*. Appendix 3 to Långtidsutredningen 2015. Official Reports of the Swedish Government 2015:48.

Borchgrevink, H., & Torstensen, K. N. (2018). *Analyser av effekter av boliglånsforskriften* [Analyses of Effects of Mortgage Regulation]. Economic Commentary Norges Bank 2018:1.

Elíasson, L., & Ragnarsson, Ö. P. (2018). *Short-term renting of residential apartments: Effects of Airbnb in the Icelandic housing market*. Working paper Central Bank of Iceland 2018:76.

European Commission. (2015). *Population projections*. Accessed May 2018, from https://ec.europa.eu/eurostat/web/population-demography-migration-projections/population-projections-data

Haughwout, A., Lee, D., Scally, J., & van der Klaauw, W. (2018). *Home prices, housing wealth and home equity extraction*. New York: Federal Reserve Bank of New York.

ING Bank. (2016, April 25). *Airbnb heeft flink opwaarts effect op Amsterdamse huizenprijzen* [Airbnb has a significant upward effect on Amsterdam house prices]. https://www.ing.nl/nieuws/nieuws_en_persberichten/2016/04/airbnb_heeft_flink_opwaarts_effect_op_amsterdamse_huizenprijzen.htm

Katinic, G. (2018). *Perspectives on housing construction*. Economic commentary 2018:2. Sveriges Riksbank.

Norges Bank. (2017). *Financial stability report*.

Nygaard, R. (2013). *Rent levels in the Norwegian rental market*. Memo Statistics Norway.

Sveriges Riksbank. (2017). *Financial stability report* 2017:2.

Chapter 12
The Relationship Between Supply Constraints and House Price Dynamics in the Netherlands

Bahar Öztürk, Dorinth van Dijk, Frank van Hoenselaar, and Sander Burgers

1 Introduction

After having sharply declined during the Great Financial Crisis (GFC), house prices in the Netherlands have been increasing strongly since 2014. There is substantial heterogeneity between regions, however. In 2018Q1, nominal house prices in Amsterdam stood 32% above their pre-crisis peak of 2008Q3, whereas in the more rural province of Friesland they were still 8% below their pre-crisis peak. Due to the relevance of house price swings for macroeconomic stability and the existence of spillover effects between regions (Teye and Ahelegbey 2017), it is of great importance for policymakers to gain a good understanding of the heterogeneity in house price developments across regions.

A typical feature of the Dutch housing market is that the price elasticity of housing supply is low, which is partly related to the relatively high population density (Caldera and Johansson 2013). Moreover, the supply elasticity is generally lower in the major cities compared to the rest of the country (Michielsen et al. 2017). If housing supply inadequately adjusts to changes in housing demand, this might lead to house prices deviating from their equilibrium values for an extended period of time (Capozza et al. 2002). In the literature, a low supply elasticity is often linked to physical supply constraints related to geography (Saiz 2010) or a rigid planning system (Hilber and Vermeulen 2016). For the Netherlands, both sources of supply restrictions are relevant. New construction is restricted by physical constraints,

This chapter is based on Öztürk, B., Van Dijk, D., Van Hoenselaar, F. & Burgers, S. (2018). The relationship between supply constraints and house price dynamics in the Netherlands. DNB Working Paper 601. The views presented in this chapter are those of the authors and do not necessarily represent the views of De Nederlandsche Bank.

B. Öztürk (✉) · D. van Dijk · F. van Hoenselaar (✉) · S. Burgers
De Nederlandsche Bank, Amsterdam, Netherlands
e-mail: b.ozturk@dnb.nl; d.w.van.dijk@dnb.nl; f.j.g.van.hoenselaar@dnb.nl

R. Nijskens et al. (eds.), *Hot Property*, https://doi.org/10.1007/978-3-030-11674-3_12

mostly in urban areas, because a considerable share of land is already developed. In addition, new housing supply is further hampered by a planning system that is fairly restrictive (Vermeulen and Rouwendal 2007).

It is often found that regions where housing supply is more restricted due to physical and/or regulatory constraints exhibit different house price dynamics. Glaeser et al. (2008) show that areas with stronger supply constraints in the United States experienced a larger housing boom in the 1982–2007 period. Extending on this research, Huang and Tang (2012) find that these areas also experienced larger housing busts during the GFC. In addition, Capozza et al. (2002), the closest work to ours, analyze house price dynamics in various US metropolitan areas and find that areas that face stronger supply constraints also experience stronger serial correlation (i.e. persistence in house price growth) and slower mean reversion of prices (i.e. the speed of adjustment to the long-run equilibrium house price). Similarly, Galati et al. (2011) find that the speed of mean reversion is the lowest in the most urbanized areas of the Netherlands. This finding seems to be in line with the findings of Capozza et al. (2002), assuming that more urbanized areas also face stronger supply constraints. However, in a somewhat more recent study, Galati and Teppa (2017) come to a different conclusion and find that mean reversion is lowest in both the least and most urbanized segments of the Dutch housing market.

The goal of this chapter is to study the interaction between supply constraints and house price dynamics in the Netherlands. Our hypothesis is that a shock in real household income will have a stronger effect on house prices in municipalities with stronger supply constraints. A well-known measure of supply constraints is developed by Saiz (2010), who measures physical supply constraints in the United States by making use of elevation in the landscape. This measure, however, is not suitable for our study as the variation in elevation levels is very low in the Netherlands. Instead, we use the measure developed by Hilber and Vermeulen (2016). Based on this methodology, we create an index for the extent of supply constraints in a given region (i.e. municipality) by relating the amount of already developed land to total available developable land. Note that physical and regulatory supply constraints are highly correlated in practice (Saiz 2010) and our observed supply constraints are driven by both physical and regulatory constraints. We divide the sample into three equally-sized groups: municipalities with weak, medium, and strong supply constraints, labeled as "least developed", "medium developed" and "most developed", respectively. We then study the relationship between house prices and income shocks, using an error correction model. Our results suggest that income shocks are associated with significantly larger increases in house prices in municipalities that face relatively strong supply constraints.

The contribution of our work to the literature is twofold. First, we employ a rich dataset that allows us to study the short- and long-run dynamics of house prices at a more granular (i.e. municipality) level than done by previous work on the Dutch housing market. Second, we add to the existing literature by studying the interaction between income shocks and housing supply constraints.

2 Data

For our dependent variable, i.e. house prices, we estimate a hedonic annual house price index at the municipality level using individual transaction data from the Dutch Association of Real Estate Brokers and Real Estate Experts (NVM), covering the period 1987 until 2016. In order to estimate the model for smaller municipalities with fewer transactions, we use the Hierarchical Trend Model of Francke and De Vos (2000) and Francke and Vos (2004). For a more detailed description of the house price index estimation method, see Öztürk et al. (2018).

We are somewhat limited in our selection of explanatory variables as these should ideally exhibit both time- and cross-sectional variation. In line with the literature, we include household income, the unemployment rate, population, construction costs, the mortgage interest rate, and the loan-to-value ratio of first-time buyers (LTV) in our analysis (Table 12.1). House prices, disposable household income, construction costs, and the mortgage rate are deflated by the Consumer Price Index (CPI). During our sample period several municipalities merged, which we account for by computing the weighted average for a merged municipality (weights based on population). For a more detailed description of this procedure see Burgers (2017). In total, we have complete data for 316 out of the 388 municipalities, determined by the availability of data on regional disposable household income.

Our main explanatory variable of interest is household income. We expect that an increase in income leads to an increase in house prices as this enables households to afford a more expensive house. The unemployment rate is expected to be negatively related to house prices since it reduces the number of people who can afford a house. Population should be positively related to house prices as the demand for housing will increase with the number of people living in a region. Construction costs should be positively related to house prices as this determines the structure value of the house, which is part of the total house price. The latter is usually defined as the sum of land and structure value (Francke and van de Minne 2017). The real mortgage interest rate is expected to have a negative relationship with house prices as debt

Table 12.1 Variables and data sources

Variable	Variation	Source
Log real house prices	Municipal, year	NVM
Log real average disposable household income	Municipal, year	CBS
Unemployment rate	Municipal, year	CBS
Log population	Municipal, year	CBS
Log real construction cost index	Year	CBS
Consumer price index	Year	CBS
Real mortgage rate	Year	DNB
LTV	Year	DNB
Share developed land	Municipal	LGN05

financing becomes cheaper when interest rates fall, driving up house prices.[1] Finally, we include the LTV of first-time buyers as a proxy for credit conditions (we assume that a higher LTV reflects looser credit standards), and expect it to be positively related to house prices. This variable is usually seen as exogenous to house prices, since first-time buyers are assumed to be credit constrained (Francke et al. 2015). For a more detailed description of this variable see Verbruggen et al. (2015). We purposefully do not employ the housing stock as an explanatory variable as it is directly related to the degree of supply constraints, which we account for by the variable share developed land. Including the housing stock would possibly absorb the heterogeneous relationship between household income and house prices across regions, which is the centroid of our research.

The data used to construct the variable share developed land, which accounts for the extent of supply constraints in a given municipality, come from the Dutch land cover map (*Het Landelijk Grondgebruiksbestand Nederland*, LGN5) and are based on aerial photos taken in 2003 and 2004. We follow Hilber and Vermeulen (2016) as closely as possible and categorize land into developed land, developable land and non-developable land. The share of developed land (termed as "share developed" below) is the amount of developed land divided by the total amount of developable land (already developed and potentially developable). Note that we only have data for one moment in time. However, we expect that the level of the share developed remains fairly constant over time. We divide our sample into three equally-sized groups (in terms of the number of municipalities) according to the variable share developed land, i.e. municipalities that are the *least* (value lower than 0.14), *medium* (value between 0.14–0.25), and the *most* (value higher than 0.25) developed.

3 Methodology

We are interested in both the long- and short-run effects of income shocks on house prices. Therefore, our framework should model both the long-run underlying equilibrium relationship and the short-run deviations. In the literature, these are usually modelled in an error-correction (ECM) framework (Francke et al. 2009). Given the fact that we are especially interested in heterogeneous cross-sectional effects, we estimate the model with panel data. In an ECM, the long-run equation estimates the underlying equilibrium relationship in levels. In the short-run, deviations from this long-run equilibrium are modeled. Important components in the short-run equation are the speed of adjustment to the long-run equilibrium value (i.e. the error-correction term, ECT) and the degree of serial correlation.

[1]Between 1987 and 2002, the real mortgage interest rate is the average 5-year mortgage rate for new mortgages and between 2003 and 2016 the rate is calculated as the average of the 1 to 5-year rate and 5 to 10-year rate on new mortgages.

As our goal is to explore the role of supply constraints on house price dynamics as mentioned above, we run our analysis for each of the three groups of municipalities (least-, medium-, and most developed) separately. In other words, we allow for the possibility that supply constraints impact house prices via their interaction with *all* explanatory variables. The main focus is, however, on the interaction of supply constraints with the income variable.

We employ a two-step Engle-Granger approach by first estimating the long-run equilibrium Eq. (12.1) and subsequently the short-run error-correction Eq. (12.2):

$$h_{it}^{*} = x_{it}\beta_{0,j} + z_t\beta_{1,j} + d_i, \tag{12.1}$$

$$\begin{aligned}\Delta h_{it} = {} & \alpha_j \Delta h_{it-1} + \delta_j\left(h_{it-1} - h_{it-1}^{*}\right) + \Delta x_{it}\gamma_{0,j} + \Delta z_t\gamma_{1,j} + d_i + \theta_{0,j}\overline{\Delta h_t} \\ & + \theta_{1,j}\overline{\Delta h_{t-1}} + \theta_{2,j}\overline{\left(h_{t-1} - h_{t-1}^{*}\right)} + \theta_{3,j}\overline{\Delta x_t} + \varepsilon_{it}.\end{aligned} \tag{12.2}$$

Here subscript i denotes the municipality for $i \in \{1, N\}$, t the year for $t \in \{1, T\}$, and j the group based on the share developed land for $j \in \{least, medium, most\}$. The dependent variable, h, is log house prices. Further, x is a 1xK row-vector of house price determinants that vary over time and municipality, β_j^0 and γ_j^0 are the Kx1 corresponding long- and short-run coefficient vectors, respectively. Additionally, z is a 1xL row-vector of house price determinants that vary over time only, β_j^1 and γ_j^1 are the Lx1 corresponding long- and short-run coefficient vectors, respectively.

Next, d_i is a municipal-specific intercept, α_j is the coefficient on lagged house price changes that represents the degree of serial correlation, and δ_j measures the speed of adjustment. The *barred* variables include the cross-sectional averages of the variables that vary over the cross-section and time, and $\theta_{(0\,\ldots\,3),\,j}$ are their respective loadings.[2]

We estimate the long-run Eq. (12.1) with Dynamic OLS (DOLS) and heteroscedasticity- and autocorrelation-consistent (HAC) standard errors clustered at the municipality level. The short-run Eq. (12.2) is estimated with OLS and HAC standard errors clustered at the municipality level. Because we correct for cross-sectional dependence in the short-run equation, we are not able to include the variables that only exhibit time-variation due to perfect multicollinearity (e.g. the mortgage rate and construction costs).

Admittedly, some of our variables might be endogenous to house prices. For our long-run equation this should not be a major issue, as this relationship is simply a long-run relationship between the variables and does not imply causality. Yet, we impose only one co-integrating relationship and do not allow for feedback effects through other variables. However, the literature on panel (V)ECMs is not very well

[2]It might be expected that there are spillovers between regions. Therefore, we correct for this possible cross-sectional dependence by including cross-sectional averages of all our explanatory variables (Pesaran 2006). We assume that this cross-sectional dependence is stationary and should therefore be accounted for in the short-run equation. Intuitively, this implies that these spillovers mainly affect the short-run dynamics of the housing market.

developed in this respect, and there is no standard accepted method as how to approach this problem. The implication for our findings is that some effects are probably over- or underestimated. For example, in our regression equations we do not allow for the housing stock to change in response to a demand shock. This implies that the effect of a positive income shock on house prices might be overstated (i.e. if supply would be able to increase in response to a positive demand shock, the long-run effect on prices would be lower). We are, however, mainly interested in the *differences* in the effect of income shocks on house prices between regions with respect to the degree of supply restrictiveness. Assuming that supply is less (more) elastic in more (less) constrained regions, the negligence of these dynamics implies that our estimates of these differences are actually on the conservative side.

4 Results

Our empirical analysis consists of two stages. First, we estimate both the long- and short-run relationship for real house prices as given by Eqs. (12.1) and (12.2) for the whole sample, without taking into account the role of supply constraints. Second, we estimate these equations separately for each of the three subsamples of municipalities, allowing supply constraints to interact with *all* our explanatory variables in an unrestricted manner.[3]

4.1 The Long-Run Relation Between Income and House Prices

We begin by estimating the long-run relationship in Eq. (12.1); the results are shown in Table 12.2. Note that all variables except for the mortgage rate, the unemployment rate, and the LTV are in logs, and can thus be interpreted as elasticities. As shown in Column 1 of Table 12.2, all variables have the expected sign. The results imply that a 1% increase in real income is associated with a 0.7% increase in real house prices in the long-run. The size of this coefficient is relatively small compared to the coefficient estimated by Kranendonk et al. (2005) (i.e. 1.4).

As a next step, we estimate the long-run price relationship for each of the three subsamples separately. The results indicate that in municipalities that are characterized by weak supply constraints ("least developed"), a 1% increase in real income leads to a 0.38% increase in house prices in the long-run (Table 12.2, Column 2.) In

[3]In this chapter, we focus mainly on the effect of income on house prices. For a more detailed discussion of the other variables, please refer to Öztürk et al. (2018).

Table 12.2 First stage (long-run) estimates

Dependent variable: Log real house price				
	(1)	(2)	(3)	(4)
Variables	Total	Least developed	Medium developed	Most developed
Real average income	0.70***	0.38***	0.75***	0.92***
	(0.06)	(0.11)	(0.11)	(0.10)
Real mortgage rate	−0.03***	−0.03***	−0.03***	−0.02*
	(0.01)	(0.01)	(0.01)	(0.01)
Unemployment rate	−0.03***	−0.04***	−0.03***	−0.04***
	(0.00)	(0.01)	(0.00)	(0.01)
Population	0.00	0.24*	−0.14***	0.06
	(0.04)	(0.12)	(0.03)	(0.07)
LTV	0.03***	0.03***	0.03***	0.03***
	(0.00)	(0.00)	(0.00)	(0.01)
Real cons. costs	0.89***	0.98***	0.89***	0.71***
	(0.05)	(0.08)	(0.08)	(0.10)
Constant	−2.66***	−4.49***	−1.48***	−3.10***
	(0.47)	(1.20)	(0.43)	(0.93)
Observations	8216	2756	2730	2730
Number of municipalities	316	106	105	105
Adjusted R-squared	0.98	0.98	0.98	0.98
Municipality FE	Yes	Yes	Yes	Yes

Heteroskedasticity-and autocorrelation-consistent (HAC) standard errors (in parenthesis) are adjusted for clustering at municipality level

*** $p < 0.01$, ** $p < 0.05$, * $p < 0.1$

Notes: All variables expect for the mortgage rate, unemployment rate and LTV are in logs. Only the coefficients of the main variables are reported here. Sample period is 1987–2016

municipalities that are characterized by medium and strong supply constraints ("medium developed" and "most developed"), a 1% increase in real income increases house prices by around 0.75% and 0.92%, respectively (Table 12.2, Columns 3–4). Figure 12.1 shows the 95% confidence intervals of these coefficients. F-tests show that the coefficients of the medium- and most developed groups are statistically significantly higher than the coefficient of the least developed group. While the point estimate for the most developed group is larger than that of the medium developed group, this difference is not statistically significant. In line with our hypothesis, the income elasticity of house prices increases with the extent of supply constraints. Intuitively, this confirms that supply elasticities in supply-constrained areas are relatively low. As a result, a given increase in income leads to a strong response in equilibrium house price that is not offset by the relative muted supply response (as it would in less constrained areas).

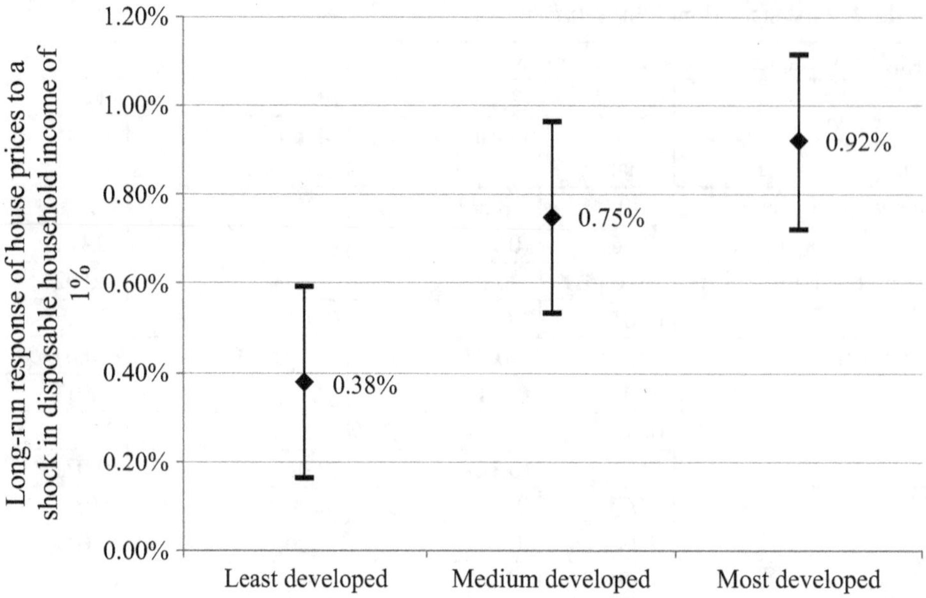

Fig. 12.1 Estimated coefficients and 95% confidence intervals on real disposable household income in the long-run equation

4.2 The Short-Run (Dynamic) Relation Between Income and House Prices

We estimate the short-run relationship for real house prices according to Eq. (12.2).[4] As in the first stage, we first run the regression on the whole sample and then separately for each of the three subsamples. Table 12.3 summarizes the main findings. As given by Column 1, the coefficient on real household income is significant and positive (0.06).

Next, we estimate the short-run price relationship for each of the three subsamples separately. The results yield statistically significant coefficients for the real income variable only for the medium and most developed group. Although the coefficients are small, our hypothesis is confirmed since the effect of an income shock on house price growth is significantly larger in these groups compared to the least developed group. That the coefficient is small might be related to the fact that the purchase of a house—often the biggest purchase item in a consumer's lifetime—requires some time for orientation, leading to a muted response of house prices in the short-run. For the other variables we do not find any heterogeneity in house price responses between municipalities with weak and strong supply constraints.

[4]In Öztürk et al., we show the results of various panel unit root- and cointegration tests which confirm that our level variables all contain a unit root (except unemployment) and that the residual (ECT) and the first differences are all stationary.

Table 12.3 Second stage (short run) estimates

Dependent variable: Δlog real house price				
	(1)	(2)	(3)	(4)
Variables	Total	Least developed	Medium developed	Most developed
Δlog real income	0.06***	0.01	0.09**	0.10***
	(0.02)	(0.02)	(0.03)	(0.03)
(Δlog real house price)t-1	0.38***	0.36***	0.41***	0.35***
	(0.02)	(0.02)	(0.02)	(0.03)
Δ unemployment	0.00	−0.00**	0.00	0.00
	(0.00)	(0.00)	(0.00)	(0.00)
Δ log population	0.12***	0.11**	0.11***	0.12*
	(0.03)	(0.04)	(0.03)	(0.06)
ECT	−0.12***	−0.12***	−0.14***	−0.12***
	(0.01)	(0.01)	(0.01)	(0.01)
Observations	8216	2756	2730	2730
Number of municipalities	316	106	105	105
Adjusted R-squared	0.91	0.93	0.92	0.90
Municipality FE	Yes	Yes	Yes	Yes

Heteroskedasticity-and autocorrelation-consistent (HAC) standard errors (in parenthesis) are adjusted for clustering at municipality level

*** $p < 0.01$, ** $p < 0.05$, * $p < 0.1$

Notes: All variables expect for the unemployment are in logs. Only the coefficients of the main variables are reported here. Sample period is 1988–2016

As mentioned earlier, the short-run relationship includes the first lag of the dependent variable to account for the degree of serial correlation (persistence). If house prices were to adjust to local economic shocks fully in the short run, the coefficient of this variable would be 0 (Capozza et al. 2002). Yet, the empirical literature has generally found a positive and large coefficient for this variable, hinting at backward-looking price setting behavior by sellers (Van Dijk and Francke 2018). As shown in Column 1 of Table 12.3, the coefficient of the first lag of the dependent variable is positive (0.38) and statistically significant, and in line with earlier findings for the United States. Capozza et al. (2002) find a serial correlation coefficient of 0.33 for the based on a panel data set of 62 US metro areas from 1979–1995. Similarly, Case and Shiller (1989) find that annual serial correlation ranges from 0.25 to 0.50 across the four cities that they study.[5] When the coefficients are estimated seperately by subsample, the coefficients of the serial correlation variable appear to be of similar size (see Columns 2–4). Thus, we do not find the degree of serial correlation to be heterogeneous across regions with different supply constraints.

[5]Atlanta, Chicago, Dallas and San Francisco.

Finally, we also look at the error-correction term to see how fast house prices converge to their long-run equilibrium, and whether this speed differs across regions with different supply constraints. For house prices to revert to their long-run equilibrium values, the coefficient of the lagged error-correction term should be negative. As shown by Column 1 of Table 12.3, the coefficient of the lagged error-correction term is indeed negative (−0.12) and statistically significant for the whole sample. This suggests that actual house prices adjust by 12% of the difference from their long-run values each year. The serial correlation coefficient (0.38) and the error-correction term together indicate how long it takes for house prices to adjust to a shock. As an example: a 10% income shock at t = 1 increases equilibrium house prices instantaneously by 7%, and first period prices by 0.6%. In the next periods, the error correction mechanism and the serial correlation coefficient will move house prices closer to their new equilibrium value until they eventually fully converge to their new equilibrium.

Figure 12.2 illustrates the effect of such a 10% shock and the adjustment process of house prices in the least, medium and most developed regions. A shock in income indeed has a larger effect on house prices in the medium and most developed regions than in the least developed regions, as expected. On the other hand, the time it takes for house prices to make up for half of the shock is more or less equal across the three groups: 4.5 years for the least, 3.5 years for the medium and the most developed regions.[6]

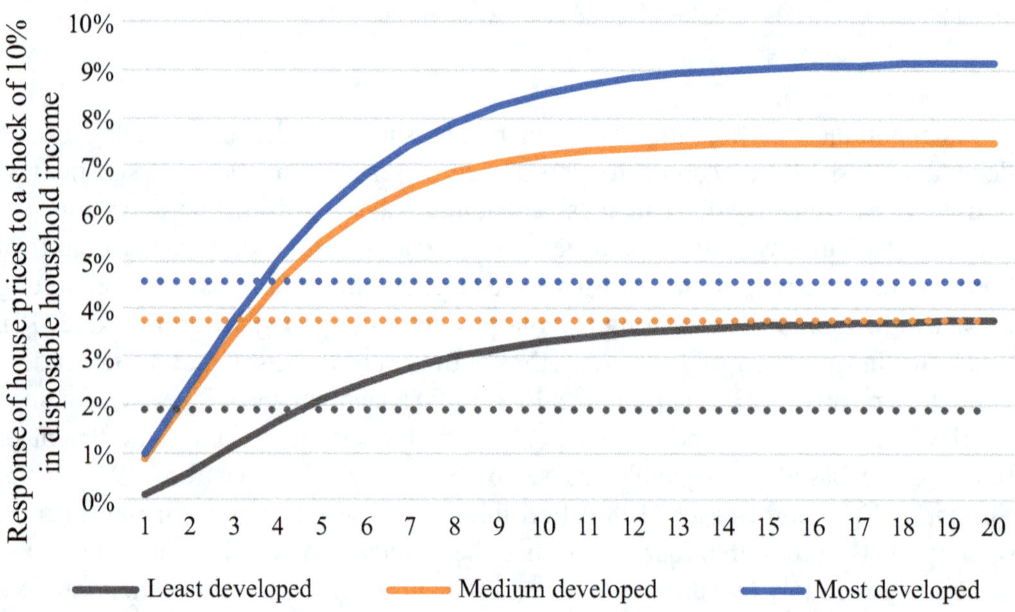

Fig. 12.2 Responses of house prices to a shock of 10% in real disposable household income. Note: The dashed lines represent half of the size of the final shock

[6]These differences are insignificant since the differences between serial correlation coefficients and error-correction terms are insignificant.

5 Conclusion and Future Research

We have shown that house price dynamics in the Netherlands differ significantly between the least and most supply constrained municipalities. Our results suggest that positive income shocks are associated with significantly larger house price increases in municipalities that face strong supply constraints compared to municipalities with weaker supply constraints.[7] The response of house prices to an income shock is found to be generally muted in the short-run, but significantly stronger in municipalities with strong supply constraints. Contrary to findings for the United States by Capozza et al. (2002), we find no difference in the extent of persistence and mean reversion of house prices across municipalities with different supply constraints. We further find that after an income shock it takes between 3.5 and 4.5 years for house prices to make up for half of their initial deviation from the equilibrium price.

Future research in this area could explore ways to refine our measure of supply constraints for the Netherlands. As was previously discussed, the ratio of developed land to developable land is an imperfect measure of supply constraints. Not only does it imperfectly capture physical constraints to construction, it cannot distinguish physical constraints from regulatory constraints. Furthermore, in an ideal setting, such a measure should be exogenous to house prices and vary over time in order to find a causal effect of supply constraints on house prices.

References

Burgers, S. (2017). Determinants of regional house price dynamics: The role of supply constraints and sales activity. *University of Amsterdam Thesis.*

Caldera, A., & Johansson, Å. (2013). The price responsiveness of housing supply in OECD countries. *Journal of Housing Economics, 22*(3), 231–249.

Capozza, D. R., Hendershott, P. H., Mack, C., & Mayer, C. J. (2002). *Determinants of real house price dynamics*. NBER Working Paper, No w9262.

Case, K. E., & Shiller, R. J. (1989). The efficiency of the market for single-family homes. *American Economic Review, 79*(1), 125–137.

Francke, M., & De Vos, A. (2000). Efficient computation of hierarchical trends. *Journal of Business & Economic Statistics, 18*(1), 51–57.

Francke, M. K., & van de Minne, A. (2017). Land, structure and depreciation. *Real Estate Economics, 45*(2), 415–451.

Francke, M., & Vos, G. (2004). The hierarchical trend model for property valuation and local price indices. *Journal of Real Estate Finance and Economics, 28*(2), 179–208.

[7] We performed various robustness checks and our main result always holds. These checks include regressions for different time periods, without unemployment (which is not I(1)), without population (since some of the long-run population coefficients were puzzling) and performed a weighted regression (with population weights).

Francke, M., Vujic, S., & Vos, G. (2009). Evaluation of house price models using an ECM approach: The case of the Netherlands. *Ortec Finance Working Paper Series*, Methodological Paper No. 2009–05.

Francke, M., van de Minne, A., & Verbruggen, J. (2015). De sterke gevoeligheid van woningprijzen voor kredietvoorwaarden. *Economisch-Statistische Berichten, 100*(4713–4714), 426–429.

Galati, G., & Teppa, F. (2017). *Heterogeneity in house price dynamics*. DNB Working Paper No. 564.

Galati, G., Teppa, F., & Alessie, R. J. (2011). *Macro and micro drivers of house price dynamics: An application to Dutch data*. DNB Working Paper No. 288.

Glaeser, E. L., Gyourko, J., & Saiz, A. (2008). Housing supply and housing bubbles. *Journal of Urban Economics, 64*(2), 198–217.

Hilber, C. A., & Vermeulen, W. (2016). The impact of supply constraints on house prices in England. *The Economic Journal, 126*(591), 358–405.

Huang, H., & Tang, Y. (2012). Residential land use regulation and the US housing price cycle between 2000 and 2009. *Journal of Urban Economics, 71*(1), 93–99.

Kranendonk, H., van Leuvensteijn, M., Toet, M., & Verbruggen, J. (2005). Welke factoren bepalen de ontwikkeling van de huizenprijs in Nederland? *CPB Document*, 81.

Michielsen, T., Groot, S., & Maarseveen, R. (2017). Prijselasticiteit van het woningaanbod. *CPB Notitie.*

Öztürk, B., Van Dijk, D., Van Hoenselaar, F., & Burgers, S. (2018). The relationship between supply constraints and house price dynamics in the Netherlands. *DNB Working Paper*, 601.

Pesaran, M. H. (2006). Estimation and inference in large heterogeneous panels with a multifactor error structure. *Econometrica, 74*(4), 967–1012.

Saiz, A. (2010). The geographic determinants of housing supply. *Quarterly Journal of Economics, 125*(3), 1253–1296.

Teye, A. L., & Ahelegbey, D. F. (2017). Detecting spatial and temporal house price diffusion in the Netherlands: A Bayesian network approach. *Regional Science and Urban Economics, 65*, 56–64.

Van Dijk, D., & Francke, M. (2018). Internet search behavior, liquidity and prices in the housing market. *Real Estate Economics, 46*(2), 368–403.

Verbruggen, J., Van der Molen, R., Jonk, S., Kakes, J., & Heeringa, W. (2015). Effects on further reductions in the LTV limit. *DNB Occasional Study, 13*(2).

Vermeulen, W., & Rouwendal, J. (2007). *Housing supply and land use regulation in the Netherlands*. CPB Discussion Paper No 87.

Part IV
Policy Responses

Chapter 13
The Dutch Housing Agenda

Kajsa Ollongren

1 Introduction

Urban Age, the Triumph of the City, the City of the Future. These are the powerful one-liners from leading institutes and opinion makers, all of whom share a single message: the future lies in the city. For these opinion makers, the fact that the future lies in the city is not merely a matter of hope but a clear fact. Cities are the driving forces behind the economy. The number of people living in a predominantly urban region or intermediate region increases. By 2050, that total will have risen to around 80% (European Union 2016). The structural migration to the cities is above all prevalent among young people (Hekwolter of Hekhuis et al. 2017). They are attracted by the high-quality education and employment opportunities, the culture and the good recreational opportunities. If you combine migration to the cities with low interest rates and rising income levels—so that people can borrow more—then you have the reasons for our attendance at De Nederlandsche Bank's 'Hot property' seminar in May 2018: London, Paris and Amsterdam are all cities with a squeezed housing market and a rising trend in house prices.

The number of homes available cannot keep pace with the rate of migration to the cities. This causes the rise of housing prices to continue. Data from Statistics Netherlands (2018) show that price rises of more than 10% are commonplace in our large cities. With the financial crisis still in mind, the question soon emerges: are we seeing an overheating housing market in our large cities?

This article is based on a speech given by Erik Jan van Kempen, Program Director General Environmental and Planning Act of the Ministry of the Interior and Kingdom Relations, at the DNB Housing Market Seminar on 24 May 2018.

K. Ollongren (✉)
Ministry of the Interior and Kingdom Relations, The Hague, The Netherlands
e-mail: postbuswoningmarkt@minbzk.nl

R. Nijskens et al. (eds.), *Hot Property*, https://doi.org/10.1007/978-3-030-11674-3_13

The study undertaken by De Nederlandsche Bank in 2017 ('The housing market in major Dutch cities') shows that the Dutch housing market, in the large cities at least, does seem to be showing signs of that phenomenon. For the time being, however, there are no real indications of a 'credit-driven bubble'. After all, people in the large cities often provide much of their own financing, when they buy a home. At the same time, it remains of key importance that we carefully protect both consumers and the financial sector against the risks of a possible housing bubble.

It is beyond doubt that rising house prices do engender another problem, namely a shortage of affordable housing, above all for those with a middle income. Without access to own funding, they have difficulty finding a home in the city.

The problems on the housing market are a complex social issue. Everyone is entitled to a home. Finding a good balance between accessibility, affordability and minimising the macro-economic risks is a huge puzzle which we in the Cabinet are currently working on. The Cabinet has for example taken steps to slow down the growth of mortgage indebtedness, making both consumers and banks less vulnerable to possible shocks in the future. We will accelerate the reduction of the mortgage interest deductibility until it reaches the level of the lowest tax bracket. In addition, since 2013, home owners have been required to make mortgage repayments, in order to be eligible for mortgage tax deduction. The rules governing mortgages were further tightened up during the last Cabinet period. For example, the loan-to-income standard was adjusted and embedded in a legal framework. Dutch LTI ratios are relatively strict, with the aim of protecting consumers and ensuring financial stability. The maximum mortgage has also been gradually reduced to not more than the value of the home. This is a requirement we plan to adhere to: a maximum loan-to-value of 100%. In our opinion, this is a responsible mortgage level, and it does not unnecessarily hinder access to the housing market for newcomers to that market. In the Netherlands, the level of mortgage payment arrears is particularly low compared to other countries.

2 Housing Affordability and Increasing Supply

This brings us to the next point: the accessibility and affordability of homes. To keep pace with the growth in demand for houses in the cities, it is essential that enough new homes are being built. People should be able to find a home they can afford in the region where they wish to live. We have no intention of deciding where houses should be built. That responsibility lies with the municipalities and provinces. On the other hand, we do wish to tackle the housing shortage in collaboration with local government and the other stakeholders. Solutions require commitment, involvement and cooperation from and between all players in the housing market. We want to take a lead in this process. On a national level, we do this through the National Housing Agenda (Ministry of the Interior and Kingdom Relations 2018). This Agenda has been achieved in order to tackle the challenges in the housing market together with stakeholders in the short and long term. The three challenges that the National Housing Agenda focuses on are increasing and accelerating the construction of housing, making better use of the existing stock, and securing the affordability of housing. However, regional differences in tightness of the housing market are large, and major aspects of housing policy, like planning the construction of new housing, are mainly the responsibility of municipalities and provinces. That is why we also tackle these challenges at a regional level by initiating discussions, reaching agreements and sharing knowledge in large urban regions where tension on the housing market is high.

First, the acceleration of the housing construction. The 2015–2025 forecast is a housing shortage of 700,000. Building 75,000 homes per year is a gauge on which parties focus and address each other. In the large urban regions, we focus on urging regional stakeholders to construct those houses in areas where demand for housing is highest. One of the reasons why there is such an urgent need to accelerate the rate of house building is that insufficient new homes were built during the crisis period. Production in the construction sector is heavily dependent on economic growth on the market, business and consumer confidence and investor sentiment. On top of these factors, the construction sector is a late-cyclic sector. In other words, the response by the construction sector lags behind economic changes. For that reason, we believe it is essential that we also focus on continuity in the construction process, next to accelerating the production. We have therefore called upon the municipalities and provinces to not only focus on the short term, but also to plan sufficiently for the medium and long term.

With respect to making better use of the existing stock, we will focus on the mid-priced rental sector. Moreover, focus will be on the reinforcement of the municipal housing policy and tackling exploitation of rental housing by landlords.

To secure the affordability of housing, the National Housing Agenda calls for the conclusion of a social rental agreement for the regulated rental sector. In this respect, we will focus on the regular rent increases and appropriate measures to stimulate the flow from the regulated sector to the non-regulated sector for the households who earn enough money to live in a non-regulated rental home.

More than half of the total Dutch housing stock consists of owner-occupied homes. The vast majority of rental homes are in the social housing sector, for which access is limited by a maximum income level. In other words, in the Netherlands we have a relatively small non-regulated rental sector. And specifically that non-regulated rental sector is becoming increasingly important. Young people no longer wish to immediately tie themselves down with an owner-occupied home, and the flexible labour market means that in particular demand for affordable rental housing is rising. Particularly in the large urban regions, limited supply and high demand for rental housing in the non-regulated sector has led to very high rent levels, mostly eliminating the existence of a mid-priced rental sector. Within the Cabinet, our priorities are focused on this mid-priced rental sector. More mid-priced rental housing is an essential precondition for a smoothly functioning housing market. More mid-priced rental housing promotes flow on the market, and that flow is needed in order to offer newcomers to the housing market and young families good-quality accommodation.

At the start of 2017, headed by the government, a start was made on bringing local parties together. Agreements were reached with those parties on creating more mid-priced rental housing. On a national level, we explored ways to provide solutions to deal with the practical obstacles at local level. One of the great hindrances was the lack of communication between municipalities and investors. A digital platform to promote specifically that form of cooperation has been launched, via which municipalities can now publish their plans for the construction of mid-rental housing.

3 Concluding Remarks

The housing market today still faces a large number of challenges, and the key question is how we should solve the problems facing the housing market as effectively as possible. Central bankers will concentrate their efforts from their position as guardians of financial stability; our efforts will be based on our role as guardian of the housing market. Our advice is to respond in a timely fashion to the dynamics of today's modern cities. We must ensure the accessibility and affordability of all regions including large urban areas and for all groups in our society. And we must protect our society form the consequences of rising purchase and rental prices, limited flow on the market and long waiting lists.

References

European Union. (2016). *Urban Europe statistics on cities, towns and suburbs*. Luxembourg: Publications office of the European Union.

Hekwolter of Hekhuis, M., Nijskens, R., & Heeringa, W. (2017). The housing market in major Dutch cities. *DNB Occasional Study*, 15(1).

Ministry of the Interior and Kingdom Relations. (2018). *Nationale Woonagenda 2018–2021*. Retrieved May 23, 2018, from https://www.rijksoverheid.nl/binaries/rijksoverheid/documenten/publicaties/2018/05/23/nationale-woonagenda-2018-2021/nationale-woonagenda-2018-2021.pdf

Statistics Netherlands. (2018). *House Price Index by region; existing own homes; 2010 = 100 1995–2017* [Data file]. Retrieved May 11, 2018, from http://statline.cbs.nl/Statweb/publication/?DM=SLNL&PA=81885ned&D1=0&D2=0,5,13,15,17,19&D3=4,29,54,79,84,89,94,99,104,109,l&HDR=T,G1&STB=G2&VW=T

Chapter 14
Financial Stability and Housing Markets in Large Cities: What Role for Macroprudential Policy?

Marco Lo Duca and Sergio Nicoletti-Altimari

1 Facts About House Price Trends in Large Cities

In recent years, residential real estate (RRE) prices in capital and large cities increased sharply and at a faster pace than country wide averages across many euro area countries (ECB 2017a). While the median growth of RRE prices across the euro area as whole was around 8% between 2013Q4 and 2017Q2, the median growth of RRE prices in capital cities was around 13% over the same period.[1] The divergence of housing price dynamics between country averages and capital cities is particularly evident in the Netherlands (+16.6% at the country level vs +47.5% in Amsterdam between 2013Q4 and 2017Q2), in Germany (+19% vs +29%) and Spain (+15% vs +30%) (Fig. 14.1).

As a result of strong increases, price misalignments might be emerging in euro area large cities. While measurement uncertainty and data gaps limit the possibility of assessing price misalignments, especially at the local level, a number of findings emerge across the euro area. According to the ECB (2017b), RRE prices appeared close or slightly above fundamental values in 2017 in the euro area as whole.

The authors would like to thank Alvaro Santos Rivera, Marek Rusnák and Cosimo Izzo for their input. The views presented in the paper are those of the authors and do not necessarily represent the views of the European Central Bank or the Eurosystem.

[1]The calculation refers to the change in nominal RRE price indexes between 2013Q4 and 2017Q2 for those countries where aggregate country indexes and indexes for capital cities were both available. These countries include FI, FR, DE, GR, IE, IT, NL, SI and ES. Between 2010Q4 and 2017Q4, the median change for country aggregate indexes was around 0, while for cities was around 20%. This suggests that the recovery in capital cities led the residential real estate cycle in the euro area.

M. Lo Duca (✉) · S. Nicoletti-Altimari
European Central Bank, Frankfurt am Main, Germany
e-mail: marco.lo_duca@ecb.int; sergio.nicoletti_altimari@ecb.int

R. Nijskens et al. (eds.), *Hot Property*, https://doi.org/10.1007/978-3-030-11674-3_14

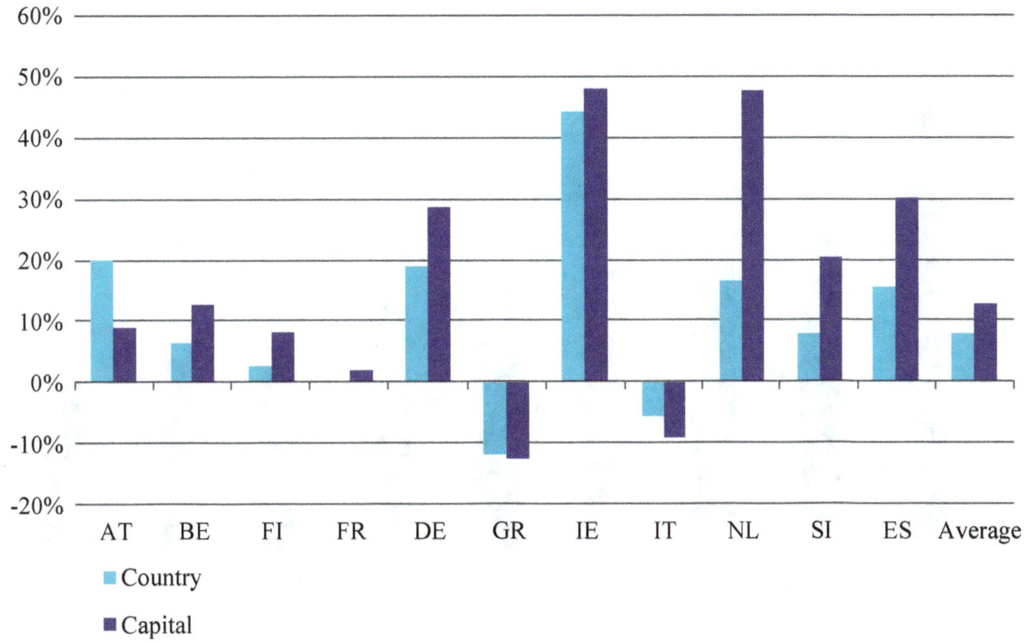

Source: Haver Analytics, ECB Statistical Data Warehouse (2018a, b) and National Statistical Offices

Fig. 14.1 Residential real estate prices across countries and capital cities (% increase between 2013Q4 and 2017Q2)

However, valuation measures were largely heterogeneous across countries, reflecting different cyclical positions. Significant heterogeneity in RRE price valuations existed across regions within countries, with the largest overvaluations seemingly concentrated in large cities (Bundesbank 2018). However, beyond anecdotal evidence, the hard evidence on the latter point is limited by data constraints. One available study on the German market (Kajuth et al. 2016)[2] compares actual house prices to their fundamental values for a number of different regional sub-aggregates using data at the regional level. It finds that apartment prices significantly exceed fundamental values, especially in large cities. A similar pattern holds for single-family houses, for which house price misalignments are generally smaller than for apartments and often not significant. Generally, the large variation in valuation metrics across German cities is evident when looking at the price to rent ratio (Fig. 14.2). Finally, also evidence from the Netherlands points to potential emerging price misalignments in large cities where price developments outpaced personal income growth (Hekwolter of Hekhuis et al. 2017).

Strong price dynamics in large cities appear to be part of a global trend, also beyond the euro area. According to the IMF (2018), RRE price growth in large cities outpaced country averages in several countries around the world since 2013. This is

[2]The study uses a regional panel dataset comprising price data for single-family houses and apartments in all 402 districts in Germany and district-specific explanatory variables. It is one of the few studies looking at fragmentation in housing markets by estimating price misalignments across districts in one country.

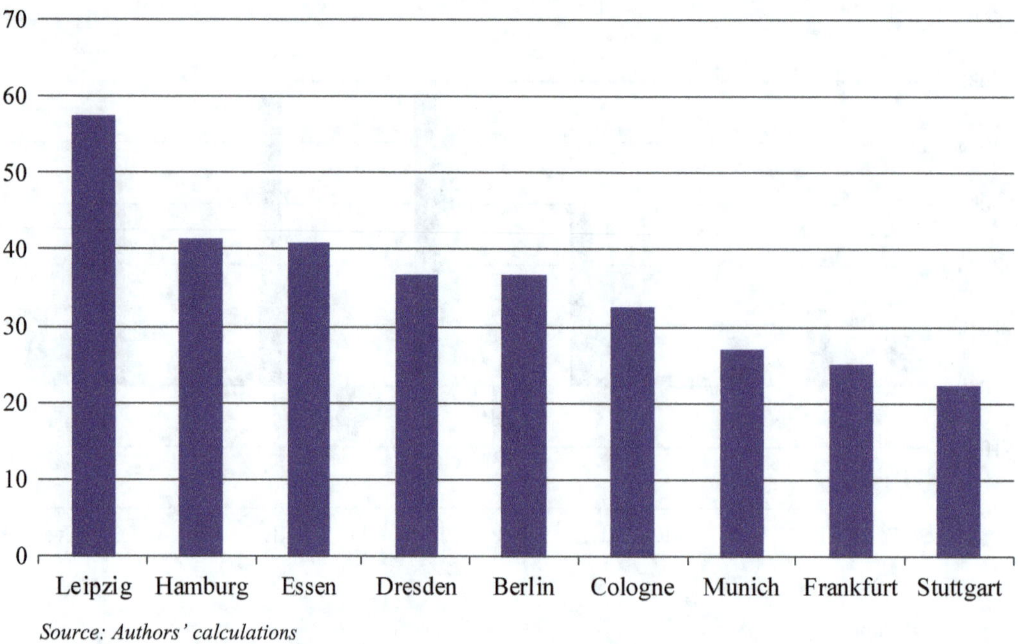

Fig. 14.2 Price to rent ratios across German cities in 2017

the case in China, New Zealand, Australia, Turkey, Japan, Hungary, Great Britain, Sweden, Denmark, and a number of other countries. Valuation metrics for prices in some large cities across the world have led analysts to talk about the potential risks of bubbles (UBS 2017).

Residential real estate prices in large cities appear to increasingly co-move across the globe. Recent analysis on house price synchronisation across countries (IMF 2018) reveals a number of interesting findings. First, the correlation among house price dynamics in large cities worldwide is currently at least as strong as the correlation among price dynamics at the country level. This is a surprising finding, as price dynamics in cities should be affected by idiosyncratic shocks, thus resulting in lower average correlations worldwide than for country aggregates. Second, according to a cluster analysis, price developments in some city pairs appear to be interlinked, while developments at the aggregate level in the countries where these cities are located are not. For example, Tokyo appears to be largely interconnected to the rest of the world, while overall price developments in Japan are not.

The remainder of this article reviews the possible determinants of housing markets in large cities and discusses the role of macroprudential policy.

2 Drivers of House Price Trends in Large Cities

Housing markets are segmented, which explains, at least partially, heterogeneous trends within countries between large cities and other areas. Regulation, market liquidity, mobility of the labour force (or population) and factors affecting the supply of housing all have a regional dimension. Moreover, as regions are also heterogeneous in terms of economic structure and financial development, regional housing markets may respond differently to common economic shocks or may be subject to different shocks. As a consequence, it is natural that price dynamics might diverge across regions.

A number of cyclical and structural factors might explain relatively strong increases in house prices in large cities versus national aggregates. Structural factors range from demographics to technological progress, while cyclical factors might relate to investors' preferences in the aftermath of the global financial crisis.

Increasing trends in house prices are a result of structural features of housing markets and of the interplay between them and other economic sectors. Generally, over long horizons, increases in nominal and real housing prices are the result of relatively limited technological progress in the housing sector compared to other sectors of the economy and of the limited supply of land which enters in the "production function" of new homes (Iacoviello and Neri 2010). In the case of large cities, other factors also play a role. For example, in recent decades, the share of population living in urban areas has increased across advanced and emerging market economies.[3]

Miles and Sefton (2017) show that persistent and strong house price increases in large cities are not new from an historical perspective. Under some circumstances, the "overperformance" of prices in large cities is also the result of household preferences and technological progress. Specifically, when the rate of improvement in transport technology slows relative to population growth and total productivity, house prices in large cities can be expected to grow persistently. Moreover, when there is little substitutability between new land and high density housing, house prices might persistently outpace income growth as well.

Observed trends in house prices in large cities might also be the outcome of cyclical forces. According to Iacoviello and Neri (2010), housing demand, housing supply and monetary factors explain a substantial part of the variation of house prices at business cycle frequencies. Regarding housing supply, in the aftermath of the global financial crisis bottlenecks in the capacity of the construction sector might have emerged due to the severity of the housing recession in some countries.[4] As the capacity of the sector gradually improves, bottlenecks and price pressures emerging

[3]Notably, preferences for urbanisation differ across age cohorts. Young generations are particularly likely to move to large cities due to the quality of institutions, jobs, culture and recreation opportunities (Hekwolter of Hekhuis et al. 2017).

[4]Hekwolter of Hekhuis et al. (2017) report that, in the Netherlands, municipalities and construction companies reduced their planning and construction capacity after the crisis. Therefore, the response to accelerating demand is currently sluggish. More generally, also the IMF (2016) points to supply shortages as a potential driver of price developments in urban areas. Hilber and Vermeulen (2016) use micro data to show that regulatory constraints have a substantive positive impact on the house price-earnings elasticity in the UK. In addition, the effect of constraints due to scarcity of developable land is largely confined to highly urbanised areas. Saiz (2010) shows that supply elasticities depend on physical and regulatory constraints. The latter in turn are endogenous to prices and demographic growth. Therefore, geography is a key factor in the contemporaneous urban development of the United States.

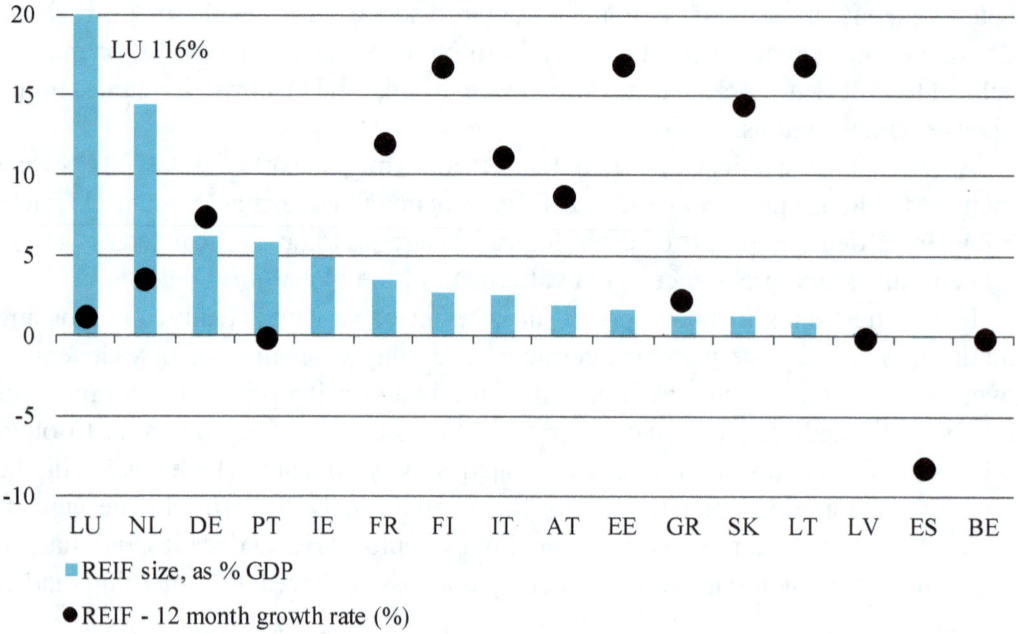

Source: ECB, Statistical Data Warehouse (2018a, b)

Fig. 14.3 Growth of REITs and REIFs in the euro area (2017Q4)

from supply constraints might fade away. Housing demand and monetary factors could also be important cyclical drivers of observed trends in house prices in large cities. First, housing demand might be stronger in large cities as job creation and income growth might be more dynamic there. Second, credit constraints might be less binding in large cities due to the underlying quality and liquidity of collateral (and concentration of financial services). Third, the demand for housing as an investment good and demand from foreign investors might also explain the strong price dynamics in large cities. In the context of the low yield environment, capital gains and the relatively high yield of buy-to-let housing vs. alternative investment opportunities might have attracted demand from a diversified pool of investors.[5] These include (domestic and foreign) high net worth individuals, domestic institutional investors (insurance companies and pension funds) and foreign investors. In most cases, foreign investment is channelled via real estate investment funds or trusts (REIFs/REITs) which have growth substantially in recent years (Fig. 14.3).

More generally, lending support to the increasing role of the foreign investors, the IMF (2018) finds that housing is increasingly behaving as a financial asset. Global financial conditions may explain synchronicity in RRE prices across countries after controlling for domestic fundamentals and other fixed and time varying factors. Most importantly, the IMF finds that the contribution of global financial conditions is stronger for large cities.

[5]In some large international cities where tourism is growing fast, many private homes are mainly rented out for short periods via websites such as Airbnb. As a result the housing stock available for rent is reduced (Hekwolter of Hekhuis et al. 2017).

3 Implications for Financial Stability and the Role of Macroprudential Policy

From a financial stability perspective, housing markets in large cities can be important for several reasons. First, in some cases the housing stock, housing wealth and general real estate activity in largely concentrated in big cities. This makes large cities "systemic" from a financial stability perspective because they constitute the largest fraction of the residential real estate market in the country. As a result, developments in residential real estate markets in large cities might have broader macro-financial implications at the country level. Second, banks might be heavily exposed to large cities via large mortgage lending portfolios and via lending to broader real estate activities. Third, in some countries a large fraction of borrowers lives in large cities. As a consequence, rising prices in large cities might affect housing affordability with the potential of weakening the balance sheet of a large fraction of the population.[6] There could be also broader implications of rising house prices on wealth inequality. Fourth, price developments in large cities might have ripple effects to neighbouring areas in good and bad times. As such, housing markets in large cities might be leading the national cycle. The spillovers of price dynamics to primary locations or large cities to other areas might be affected by country specific factors, including mobility of the labour force and transport infrastructure. Analysis on this type of spillovers within one country is fairly limited.

While developments in large cities might be important from a financial stability perspective, a number of considerations suggest that the role that macroprudential policy can play to address local vulnerabilities might be limited. First, macroprudential policy should not lose sight of the key goal of preserving overall financial stability. In some situations, the attention to developments that are of local nature might result into overly ambitious attempts of micro-managing the economy that are only loosely linked to the overall financial stability goal. Second, a number of factors constrain the role of macroprudential policy in this field. These include data limitations, impact of other policies and limited effectiveness of some macroprudential policy instruments to address local vulnerabilities.

Currently a number of data gaps limit the role of macroprudential policy in addressing housing vulnerabilities in large cities. Macroprudential policy should be supported by granular data in order to identify key vulnerabilities and decide on policy responses. In the context of housing markets in large cities, data should focus on specific geographical areas and ideally cover prices, lending conditions, borrowers' balance sheets and bank exposures. In this context, bank data on local lending and exposures, and information on the balance sheets of borrowers are not easily available across countries (ESRB 2016). In some cases, while this information is available, it cannot be easily accessed by macroprudential authorities. In the euro area, a number of initiatives are in place which could lead to better data in the future.

[6]Although the relevance of this point for financial stability depends on structural features of housing markets, including the share of home ownership in one country.

These include the "analytical credit datasets" or AnaCredit which will cover data on individual bank loans in the euro area.

Depending on the specific sources and nature of the observed imbalances, other policies outside the macroprudential domain might be better positioned to address local vulnerabilities in housing markets. For example, zoning restrictions for residential real estate development limit the supply of new housing. Lifting zoning restrictions might ease upside pressures on prices, especially when the latter emerge from structural factors as, for example, demographic trends towards urbanisation. Rental regulations strongly affect the demand for buy-to-let housing and have a large impact on prices. Developing transport infrastructure might also ease price pressures in specific areas by addressing housing demand stemming from urbanisation and from the preference of living close to "job centres". Similarly, decentralisation of job places may act in the same direction. Fiscal measures (e.g. property taxes, transaction taxes, mortgage tax deductibility, etc.) also affect housing demand and transaction volumes, thereby impacting pricing and activity in the market. As a result, fiscal measures can be flexibly used to address price pressures emerging from cyclical factors (e.g. speculative demand), including demand from foreign investors in search for yield. As some of the abovementioned measures can often be applied to specific geographical areas and are often under the control of local authorities, they appear to be the first line of defence in order to address vulnerabilities in local housing markets.

Against this background, a first line of action for macroprudential policy could entail a communication strategy to raise public awareness on risks in housing markets in order to limit potential demand emerging from speculative motives. Moreover, it could raise awareness about the role that other policy areas can play in addressing local housing market vulnerabilities when they become a threat.

In case of need, macroprudential policy can make a selective use of policy instruments while being mindful of their limitations. Policy options in this context include borrower based measures, capital measures, and limits to exposures.

In general terms, borrower based measures[7] can be used to limit new mortgage lending and ensure the good credit quality of it, thereby slowing credit growth and keeping household balance sheets sound in the medium term. In the context of addressing housing market vulnerabilities in large cities, borrower based measures might be effective in a "text book" situation when RRE price pressures emerge as a result of "leveraged demand" from local households. This is the case when housing price dynamics occur in the presence of strong mortgage lending (potentially rising household indebtedness) and deteriorating bank lending standards. Ideally, a policy measure could take the form of a combination of borrower based instruments targeting all lending flows that are collateralised with real estate assets in a specific geographical area. In this context, it is worth noting that "flat" borrower based measures imposed at the country level imply different binding restrictions across

[7]Borrower based measures include loan to value (LTV) limits, loan/debt to income (L/DTI) limits, debt service to income (DSTI) limits, maturity limits, amortisation requirements etc.

regions. Preliminary evidence (Hekwolter of Hekhuis et al. 2017; Faykiss et al. 2017) seem to indicate that borrower based measures are more binding outside urban areas where income levels are lower. This evidence lends support to the potential introduction of regional policies in the form of diversified borrower based limits between large cities and other areas.

In some situations, however, there might be limitations to borrower based measures in addressing local vulnerabilities. When housing price developments are the result of demand from foreign investors or large investors for buy-to-let purposes, borrower based measures might be ineffective and even counterproductive for the following reasons.[8] First, key investors might be able to rely on funding sources (e.g. bond markets or foreign banks, which are not subject to domestic regulation) that are out of the scope of domestic borrower based measures. Second, borrower based measures might affect only some market players (e.g. local buy-to-let business that rely on bank finance), thereby un-levelling the playing field (e.g. in the buy-to-let business). Third, borrower based measures might unduly compromise housing affordability for households when the driver of price growth is not leveraged demand from households. In this situation, borrower based measures would not be effective in taming the cycle.[9] Furthermore, cycles induced by foreign investors might have higher amplitudes and shorter duration than "text book" housing cycles driven by household leverage. This limits the effectiveness of borrower based measures which act on flows and require time to affect the credit quality of the stock of lending. Against this backdrop, macroprudential authorities could ensure key market players remain sound and do not amplify the cycle. For example, authorities could ensure that real estate investment funds are well managed and able to contain risks emerging from liquidity mismatches in line with the recent recommendations from the Financial Stability Board (FSB 2017).

Finally, macroprudential policy could focus on strengthening banks with capital measures or dis-incentivizing banks' exposure concentration to some geographical areas. When house price developments reflect underlying demand forces that cannot be easily addressed with borrower based instruments, containing the build-up of vulnerabilities might be out of reach for macroprudential authorities. In this context, the latter could primarily focus on ensuring that banks remain resilient when credit risks materialise. This can be done by capital measures or by imposing limits to the exposures of certain types of borrowers and/or to certain geographical areas. If the

[8]Generally, also demand from commercial real estate players might affect housing prices, when commercial real estate and residential real estate demand compete for the same space.

[9]Borrower based measures might be able to ensure that household credit risk remains contained, although this policy objective does not appear a crucial policy goal in the above scenario of rising prices, due to demand outside the household sector. This is because if adverse developments materialise (e.g. house price declines), households might not necessarily be the primary source of credit risk for banks. The credit quality of other borrowers as, for example, real estate developers, might be a more important source of risks. Further, increasing household resilience by imposing borrower based measures comes at the cost of lower housing affordability and potentially increasing inequality (Grossmann et al. 2018).

source of concern is credit risk of certain categories of borrowers that are exposed to developments in specific geographical areas, higher risk weights on the exposures to these borrowers could be applied. Alternatively, exposure limits could be applied.

4 Conclusions

Macroprudential authorities need to monitor developments of real estate markets in large cities given their systemic importance in terms of activity, bank exposures and share of population, and the possibly large spillover effects of house price dynamics from large cities to the rest of the country. Containing excesses in the housing cycle in large cities might be difficult for macroprudential authorities when global factors are the key drivers. In some circumstances, borrower based measures might have limited effect. This is the case, for example, when housing price dynamics are driven by investors that have access to non-bank sources of funding. In these cases, authorities can still contribute to addressing housing vulnerabilities in large cities by raising public awareness about risks and the role that other policy areas can play. Moreover, macroprudential authorities should ensure that no disruptions in the financial system occur when credit risks materialise. This can be done by strengthening banks with capital measures, by improving lending standards or by limiting banks' exposure concentration to some geographical areas.

References

Bundesbank. (2018, February). *Housing prices in Germany in 2017*. Deutsche Bundesbank monthly report.

ECB Statistical Data Warehouse. (2018a). *House prices and house price valuation indicators*. Accessed July 1, 2018, from https://sdw.ecb.europa.eu/browse.do?node=9689359

ECB Statistical Data Warehouse. (2018b). *Real estate funds*. Accessed July 1, 2018, from https://sdw.ecb.europa.eu/browse.do?node=9691339

European Central Bank. (2017a, May). *Residential real estate prices in capital cities: A review of trends*. Box 3, p 50, Financial stability review.

European Central Bank. (2017b, November). *Financial stability review*.

European Systemic Risk Board. (2016). Recommendation of the European Systemic Risk Board of 31 October 2016 on closing real estate data gaps (ESRB/2016/14).

Faykiss, F., Nagy, M., & Szombati, A. (2017). *Regionally-differentiated debt cap rules: A Hungarian perspective* (BIS papers No. 94).

Financial Stability Board. (2017, January). *Policy recommendations to address structural vulnerabilities from asset management activities*.

Hekwolter of Hekhuis, M., Nijskens, R., & Heeringa, W. (2017). The housing market in major Dutch cities. *De Nederlandsche Bank Occasional Studies*, 15(1).

Hilber, C. A. L., & Vermeulen, W. (2016). The impact of supply constraints on house prices in England. *The Economic Journal, 126*, 358–405.

Iacoviello, M., & Neri, S. (2010). Housing market spillovers: Evidence from an estimated DSGE model. *American Economic Journal, 2*, 125–164.

International Monetary Fund. (2016, November). *Global housing watch report*.

International Montery Fund. (2018, April). *Global financial stability report.*

Kajuth, F., Knetsch, T., & Pinkwart, N. (2016). Assessing house prices in Germany: Evidence from a regional dataset. *Journal of European Real Estate Research, 9*(3), 286–307.

Miles, D., & Sefton, J. (2017). *Houses across time and across place* (CEPR discussion paper no. 12103).

Saiz, A. (2010). The geographic determinants of housing supply. *The Quarterly Journal of Economics, 125*(3), 1253–1296.

Grossmann, V., Larin, B., Löfflad, H. T., & Steger, T. (2018). *The macroeconomics of housing and the dynamics of wealth inequality* (CEPR working paper).

UBS. (2017). *The UBS global real estate bubble index.*

Chapter 15
Soaring House Prices in Major Cities: How to Spot and Moderate Them

Grégory Claeys, Konstantinos Efstathiou, and Dirk Schoenmaker

1 Introduction

Rapidly rising house prices are a well-known source of financial instability. When fuelled by credit booms, asset price bubbles increase the risk of a financial crisis, and the collapse of such bubbles tends to be followed by deeper recessions and slower recoveries (Jordà et al. 2015). Debt-financed house price bubbles have emerged as a particularly dangerous phenomenon for two reasons. First, mortgages that are not repaid cause losses for the financial system. Second, households in negative equity (i.e. when the value of the house is lower than the outstanding mortgage) reduce their consumption significantly to rebuild their equity position. This deepens the economic downturn (Mian et al. 2013). By the same token, households increase their consumption when house prices are rising. Housing can thus be a strong pro-cyclical force in the economy, as housing boom-bust cycles in Spain and Ireland have made abundantly clear.

The cyclical pattern of house prices is very strong because households, as non-professional investors, mainly base their house price expectations on current price developments, even if these expectations look unrealistic from an ex-post perspective (Schoenmaker and Wierts 2017). Such expectations have a reinforcing effect both when house prices are rising and when they are falling. More remarkably, these price expectations are mainly local: in some cities, house prices might increase, but not in others, as Shiller (2008) shows.

G. Claeys · K. Efstathiou
Bruegel, Brussels, Belgium
e-mail: gregory.claeys@bruegel.org; konstantinos.efstathiou@bruegel.org

D. Schoenmaker (✉)
Bruegel, Brussels, Belgium

Erasmus University Rotterdam, Rotterdam, The Netherlands
e-mail: schoenmaker@rsm.nl

R. Nijskens et al. (eds.), *Hot Property*, https://doi.org/10.1007/978-3-030-11674-3_15

This chapter examines whether there are regional differences in house price growth within European countries and, if so, whether this warrants more targeted measures to address vulnerabilities. The monitoring of vulnerabilities and potential imbalances in European housing markets is carried out jointly by the European Systemic Risk Board (2015 and 2016) and by national authorities. Their analyses are done mainly at the country level. Though essential, tracking only national indicators means that these analyses might miss imbalances developing within countries. In Denmark, for example, the International Monetary Fund noted the growing divergence of house prices within the country and found evidence of signs of overvaluation in Copenhagen (Chen et al. 2016).

We focus on the division in terms of house prices between the capital cities and the rest of the territories of six EU countries for which there are sufficiently long series of house price indices (HPI) at the regional level. Capital cities are important because they tend to be large and densely populated and because they possess structural (supply-side) characteristics that can amplify the response of prices to shocks. We do not examine the drivers of property prices at the regional level, nor do we set out to identify potential bubbles, which is very difficult in real time. Instead, we calculate indicators that can be used by policymakers to gauge the level of overvaluation of residential housing separately for national capitals and the rest of the country, in order to see if there are significant divergences between the two.

A stronger cyclical pattern of property prices—coupled with slower growth of household disposable income in capital cities—would represent an additional source of financial vulnerability. This combination could lead households in capital cities to carry heavier debt (compared to their income) and thus be more vulnerable to economic shocks, with implications for financial stability if those households are not able to repay their mortgage. Moreover, price developments in the capital region might spill-over to neighbouring regions within each country, causing price changes that might be even less justified by the fundamentals of these regions.

A stronger cyclical pattern in capital cities compared to other regions within each country would indicate a clear rationale for regional-level tools. The usual instrument to dampen cycles is the central bank's interest rate, but its effects are felt economy-wide. Moreover, since the creation of the single currency, the euro area has one interest rate for the area as a whole, without differentiation between countries, let alone regions. That makes national and/or regional instruments to dampen financial cycles even more necessary. An instrument that could be used locally is tax. However, even though property taxes or stamp duties could be targeted regionally, adjusting taxes often to dampen house prices would be very difficult. The political decision-making and subsequent administrative implementation process is usually very slow, so that changes in the levels of the tax might even become procyclical. Structural measures to adjust the housing supply, such as relaxing planning restrictions, could also be useful to alleviate the pressure on house prices, but have typically a long lead time.

An alternative to address house-price imbalances is to use loan-to-value (LTV) and debt-to-income (DTI) limits. These borrower-based macroprudential instruments can be tightened to curb excessive house-price rises. Borrower-based instruments target homebuyers who need a mortgage, but not cash buyers. Mortgage buyers are particularly vulnerable to house-price shocks, because of their outstanding mortgage. Borrower-based instruments will still have (partial) impact on house prices, as the number of buyers on the market is reduced. So far, the use of borrower-based instruments in the European Union has only been based on the evolution of national house-price indices and applied at the national level. But regional use of these instruments might be desirable and is technically feasible, because houses are immovable and recorded in the land registry, which makes circumvention of regional policies difficult.

2 Are Capital Cities Different from Other Regions?

To assess the risks of regional differences in house price developments in the European Union (EU), house price index (HPI) data at the regional level for EU countries is needed. Most analyses focus on how house prices evolve in terms of national averages, and little attention is paid to differences in house price growth that might develop within a country. Whereas some factors influencing house prices are national (e.g. the availability of credit and the central bank's policy rate), housing markets are by definition tied to location and thus involve a component of supply and demand that is local in nature.

In a working paper, we explain our methodology to decompose national house price indexes into an index for the capital and an index for the rest of the country (Claeys et al. 2017). In this chapter, we present house price data from six EU countries for which more than 20 years of data is available to identify patterns: Denmark, Finland, France, the Netherlands, Sweden and the United Kingdom (UK). The working paper provides additional information on Austria, Germany, Greece, Ireland and Lithuania, for which less than 20 years of data is available.

The capital cities of Denmark, Finland, France, the Netherlands, Sweden and the UK are those countries' most populous urban centres, giving their associated local housing markets national importance. We focus on house price growth and price-to-income ratios at the regional level for these countries. These two metrics are widely-used and have a good record of performance in highlighting vulnerabilities. For macroprudential policy purposes, Goodhart (2011) refers to the monitoring of a set of early warning *"presumptive indicators"* including "*a rate of growth of housing (and property) prices which is significantly faster than normal and above its normal trend relationship with incomes*".

Moreover, the European Systemic Risk Board has undertaken a comprehensive study assessing the predictive capacity of a set of early-warning indicators (Ferrari et al. 2015). In an EU-wide setting, nominal house price growth and price-to-income gaps were ranked among the most reliable early-warning indicators of unsustainable bubbles.

Figure 15.1 compares house price developments in the capitals and the rest of the territory in the six countries of our sample, relative to house prices at the start of the

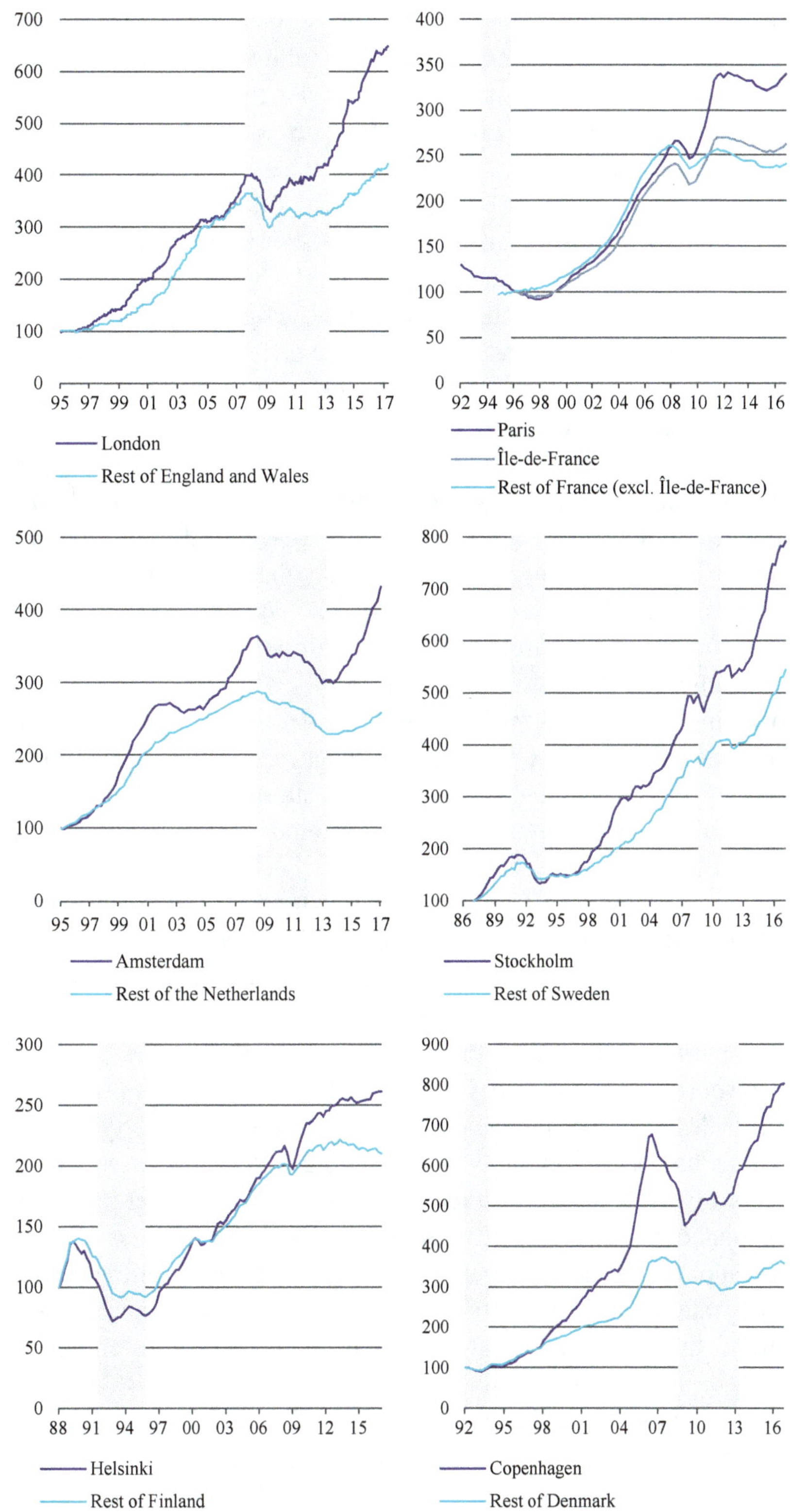

Source: Claeys et al. (2017)

Fig. 15.1 House price indices, beginning of period = 100. Note: The shaded areas represent periods of real estate-related banking crisis, based on a table from Ferrari et al. (2015). For France, we included the series for Paris (apartments only) for illustration purposes

period in each case. Because the HPI data tracks house price growth (not absolute price levels) relative to a certain point in time, it follows that it is important to know the conditions prevailing at the start point in order to understand the influence of base effects. The shaded areas in Fig. 15.1 show periods of housing crises (using the dating convention from Ferrari et al. 2015). In the early 1990s, when most of the series began, all of the countries of our sample with the exception of the Netherlands went through housing crises, meaning the series start in the trough of the cycle.

Figure 15.2 shows year-on-year HPI growth rates while Table 15.1 lists some of the descriptive statistics of the HPI growth rates. Higher average price growth in capitals over the longer run suggests that the price differential has structural features, such as persistently higher demand and less-responsive housing supply caused by restricted land supply and/or stricter planning rules in capitals. The price growth differential between the capitals and the other parts of each country ranges from 0.6% to 3.5% points. Interestingly, house prices in capitals also seem to have a stronger cyclical component, with higher upturns and deeper downturns. This stronger cyclical pattern is confirmed by more volatile year-on-year growth rates in capital cities, with the exception of London. As can be seen in Table 15.1, standard deviations and max/min of the price growth in 1 year are clearly higher in capital cities than in the rest of the countries.

As shown in Claeys et al. (2017), another striking feature of the data is the different responses of house prices after the most recent downturn. Within-country differences in growth rates have widened in the latest phase of rising house prices, mainly as a result of price growth outside the capitals remaining below its previous average.

Rapidly increasing property prices can be a sign of overheating in the housing market and raise the possibility of a housing bubble forming. At the heart of these risks is a misalignment between prevailing market prices and the value of residential housing assets justified by economic fundamentals.

As a first pass, we looked at price-to-income ratios (house prices relative to household disposable income) in Claeys et al. (2017). A rising price-to-income ratio indicates less affordable housing, with residential property prices growing faster than the disposable income of households. As with price growth, recent developments in price-to-income ratios point to growing divergences and strong growth in capital cities. Affordability has decreased in capital cities with the ratio for capital cities at or above its historical peak in all our sample countries. This contrasts with relatively stable price-to-income ratios in areas outside the capitals in recent years. There is, thus, evidence of a decoupling between capitals and the rest of the country.

Persistently decreasing affordability in capital cities is relevant for financial stability, to the extent that it could lead households in capitals to become excessively leveraged, thereby bringing into question their ability to service their debts in case of shocks (such as changes in interest rates or income levels). These diverging trends in affordability between parts of countries call for a differentiated approach in instruments, which we consider in the next section.

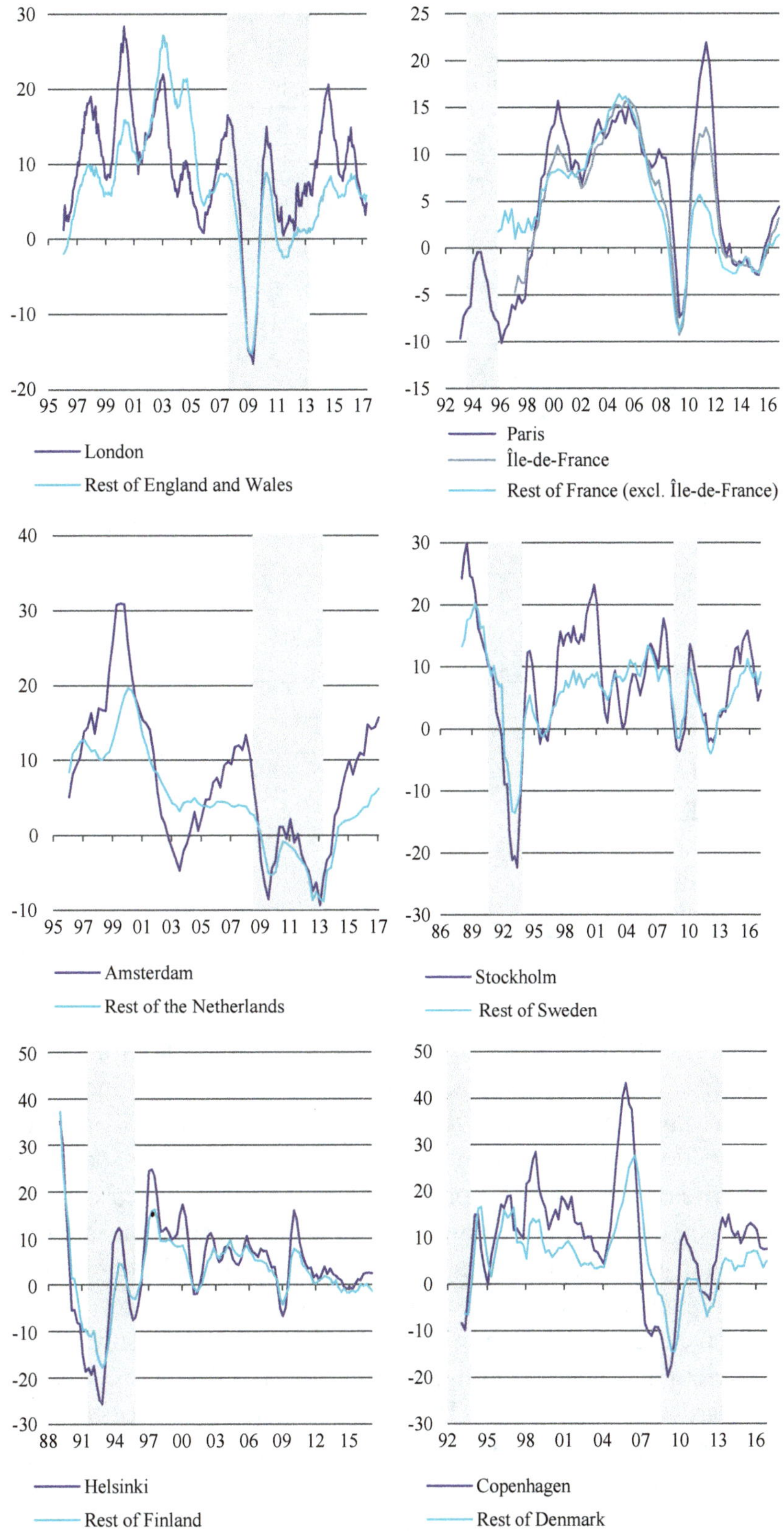

Source: Claeys et al. (2017)

Fig. 15.2 HPI year-on-year growth rates (%). Note: See Fig. 15.1

Table 15.1 House prices, descriptive statistics, year-on-year changes (%)

	Average annual growth rate	Standard deviation	Min of annual growth rate	Max of annual growth rate
Denmark				
Copenhagen	9.78	12.10	−19.89	43.13
Rest of Denmark	5.86	8.09	−14.47	27.64
Finland				
Helsinki	3.62	10.33	−25.61	35.22
Rest of Finland	2.57	7.84	−17.78	37.17
France				
Paris	3.70	7.63	−11.26	17.97
Ile de France	4.53	6.04	−10.25	13.65
Rest of France	3.96	5.59	−9.85	14.06
Netherlands				
Amsterdam	7.17	9.38	−9.34	30.96
Rest of the Netherlands	4.53	6.72	−8.88	19.61
Sweden				
Stockholm	7.45	9.47	−22.32	30.67
Rest of Sweden	5.91	6.29	−13.63	20.23
United Kingdom				
London	9.34	7.84	−16.66	28.34
Rest of England and Wales	7.14	7.96	−15.35	27.15

Source: Claeys et al. (2017)

3 Policy Recommendations

It is clear that more rapidly rising house prices in capital cities are partly related to structural factors. These include faster population growth than areas outside the capitals, which is related to movement of labour from the provincial areas to the main cities and migration (migrants tend to concentrate in the most-populated urban areas). Combined with a shortage of new homes in capital cities, the extra demand leads to price rises if the supply is not elastic, which is often the case in capital cities which are already densely built-up and where planning restrictions are often stricter than in the countryside (Hsieh and Moretti 2018). Some of these restrictions could be relaxed to reduce the supply constraint, but, as our results show, house prices in capitals are also more volatile than in other areas. Structural measures by themselves might not be enough to moderate house price cycles in capital cities. Macroprudential measures, in particular borrower (DTI/loan-to-income/debt-service-to-income ratios, amortisation) and collateral-based (LTV) instruments, appear to be more adequate to tackle the cyclical nature of the problem. However, are policies based on national house price indices appropriate for dealing with the specific overly-cyclical pattern of capital cities?

Section 3.1 briefly describes the current frameworks in which such macroprudential measures are applied in the countries analysed in Sect. 2. Section 3.2 provides policy options going forward.

3.1 Country Experiences

In the **Netherlands**, the maximum LTV in 2010 was 112%. It has been undergoing a gradual reduction to 100% by 2018. The Dutch Financial Stability Committee has advised future governments to continue the gradual lowering of the LTV limit for mortgage loans after 2018 towards 90%, by reducing it by one percentage point per year. With house prices rising by 6% per year across the Netherlands, this advice appears sensible and there is no reason for macroprudential policies to intervene more forcefully. Moreover, high price rises of 15% per year in Amsterdam might justify further macroprudential action to take the heat out of that particular market. Nevertheless, the government has decided to keep the LTV limit at 100%.

Private home-owners in **Denmark** are required to make a down-payment of at least 5% when taking out a loan. Moreover, owing to the within-country divergence in house prices, the Danish Financial Supervisory Authority (Finanstilsynet) has seven best practice guidelines, to apply only in areas with high price levels and increases. In March 2017, the Danish Systemic Risk Council recommended a cap on the flow of new mortgages (15%) to borrowers with high debt-to-income (DTI) ratios (400% or greater) in high-price areas, which include the city of Copenhagen and its environs, and the city of Aarhus. The government has called on banks to follow the Council's recommendations.

An 85% LTV limit was introduced in **Sweden** in 2010. In 2016, the Swedish financial services authority (Finansinspektionen) decided to impose amortisation requirements on new collateralised lending to highly leveraged borrowers (LTV exceeding 50%). Specifically, mortgages with an LTV ratio of more than 70% must be amortised at an annual rate of at least 2% of the original amount, with that rate falling to 1% when the LTV is between 50% and 70%. This measure was initially slated to be put in place in 2015 but its implementation was halted because of doubts about the compatibility of such measures with the Finansinspektionen's mandate. Finally, in May 2017, the Finansinspektionen announced its proposal to tighten further amortisation requirements by an additional 1% annually if DTI ratios exceed 450%.

In **Finland**, a maximum LTV ratio was introduced in 2016 at 90%, with 95% for first-time buyers. The financial services authority (Finanssivalvonta) may reduce the limit by 10% if tightening is deemed appropriate.

In the **UK**, a cap on the quarterly flow of new lending (15% of the number of loans) to borrowers with high DTIs (above 450%), similar to that in Denmark, is in effect. The Bank of England Financial Policy Committee also requires lenders to apply an interest rate stress test before granting a mortgage. The test assesses whether borrowers can still afford the mortgage if the interest rate increases by 3% anytime in the first 5 years of the loan.

France has no borrower-based or collateral-based macroprudential measures in place. However, although there is no official limit, in practice French credit institutions have all adopted a standard whereby all repayments of housing loans (including interest rates payments) must not exceed one-third of the borrower's gross income (Haut Conseil de Stabilité Financière 2017).

3.2 Policy Options

All the policies described in Sect. 3.1 (except in Denmark) are implemented at the national level and do not take into account divergences between capital cities and the rest of the countries in our sample. National policies, based on average house price growth, can be too blunt to dampen excessive house price growth in capital cities, and too tight for the rest of the country where house price growth is subdued. This could be tackled through taxes or structural measures, but these would require a long lead-time and would play out over the long term. Instead, a differentiated macroprudential policy could be implemented through different LTV or DTI ratios for mortgages in capital cities and in the rest of the countries. But where and when should these measures be applied?

Where to Differentiate

The first step would be to determine whether there are significant differences between capital cities and the rest of a country. If this were the case, a differentiated approach would be warranted. One country that already does this is Korea, which 15 years ago put in place a differentiated application of LTV and DTI ratios according to zip-codes, in order to tighten policy more quickly in areas more prone to overheating. In areas considered 'bubble-prone', the Korean Financial Services Commission implements tighter LTV ratios, regardless of types of housing, or the amount and maturity of new mortgages. LTV ratios are relaxed for first-time buyers and low-income households (Financial Services Commission 2017).

An area is designated as a 'speculative zone' where special measures might be required if both the following two criteria are satisfied (Igan and Kang 2011):

- The monthly HPI rose more by than 1.3 times the nationwide CPI inflation rate during the previous month;
- Either (i) the average house price growth rate in the previous 2 months was more than 1.3 times the average national rate in the previous 2 months, or (ii) the average of the month-on-month house price growth rates over the previous year was higher than the average of the month-on-month national rate over the previous 3 years.

Since 2002, the Korean authorities have imposed tighter limits on LTV and DTI ratios in specific areas on several occasions, and have succeeded in taming local house price booms, in terms of both prices and number of transactions (Igan and Kang 2011).

A similar framework could be applied in EU countries to prevent overheating of local housing markets and its consequences. In Claeys et al. (2017), we apply the criteria used in Korea to the six countries in our sample and show that the capital city in each case would qualify as a 'speculative zone' most of the time, especially in periods of rising prices.

When to Differentiate

With these criteria in place, the second step would be to monitor house prices at the regional level to decide when to tighten or to loosen the policies. When house price growth is considered to be excessive in a particular region, the responsible authority would impose measures or explain why measures are not taken. The 'comply or explain' strategy was also advocated by Ingves (2017) endorsing the presumptive indicators formulated by Charles Goodhart (2011).

However, it is difficult to set a specific house price growth trigger point beyond which action might be taken, in contrast to consumer price index inflation in monetary policy (Ingves 2017). For the responsible authority, it is hard to know what constitutes the correct price growth rate at a given time, because house prices are determined by a range of different factors that are both cyclical and structural in nature. Indicators are therefore necessary to know when to take action, as house prices are very important for financial stability.

Appropriate ranges for the indicator can be established precisely using historical data. As a starting point, we suggest that the five to 10% annual house price growth range would warrant close monitoring, with potential for action if deemed appropriate. The 10% or more range would set off a 'comply or explain' regime: 'comply' meaning macroprudential measures at the regional level would be tightened, and 'explain' meaning provision of a justification for the lack of measures. The macroprudential authority can publish the indicators and the measures (or the lack of them) in its semi-annual financial stability report. Tightening of macroprudential policies can be done through lowering LTV and/or DTI limits. In that way, the housing boom-bust cycle might be dampened.

References

Chen, J., Geng, N., Ho, G., & Turk, R. A. (2016). *Denmark: Selected issues* (IMF Country Report No. 16/185). International Monetary Fund.

Claeys, G., Efstathiou, K., & Schoenmaker, D. (2017). *Spotting excessive regional house price growth and what to do about it* (Bruegel Policy Contribution No. 26). Brussels.

European Systemic Risk Board. (2015). *Report on residential real estate and financial stability in the EU.*

European Systemic Risk Board. (2016). *Vulnerabilities in the EU residential real estate sector.*

Ferrari, S., Pirovano, M., & Cornacchia, W. (2015). *Identifying early warning indicators for real estate-related banking crises* (ESRB Occasional Paper Series No. 8). European Systemic Risk Board.

Financial Services Commission. (2017, August 2). *FSC tightens mortgage rules to curb speculative demand in housing market* (Press release).

Goodhart, C. A. (2011). The macro-prudential authority: Powers, scope and accountability. *OECD Journal: Financial Market Trends, 2011*(2).

Haut Conseil de Stabilité Financière. (2017). *Rapport annuel.*

Hsieh, C., & Moretti, E. (2018). *Housing Constraints and Spatial Misallocation* (CEPR Discussion Paper No. 12912).

Igan, D., & Kang, H. (2011). *Do loan-to-value and debt-to-income limits work? Evidence from Korea* (Working Paper 11/297). International Monetary Fund.

Ingves, S. (2017, May 11–12). Avoiding collective amnesia, speech to the conference. *Should macroprudential policy target real estate prices*. Vilnius, Lithuania.

Jordà, Ò., Schularick, M., & Taylor, A. M. (2015). Leveraged bubbles. *Journal of Monetary Economics, 76*(Suppl), S1–S20.

Mian, A., Rao, K., & Sufi, A. (2013). Household balance sheets, consumption, and the economic slump. *Quarterly Journal of Economics, 128*(4), 1687–1726.

Schoenmaker, D., & Wierts, P. (2017). *The mortgage credit cycle*, mimeo.

Shiller, R. J. (2008). Understanding the recent trends in house prices and home ownership. In *Housing, housing finance and monetary policy*. Jackson Hole Conference Series, Federal Reserve Bank of Kansas City.

Chapter 16
The Korean Housing Market: Its Characteristics and Policy Responses

Ho Soon Shin and Hyun Chang Yi

1 Recent Housing Market Developments

1.1 Housing Price Trends

Korea experienced only a limited drop in housing prices after the global financial crisis, unlike advanced economies that experienced sharp price declines (Fig. 16.1a). Prices began to recover in 2014 when the government eased real estate regulations, and have since then remained on an upswing. From the first quarter of 2014 to the second quarter of 2017 the rise in housing prices (10.5%) was concentrated primarily in the capital area (the SMA[1]), similar to the cases in other advanced countries such as the Netherlands and Australia. Figure 16.1b shows that the gap in the rates of housing price increases in Seoul and in the nation as a whole was 6.9 percentage points (pp) during this period.

Apartments account for 60% of all housing in Korea,[2] and since 2014 apartment prices in the SMA have risen far faster than those in the NSMA (Fig. 16.1c). In

[1]The SMA includes Seoul, Incheon and Gyeonggi (GG). The non-SMA region, NSMA, consists of five major cities and eight provinces. The five major cities are Busan, Daegu, Daejeon, Gwangju and Ulsan, and the eight provinces Gangwon (GW), Chungbuk (CB), Chungnam (CN), Jeonbuk (JB), Jeonnam (JN), Gyeongbuk (GB), Gyeongnam (GN) and Jeju (JJ).

[2]In Korea, apartments refer to five or more story residential buildings. Most apartment complexes have facilities nearby such as supermarkets, schools and district offices as well as easy access to public transport.

H. S. Shin
Bank of Korea, Seoul, Republic of Korea

H. C. Yi (✉)
Financial Stability Department, Bank of Korea, Seoul, Republic of Korea
e-mail: hyunchang.yi@bok.or.kr

R. Nijskens et al. (eds.), *Hot Property*, https://doi.org/10.1007/978-3-030-11674-3_16

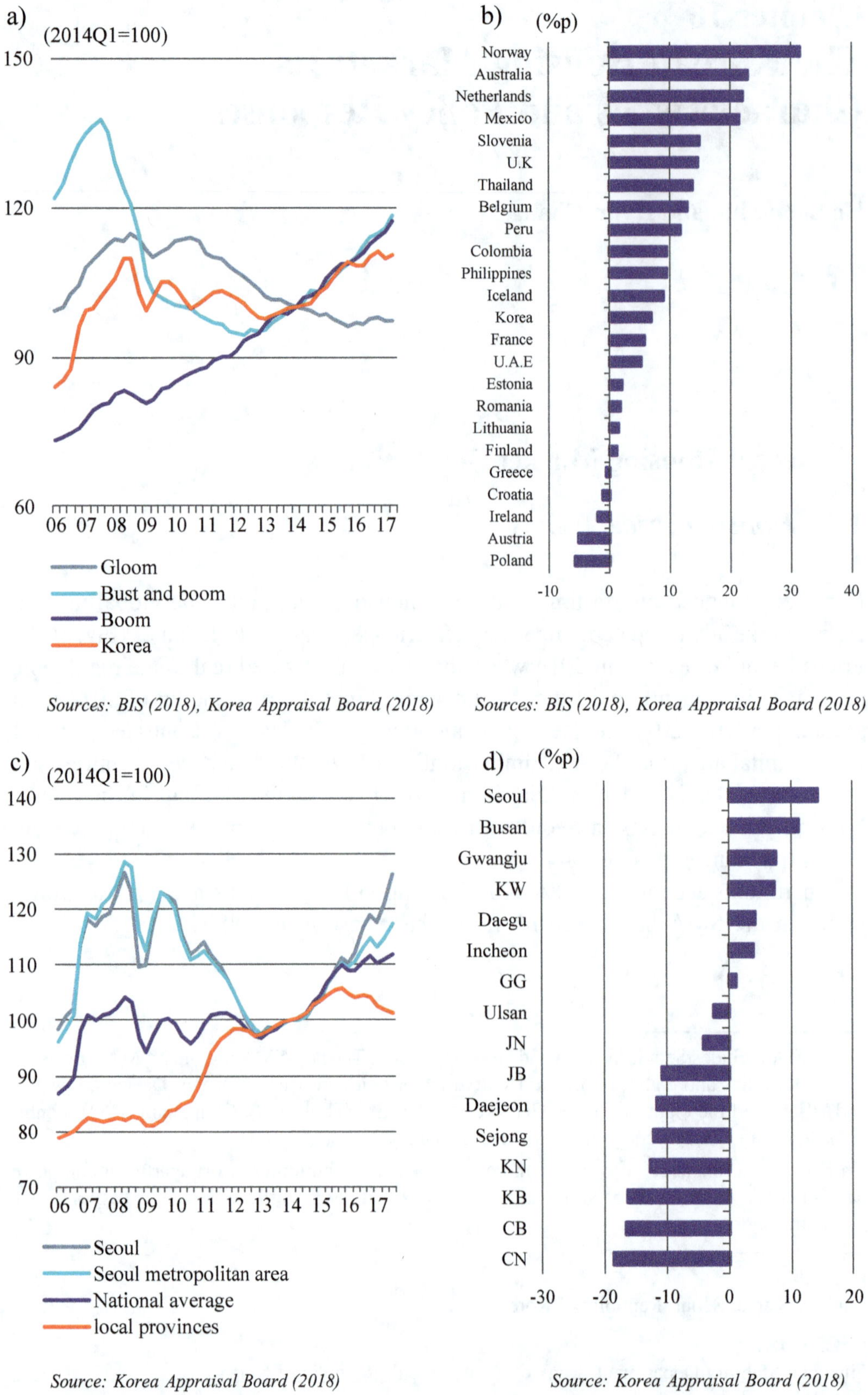

Fig. 16.1 (**a**) Real housing price index. Note: Gloom: Netherlands, China, etc; bust and boom: US, UK, etc; boom: Australia, Canada, etc. The classification is from IMF (2017). (**b**) Gaps in real housing price growth between capital cities and nations overall. Note: From Q1 2014 to Q2 2017.

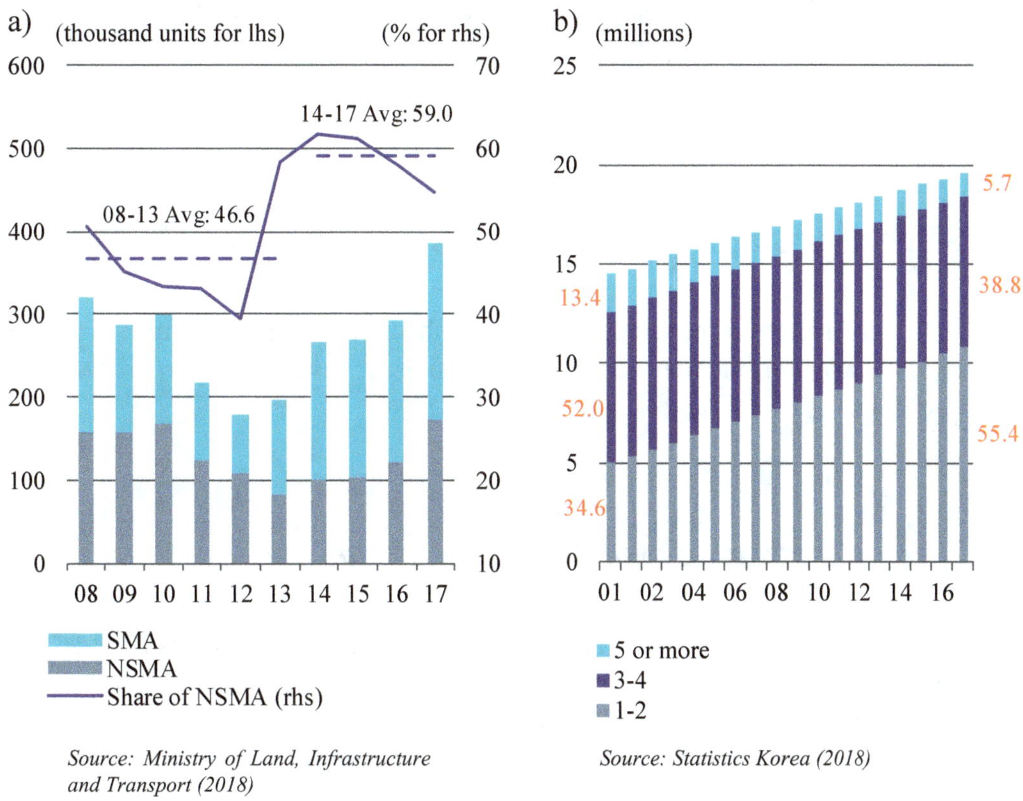

Fig. 16.2 (**a**) Number of apartments constructed. Note: SMA is the Seoul metropolitan area and NSMA is the rest of the country. (**b**) Number of households by household size. Note: Figures are the percentage proportions

particular, the growth rate in Seoul from the first quarter of 2014 to the fourth quarter of 2017 (31.2%) exceeded the national average (12.6%) by 18.7pp (Fig. 16.1d).

1.2 *Supply and Demand*

Housing supply, which had fallen amid the post-crisis housing market slump, began to increase with the real estate deregulation in 2014, led by the NSMA. The quantity of new apartments completed in 2017 stood at 385,000 units, greatly exceeding the 6-year average (2008–2013) of 250,000 (Fig. 16.2a). The supply in the NSMA accounted for 59.0% of all new apartments between 2014 and 2017, sharply up from 46.6% between 2008 and 2013.

The demand for housing has grown with the rise in the number of one- and two-person households (Fig. 16.2b) as a result of, for example, shrinking household size in the course of population aging (Oh et al. 2017). In particular, the annual rate

---

Fig. 16.1 (continued) (**c**) Regional real apartment price index in Korea. (**d**) Gaps between regional and national real apartment price growth rates. Note: From Q1 2014 to Q4 2017

of growth in the number of households is higher in the SMA (2.1%, 2000–2017) than the national average (1.8%), due to the faster growth in one- and two-person households there.

2 Structural Characteristics of the Korean Housing Market

The Korean housing market is characterized by the dominance of apartments among housing types, by considerable demand for housing for investment purposes, and by household-led supply of rental housing.

2.1 *Apartments as a Dominant Form of Housing*

As of 2016, apartments accounted for 60% of all housing units in Korea (Fig. 16.3a). On the supply side, apartments came to predominate because they could be more effectively supplied and managed than other types of housing in response to the growing overpopulation of the SMA and other large cities during the past periods of industrialization and urbanization.

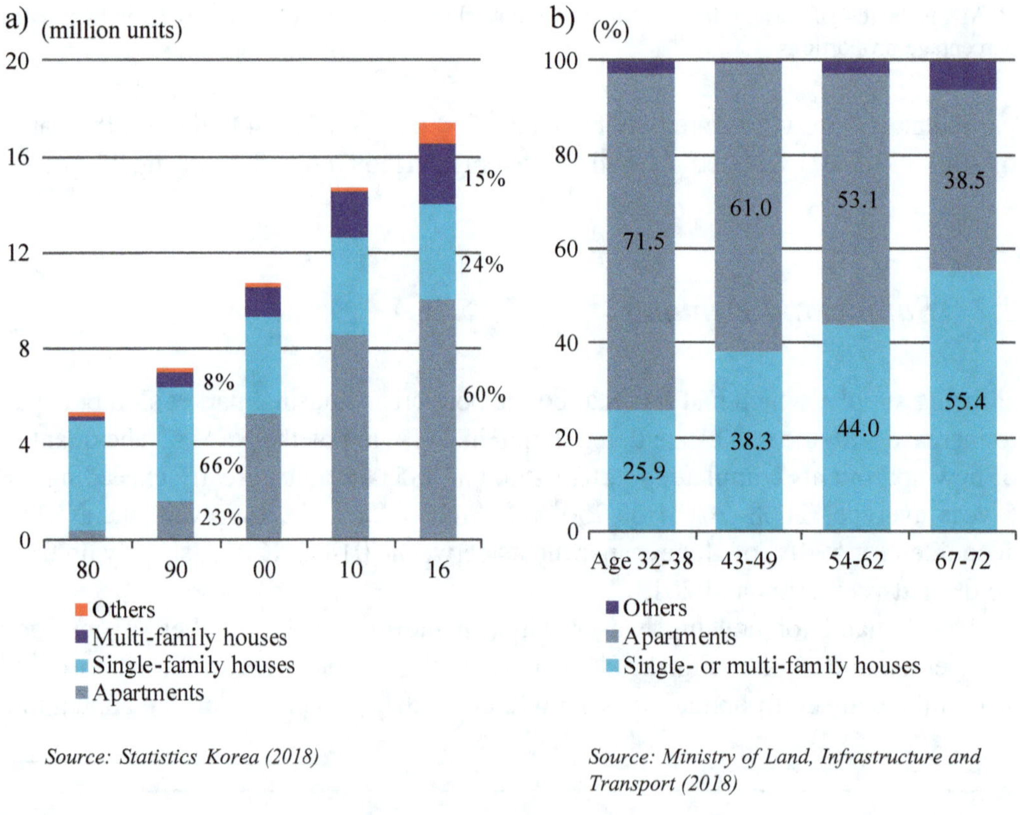

Fig. 16.3 (**a**) Number of houses by type. Note: Figures are the percentage. (**b**) Housing preferences by generation. Note: 2016 survey

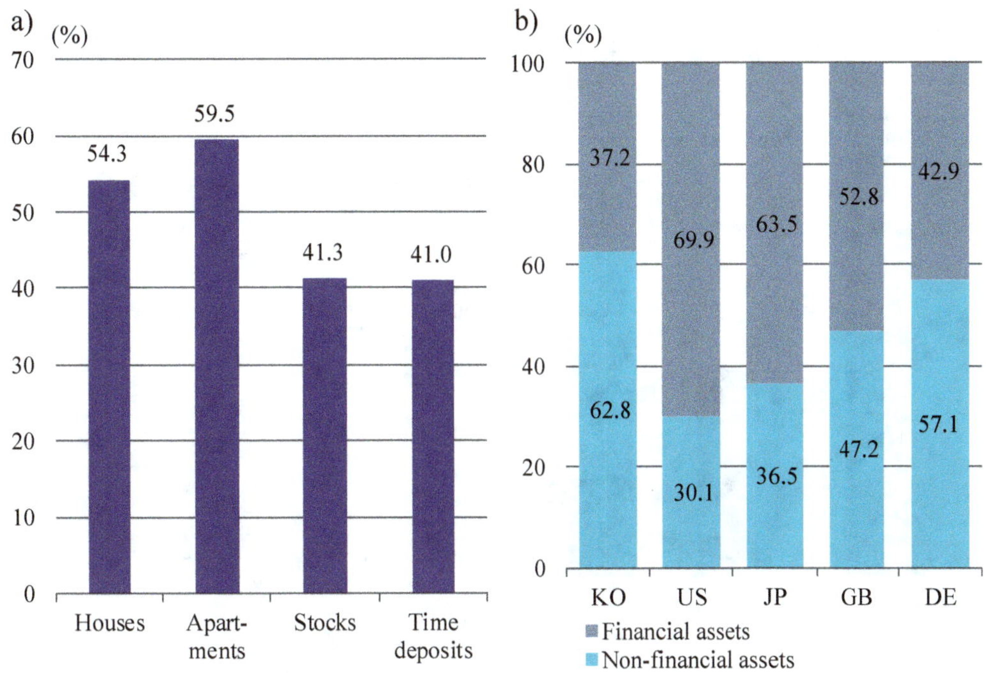

Sources: Author's calculation based on data from KB Kookmin Bank, Bank of Korea (2017)

Sources: Bank of Korea (2017)

Fig. 16.4 (**a**) Cumulated returns by asset type. Note: Between 2007 and 2016 figures for houses and apartments are based on samples from KB Kookmin Bank, and time deposits are based on one-year maturity. (**b**) Compositions of household assets in major countries. Note: Figures for Korea and the US are based on the national balance sheets in 2016 (and those for other countries on their national balance sheets in 2015)

On the demand side, the younger generations prefer apartments, as do the middle-aged because of apartments' high liquidity (Fig. 16.3b). They can cash in their property assets after retirement. The proportion of apartments is considerably higher in the SMA (63.2%) and other large cities (63.9%) than in the rest of the country (57.5%).[3]

2.2 *Demand for Housing as an Investment*

Korean households have a strong tendency to own houses not only for residential but for investment purposes as well. Apartments in Korea are highly preferred as an investment because they yield high and stable profits, and are highly liquid[4] (Fig. 16.4a). As a result, non-financial assets, such as homes and commercial

[3]The large cities include Seoul and six major cities (Incheon, Busan, Daegu, Daejeon, Gwangju and Ulsan).

[4]Since apartments in Korea are standardized, they have advantages in terms of being sold and leased out.

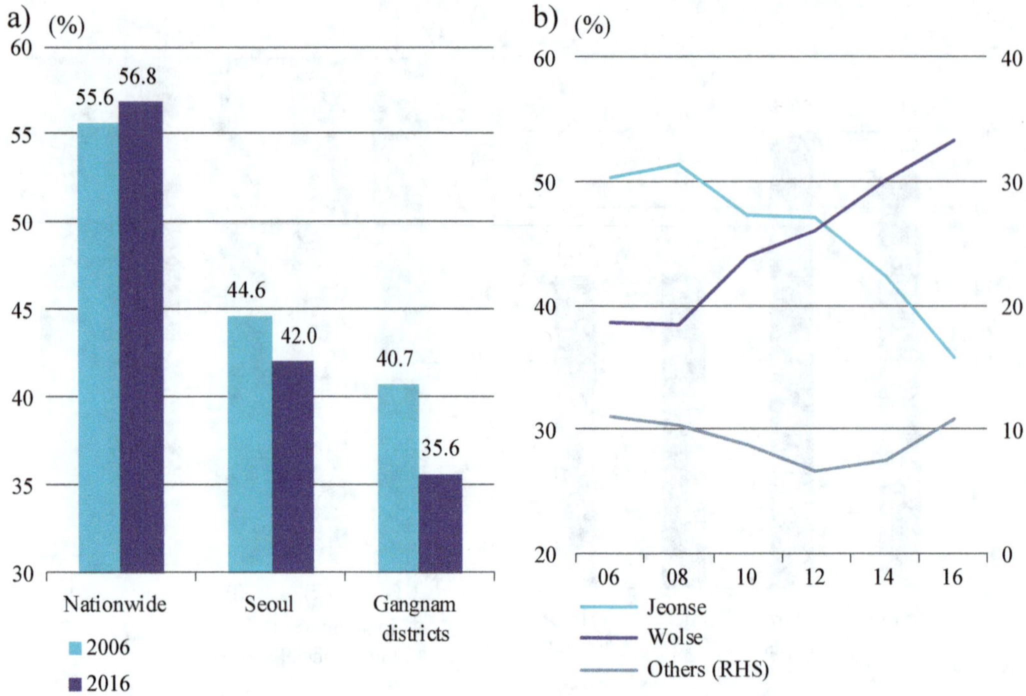

Source: Statistics Korea (2018)

Source: Ministry of Land, Infrastructure and Transport (2018)

Fig. 16.5 (**a**) Shares of owner-occupiers by region. Note: The Gangnam districts include three districts in southern Seoul (Seocho, Gangnam and Songpa). (**b**) Shares by rental housing type. Note: Wolse is a rental contract based on a deposit plus the payment of monthly rent

buildings, accounted for 62.8% of total household assets in Korea at the end of 2016, far exceeding the figures seen in other major advanced countries (Fig. 16.4b).

Meanwhile, the popularity of jeonse,[5] a leasehold deposit system unique to Korea, tends to make it easy to purchase homes for investment purposes through so-called gap investment. It allows home buyers to easily finance a sizeable portion of the purchase price in the form of the deposits they receive for leasing the housing out. The amount of deposit is referred to as jeonse price.[6]

Demand for housing as an investment is more concentrated in Seoul. As of 2016, housing units held by multi-home owners (households owning two or more homes) accounted for 53% of total housing units in Seoul, a proportion higher than the national average (49.9%). In reflection of this, the share of owner-occupiers in Seoul stood at 42.0%, well below the national average (56.8%) (Fig. 16.5a). Nationwide, the share rose from 55.6% in 2006 to 56.8% in 2016, while in Seoul it has been falling from 44.6% to 42.0% over the same period.

[5]Under this system, a homeowner rents a housing unit upon receiving a certain leasehold deposit from the tenant, and returns the deposit once the contract period ends.

[6]In 2017 the national average jeonse-to-sales price ratio for apartments was 74.6%.

2.3 Household-Led Supply of Rental Housing

The Korean rental housing market differs from those in other major countries in that the household sector, more so than the public or corporate sectors, plays the main rental housing supplier role. Korean households supplied 78.9% of total rental housing at the end of 2015 (compared to 13.7% by the public sector, and 7.4% by the corporate sector), well above the figures in major countries such as the US (56.3%), the UK (53.1%), Germany (64.1%), and Japan (66.5%).

Meanwhile, jeonse tenancies, which do not occur in other major countries, accounted for 35.9% of the total rental housing supplied by households in 2016 (Fig. 16.5b). The share of jeonse is also much higher in Seoul (45.3%) and the SMA (42.0%, regional average) than in the NSMA (25.0%).

3 Recent Buoyancy in the SMA Housing Market

The buoyancy of the housing market in recent years, particularly in the SMA, has been driven by three factors—the persistently low interest rates, the easing of real estate regulations, and the stronger incentives for financial institutions to supply mortgage loans.

3.1 Persistently Low Interest Rates

With low interest rates having continued for a prolonged period of time, demand for investment in housing has increased. This demand has particularly increased in the SMA, as expectations of housing price growth have spread there. Housing purchases in the form of gap investment[7] have been on the rise (Fig. 16.6a), particularly in the SMA where rental demand is higher than in other areas due to the favorable educational and cultural conditions. Figure 16.6b shows how the investment in housing in Seoul by non-Seoul residents has also grown since 2014.

Meanwhile, as jeonse prices for homes have increased faster than their sales prices, and borrowing costs have become lower, demand from households switching from rental to ownership of housing has also grown. The proportion of jeonse tenants purchasing their own units rose from 7.4% in 2013 to 10.4% in 2016.

[7]When the gap between the housing sales and jeonse prices is small, investors purchase homes by only investing this difference (gap). They then lease the homes and later gain profits by selling them when their sales prices rise.

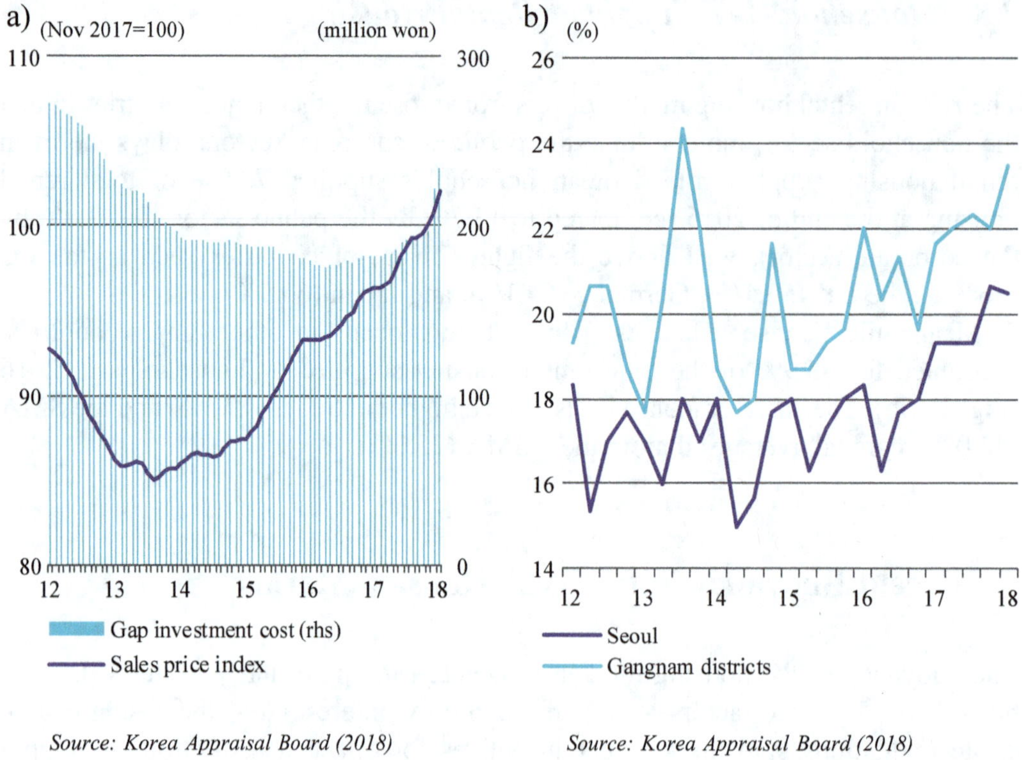

Fig. 16.6 (**a**) Apartment sales price and gap investment cost in Seoul. Note: The gap investment cost is the difference between the housing sales and jeonse prices. (**b**) Proportion of housing purchases in Seoul by non-residents

3.2 *Easing of Real Estate Regulations*

In an effort to boost the real estate market, the Korean government eased the housing market-related regulations drastically in 2014. In the SMA the LTV and DTI ratios were raised by up to 20pp (50% → 70%) and 10pp (50% → 60%), respectively.[8] This led to stronger expectations of housing price rises, and demand for housing purchases increased as a result. In addition, with the shortening of the years required before apartments are eligible for reconstruction,[9] and the easing of qualifications for having first priority to bid in new apartment pre-sale markets,[10] investor demand flowed into homes in Seoul scheduled for reconstruction as well as into new apartment pre-sale markets (Fig. 16.7a).

[8]Here, the debt-to-income ratio is calculated by dividing the sum of annual principal and interest payments of a mortgage and annual interest payments of other debts by annual income.

[9]Previously apartments had to be at least 40 years old to be eligible for reconstruction, but the government has eased that threshold to 30 years for apartments in the SMA and other large cities. This has significantly expanded the range of apartments eligible for reconstruction.

[10]In order to purchase a new apartment in Korea, one must be selected from a pool of subscribers. The qualifications for being prioritized to bid in new apartment pre-sale markets were eased to attract more demand.

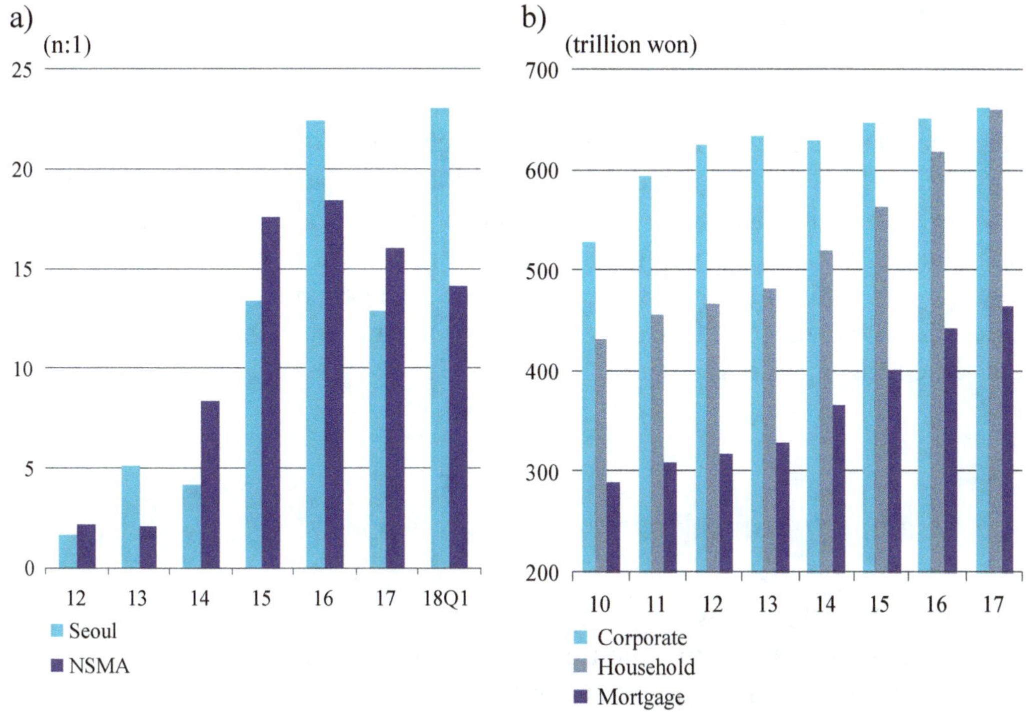

Sources: Bank of Korea (2017), commercial banks' business reports

Fig. 16.7 (**a**) Apartment subscription rate. Note: Subscriptions by those having first priority. (**b**) Household and corporate lending by depository institutions

3.3 Stronger Incentives for Financial Institutions to Provide Mortgage Loans

The incentives for financial institutions to provide mortgage loans have strengthened, due largely to the low risk weights applied to household loans for BIS capital ratio purposes,[11] as well as to rising credit risks in the corporate sector in line with its ongoing restructuring.

These stronger incentives for financial institutions to provide mortgage loans, combined with expectations of higher housing prices, have worked as major factors contributing to the surge in household debt (Fig. 16.7b). As the supply of new homes expanded in line with the easing of real estate regulations, the related mortgage lending has also increased, leading to a sharp rise in household debt.[12]

[11]The risk weights on household and home mortgage loans averaged 22.5% and 19.2%, respectively at the end of 2017, far below 55.5% for corporate loans.

[12]In line with the strength of the housing market since 2014, Korean household debt grew by 10.9% in 2015 (year-end basis) and by 11.6% in 2016, but the growth slowed to 8.1% in 2017 on the effects, for example of the government measures to stabilize the housing market (of August 2) and curb household debt growth (of October 24). Despite this slowdown, the pace of growth in debt still

4 Policy Responses

The Korean government has introduced comprehensive and tailored policy measures since the second half of 2017 in order to stabilize the housing market in the SMA and curb the sharp rise in household debt (FSC 2017a, b). The government's responses have been sweeping, and cover macroprudential, housing and tax policies related to household debt and the housing market. Further, in order to enhance policy effectiveness and minimize any negative side effects, the government has devised measures that vary in range and intensity depending on the target regions, the households concerned, and the types of housing demand.

4.1 Comprehensive Measures

Macroprudential Policies

In an attempt to manage total household debt and curb financing for speculative purposes, the government has been active in using macroprudential policies, including tightening of the regulations on all financial institutions and loans, while also developing comprehensive and systematic criteria for loan screening.

The government has tightened the LTV and DTI requirements greatly (from 70% to 40%) in August 2017, and has limited the number of home mortgage loans per household, for example from one loan per borrower to one loan per household in speculation-prone areas. To prevent any leakage from the home mortgage loan regulations, a debt service ratio (DSR) has been introduced to mandate comprehensive assessment of borrowers' debt servicing capacities for all financial institutions' loans, and will be effective from October 2018. In addition, to limit financial institutions' incentives for supplying excessive household loans several regulations have been introduced in January 2018, including an upward adjustment of the Basel risk weight from 35% to 70% for high-risk home mortgage loans with LTVs over 60%.

Housing Policies

The government has implemented policies to curb speculative demand for new apartments and for apartments scheduled for reconstruction, as that has been a main factor behind the rise in housing prices in the SMA. It has tightened the criteria for top-priority subscribers for new apartment purchasing rights, while limiting their resales by imposing a higher capital gains tax on them. The government has also tightened the requirements for apartment reconstruction, by for example revising the safety criteria for approving reconstruction projects.

---

outstrips that in income, and Korea's household debt-to-nominal GDP ratio (household credit statistics basis) has thus continued to increase, from 73.0% at end-2014 to 81.8% at end-2016 and 83.8% at end-2017.

Tax Policies

The taxation of housing investment has been strengthened, to curb demand for investment purposes and to heighten tax fairness. The government has raised the transfer income tax on owners of multiple homes, which became effective from April 2018, and imposed levies on excess earnings from reconstruction in January 2018. Discussions on revising the property holding tax on owners of multiple homes and expensive homes are also ongoing. This could be a more effective means of controlling housing demand for investment.

4.2 *Tailored Responses*

By Region

The target regions for the tighter regulations are sub-divided into speculative investment zones, overheated zones and adjustment-required zones, depending upon their respective degree of housing price rises and overheating. Each zone is subject to a different level of regulation.[13] The Gangnam districts in Seoul were designated as speculative investment zones, and are subject to the strongest regulations. Other parts of the SMA and the provincial cities are subject to relatively relaxed regulations.

By Household

The level of regulations applied to households varies depending upon whether they own multiple homes, or have taken out home mortgage loans. Households that own multiple homes are subject to a 10–20pp transfer tax add-on. Households owning only single housing units benefit from tax exemptions only after they have lived in their homes for two or more years. When a household with an existing home mortgage loan seeks an additional loan for a housing purchase, the applicable LTV and DTI ratios will be tightened by 10pp each.[14]

By Housing Demand

Housing demand is categorized into demand for speculative and for residential purposes. The government strictly regulates speculative demand, while providing active support for residential demand. Speculative demand is strictly controlled through tighter screening of the financing methods involved and checking on the owner-occupancy status of the borrower. On the other hand, LTV and DTI ratios are relaxed for low-income households purchasing homes for residential purposes, in order to alleviate their financing difficulties.

---

[13]See appendix for a detailed explanation.

[14]When a home mortgage loan borrower purchases an apartment in one of the overheated regions, the borrower will be subject to tighter LTV and DTI ratios (30% instead of 40%).

5 Policy Evaluation

Thanks to the government's comprehensive and tailored policy responses, the growth in household debt has slowed since the second half of 2017, and the housing market in the SMA has been gradually stabilizing in 2018. The rate of household debt growth was 8.1% (at year-end) in 2017, down significantly from the figures of around 10% in 2015 and 2016, in line with the tightening of the LTV and DTI limits and the other policy measures implemented in 2017 (Fig. 16.8a).

Despite the government's announcement of its housing market stabilization plan in August 2017, and its partial implementation thereof, housing prices in the SMA continued to rise for some time. In 2018, however, they have shown slower growth as the effects of the government's policies have begun to take hold (Fig. 16.8b).

For long-term housing market stability it should be noted, however, that demand-reduction policies alone cannot stabilize the housing market in the SMA. There is a structural imbalance between the limited supply of new housing in that area, and the continually growing demand for it.

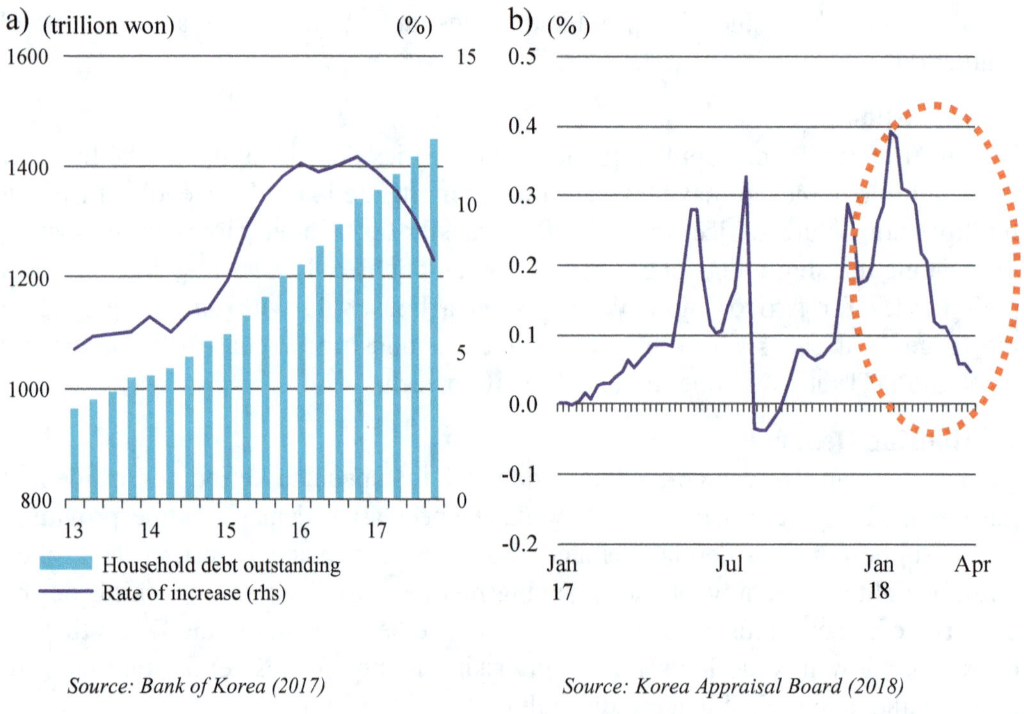

Fig. 16.8 (**a**) Volume and growth rate of household debt. Note: Quarter-end basis; year-on-year. (**b**) Growth rate of apartment prices in the SMA. Note: Week-on-week

Appendix

Table 16.1 Housing market regulations by region

Zones	Major regulations	Areas
Speculative investment	– Tighter LTV/DTI requirements (40/40%) – Limit on the number of mortgage loans – Transfer tax add-on (+10%p)	11 districts in Seoul (including Gangnam districts), Sejong
Overheated	– Tighter LTV/DTI requirements (40/40%) – Tighter requirements for apartment reconstruction and top-priority subscribers for new apartment purchasing rights – Tighter screening of the financing methods	All 25 districts in Seoul, Sejong, 1 city in Gyeonggi, 1 district in Daegu
Adjustment-required	– Tighter LTV/DTI requirements (60/50%) – Tighter requirements for apartment reconstruction and top-priority subscribers for new apartment purchasing rights – Transfer tax add-on (+10–20%p)	All 25 districts in Seoul, Sejong, 7 cities in Gyeonggi, 7 districts in Busan

Note: As of May 2018; designation of speculative investment zones was repealed in April 2018 upon the introduction of transfer tax add-on in adjustment-required zones
Source: FSC 2017a, b

References

Bank for International Settlements. (2018). *Residential property prices: Selected series (nominal and real)*. Accessed July 1, 2018, from https://www.bis.org/statistics/pp_selected.htm

Bank of Korea. (2017). *Financial Stability Report 2017(6).*

Financial Service Commission. (2017a). FSC tightens mortgage rules to curb speculative demand in housing market. *Financial Service Commission Press Release 2017(8).*

Financial Service Commission. (2017b). Comprehensive measures for household debt management. *Financial Service Commission Press Release 2017(10).*

IMF. (2017). *Global Housing Watch 2017(Q1).*

Korea Appraisal Board. (2018). Accessed July 1, 2018 from http://www.kab.co.kr/kab/home/eng/main.jsp

Ministry of Land, Infrastructure and Transport. (2018). Accessed July 1, 2018 from http://stat.molit.go.kr

Oh, K., Kim, S., Yoon, J., Ahn, S., & Kwon, D. (2017). Impact of population aging on the housing market. *Bank of Korea 2017-25.*

Statistics Korea. (2018). Accessed July 1, 2018 from http://kostat.go.kr/

Chapter 17
House Prices and Financial Stability: An Australian Perspective

Michele Bullock and David Orsmond

1 Introduction

As in a number of countries, housing prices in Australia have increased at a rapid pace over the past couple of decades, particularly in the major cities. These price rises have raised a range of concerns, including for housing affordability. As a result, there has been much debate about the types of policies that could ease the growth in housing prices.

While acknowledging the broader societal impacts of high and rising housing prices, the Reserve Bank of Australia (RBA) has not seen managing the pace of housing price rises per se as within its policy remit. Rather, the RBA's concern has been that the associated build-up in household debt and other dynamics in the housing sector have raised concerns about the health of borrowers' balance sheets and, therefore, financial stability. If realised, these risks could have a detrimental impact on the broader economy. Like many other countries, the RBA and other policymakers have considered various ways to address these risks. This chapter outlines this approach and recent experiences.

2 The Housing Market in Australia

Australia is a large country geographically but its population is concentrated in a small number of cities. From a population of close to 25 million, around 15 million live in the largest five cities, with 10 million people in Sydney and Melbourne alone.

M. Bullock
Financial System Group, Reserve Bank of Australia, Sydney, NSW, Australia
e-mail: bullockm@rba.gov.au

D. Orsmond (✉)
Financial Stability Department, Reserve Bank of Australia, Sydney, NSW, Australia
e-mail: orsmondd@rba.gov.au

R. Nijskens et al. (eds.), *Hot Property*, https://doi.org/10.1007/978-3-030-11674-3_17

In the decade to mid-2017, the combined population of the five largest cities grew by 22%, accounting for around three-quarters of Australia's population growth, which was one of the fastest within the OECD. It is unsurprising then that there has at times been pressure on the housing stock, particularly in Sydney and Melbourne.

Housing prices in Australia have risen substantially since the 1980s. Part of this reflects the strong growth in the economy and household incomes over the past few decades. But housing prices have also increased relative to incomes. The factors driving this upward shift in the relative price of housing were primarily twofold (Kohler and van der Merwe 2015; Reserve Bank of Australia 2003, 2014). First, the decline in average nominal interest rates as a result of the structural decline in inflation in the 1990s meant that borrowers could service larger loans out of their current income than they had been able to in the past. Second, deregulation of the financial system reinforced this trend by removing many of the previous constraints on credit supply to households. By the mid-2000s, this structural transition seemed largely complete and the average housing price settled at around four times average household disposable incomes (Fig. 17.1).

In more recent years, however, housing prices have grown quite strongly again, particularly in Sydney and Melbourne (Fig. 17.2). Low interest rates, relatively strong population growth and interest by investors (foreign and domestic) all contributed to a strong demand for residential property. Coupled with zoning

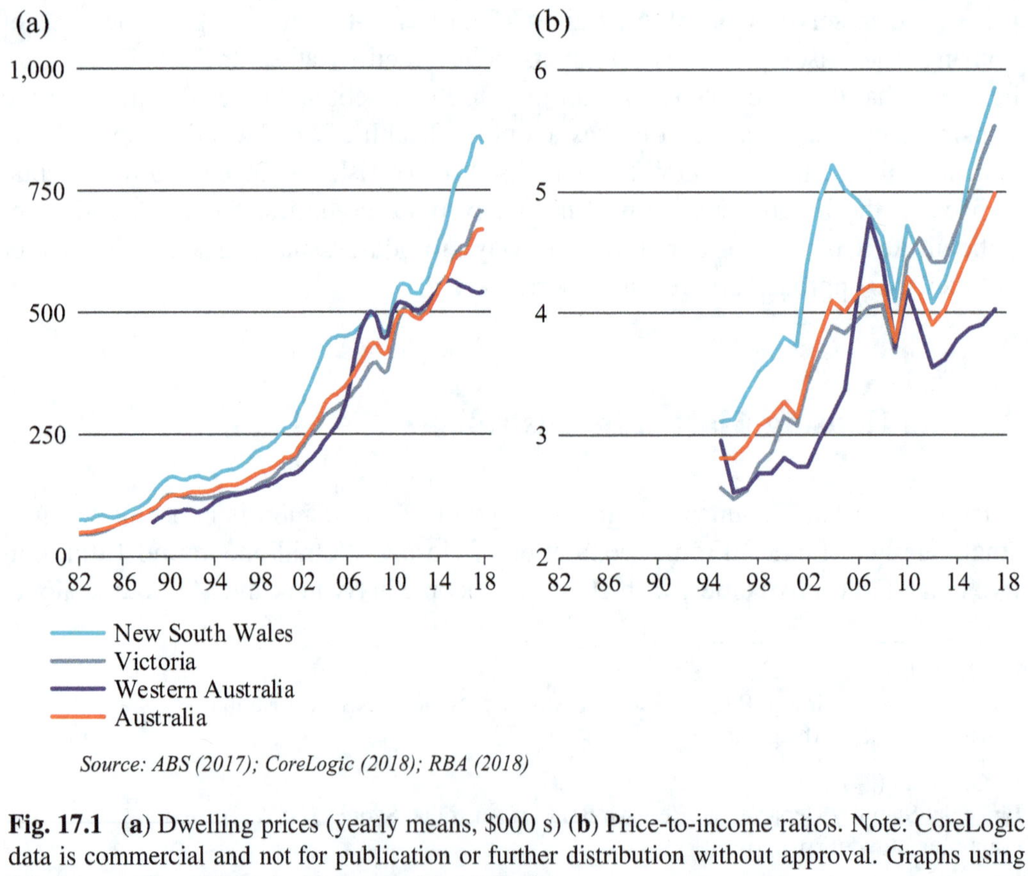

Fig. 17.1 (**a**) Dwelling prices (yearly means, $000 s) (**b**) Price-to-income ratios. Note: CoreLogic data is commercial and not for publication or further distribution without approval. Graphs using this data can be published with appropriate attribution

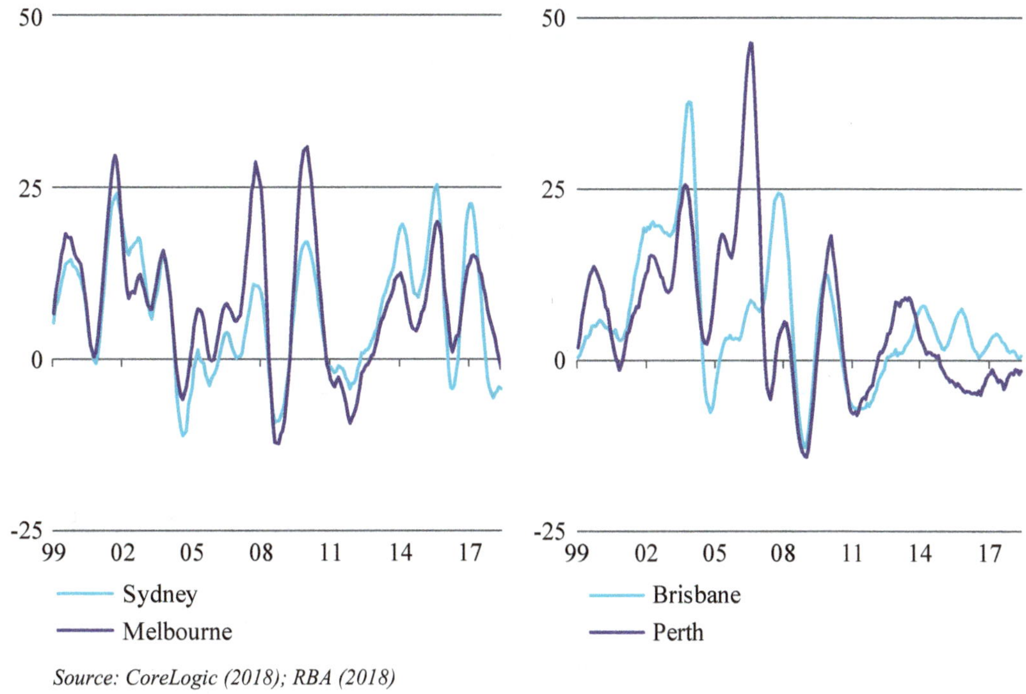

Fig. 17.2 Housing price growth (6-month-ended annualised; seasonally adjusted). Note: CoreLogic data is commercial and not for publication or further distribution without approval. Graphs using this data can be published with appropriate attribution

restrictions and other supply constraints, this resulted in housing prices increasing by around 20% a year in Sydney and Melbourne in 2013 and 2014 (Hsieh et al. 2012). While the pace of growth of overall housing credit was more modest than in previous housing cycles, investor credit was starting to rise rapidly. Housing price growth eased in 2015 but increased again through 2016 and 2017. By the end of 2017, the average price was around five times average household incomes. In contrast, the slowdown in the mining investment boom saw housing price declines in Perth and, to a lesser extent, Brisbane, which are both located in the more mining-intensive states of Australia.

These developments have generated a lot of attention. Housing affordability has consistently been a topical issue in Australia, with much discussion around issues such as how to ease constraints on supply, policies to assist first home buyers, tax incentives for investors and the impact of foreign buyers on the housing market.[1] The RBA's concerns, however, have been focused on the potential implications of broad developments in the housing sector for financial stability and macro-financial risks. There have been a couple of elements to this.

First, the rise in housing prices has been accompanied by a rise in the ratio of household debt to income. After stabilising at around 120% of income from the mid-2000s, the household mortgage debt ratio has since risen to 140% (Fig. 17.3).

[1]For the RBA submissions to the various inquiries into housing and housing finance over the past decade that outline these issues, see https://www.rba.gov.au/publications/submissions/housing-and-housing-finance/

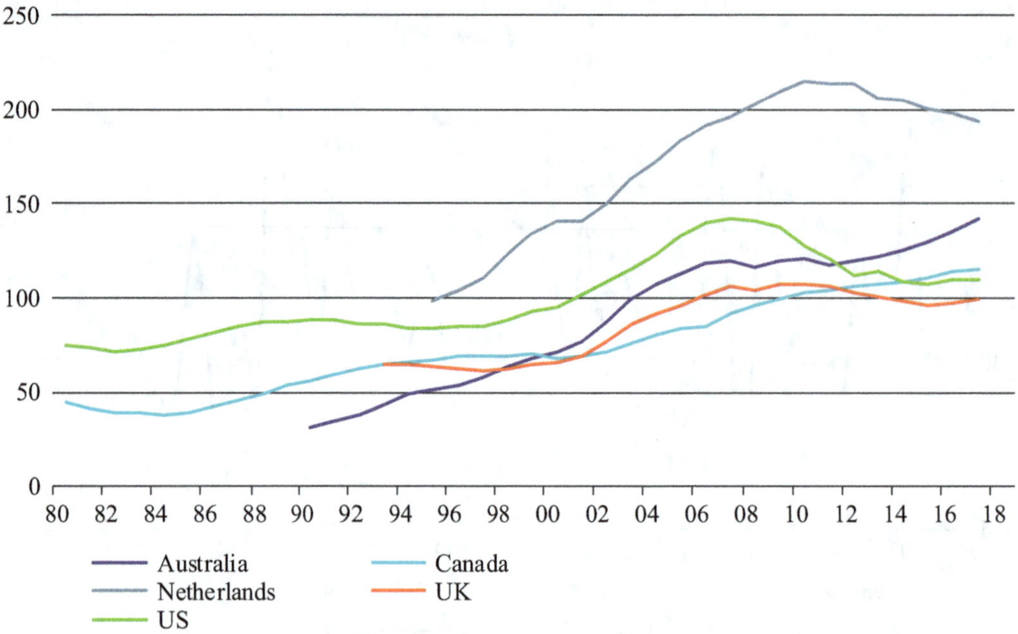

Source: National central banks and statistical offices; RBA (2018); OECD (2018); Thomson Reuters; ABS (2018); Bank of England (2018); Statistics Canada (2018); Statistics Netherlands (2018); US Federal Reserve (2018)

Fig. 17.3 Household mortgage debt-to-income ratio

This ratio is high relative to many other (but not all) advanced economies and raises issues about the resilience of household balance sheets in the event of an adverse shock to the housing sector and/or the economy.

Second, the Australian financial system is heavily weighted towards housing lending. Over the past decade, the largest Australian banks (which account for around 80% of the assets of the deposit-taking institutions) have steadily increased their exposure to housing so that around 60% of banks' lending is now for mortgages (Fig. 17.4). There have also been concerns that strong competition among mortgage lenders has resulted in lending standards becoming too relaxed. While stress tests indicate that banks are sufficiently well capitalised to handle a rise in loan delinquencies combined with a large fall in housing prices, a substantial downturn in the housing market could have implications for the economy more broadly.

These risks might be realised in a number of ways. First, while households often have sizeable pre-payment buffers, the high debt-to-income ratio can make them vulnerable to an adverse economic shock, with implications for household consumption. Households might also become forced sellers, resulting in downward pressure on housing prices and possibly inducing further selling. In addition, there has been a significant increase in the amount of interest-only lending, which can leave households with higher debt than for principal-and-interest loans and, in the event of sharp downturn in the housing market, possibly with negative equity. These developments would also weigh on banks' asset performance and profitability.

Second, investor activity could amplify the housing cycle. Unlike in many other countries, most of the rental stock of housing in Australia is owned by households as an investment, which boosts the level of household debt. Through 2013 and 2014,

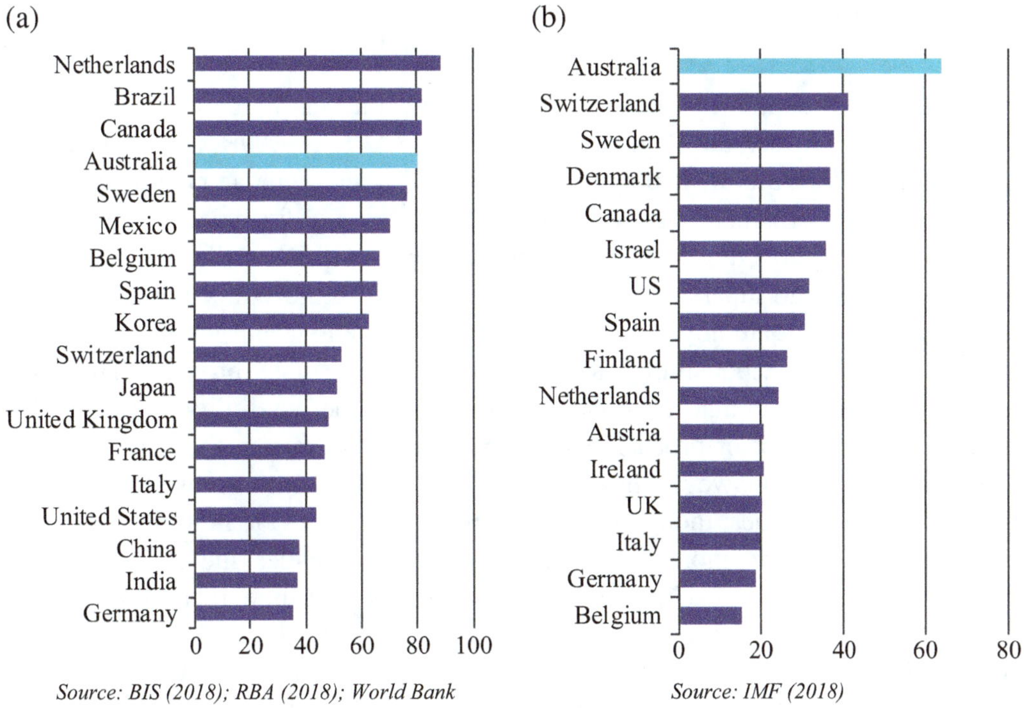

Fig. 17.4 (**a**) Banking system concentration (market share of the five largest banks) (**b**) Mortgage lending concentration

as the housing market was picking up, growth in lending to housing investors was rising by over 10% a year. In Australia, the tax deductibility of interest on investment loans and favourable rate of capital gains tax encourage households to borrow to purchase investment properties and not to pay down the principal. The substantial growth in investor lending therefore raises concerns about possible pro-cyclical behaviour of housing investors—the more housing prices rise, the more investors borrow to invest, potentially pushing up housing prices and debt levels further. If the housing market then turns down, and the prospect of capital gains diminish, these investors might sell ahead of expected price falls, amplifying the housing cycle (Reserve Bank of Australia 2017). This would have wider flow-on effects to owner-occupier households, which would find the price of their most important asset falling while they have a high level of debt.

Finally, the residential development cycle might also exacerbate the housing cycle, particularly for medium- and high-density apartment buildings, whose share has increased in recent years from around one-quarter to one-half of the new housing stock. High prices typically bring forth a supply response. But the lag in supply of new apartments coming on stream can mean that by the time it does, there is an oversupply. If the oversupply is significantly large, it would have implications for developers, and hence the performance of banks' property books. It would also have implications for households if they have contracted to purchase property in advance of construction on the expectation of making a subsequent capital gain. Again, this would have implications for bank balance sheets.

3 The Policy Response

In Australia, prudential regulation of financial institutions is the responsibility of the Australian Prudential Regulation Authority (APRA). APRA is tasked with protecting the interests of depositors, policyholders and superannuation (pension) fund members by maintaining the safety and soundness of financial institutions. Its mandate also requires it to promote financial stability more broadly. APRA has the usual regulatory and supervisory tools at its disposal to achieve this, but can also use these tools for what are now often-termed 'macroprudential' purposes.

The RBA has responsibility for financial stability more broadly. The RBA interprets this to mean that it should aim to minimise the possibility that instability in the financial sector or broader macro-financial risks threaten the real economy. The RBA does not, however, have any specific tools that it can use to deal with financial stability issues, though in stress periods it can provide liquidity to solvent institutions. While its monetary policy framework provides the RBA with the flexibility to set policy to achieve its broad objectives over time, including financial stability, addressing systemic risk typically involves identifying and communicating risks and working with other financial regulators to address them. The Council of Financial Regulators (which comprises the RBA, APRA, the Australian Securities and Investments Commission (ASIC) and the Australian Treasury) plays an important role by providing a forum for the sharing of information and views in this regard. It meets quarterly, although ongoing interactions are undertaken more frequently at all levels of these agencies. The Council has no powers of its own. So if stability risks are building, it is usually APRA that has the most appropriate tools to deal with not only risks to individual institutions but also risks to the system as a whole.

The financial stability risks associated with the recent increase in household indebtedness and housing prices generated a number of policy responses. As has historically been the case, the main approach by the regulators was to focus on setting appropriate lending standards. In response to the emerging risks in the housing sector, at end 2014 APRA announced that it would increase its supervisory oversight on mortgage lending (APRA 2014). Specifically, it indicated that it would be paying increased attention to higher-risk mortgage lending such as high loan-to-income loans, high loan-to-valuation (LVR) loans, interest-only loans to owner occupiers and loans with very long terms. It set out clear prudential expectations that lenders' serviceability tests for new borrowers must incorporate an interest rate buffer that was comfortably above (by at least 2 percentage points) the prevailing loan product rate. APRA also indicated that the prevailing strong growth in lending to property investors was a particular area of concern and set a new benchmark where growth in an institution's portfolio of investor loans of more than 10% would be an 'important risk indicator for APRA supervisors in considering the need for further action'. At the same time, ASIC took steps to reinforce the 'responsible lending' obligations that cover all lenders and ensure that loan serviceability is assessed to ensure that new borrowers do not overstretch their financial capacity to purchase property or need to rely on expectations of future increases in housing prices to enable them to do so.

These policy steps were primarily designed to dampen the most risky competitive pressures and encourage banks to lend more prudently. But they also helped to improve the resilience of household balance sheets, essentially reducing the maximum loan size and ensuring that the borrowers that received loans were in the best position to service the loans thereafter. Growth in lending to property investors subsequently fell from over 10% to less than 3% annually while growth in credit to owner-occupiers actually increased (Fig. 17.5). The share of loans at LVRs of over 90% declined from 12% to 7%. Growth in housing prices also eased.

Nevertheless, by 2016, housing activity was picking up again in Sydney and Melbourne, household debt was still rising faster than incomes, and growth in lending to property investors had started to rise again. So in early 2017, APRA, with the support of the Council of Financial Regulators, introduced further measures to bolster residential mortgage lending practices (APRA 2017). Apart from tightening somewhat further its 2014 guidelines on lending standard expectations, APRA indicated that it expected financial institutions to limit the flow of new interest-only lending for housing to 30% of their new lending (Fig. 17.5). To limit the risk of leakage, APRA also noted that it would be carefully examining trends in the level of warehouse funding by banks to non-bank lenders.

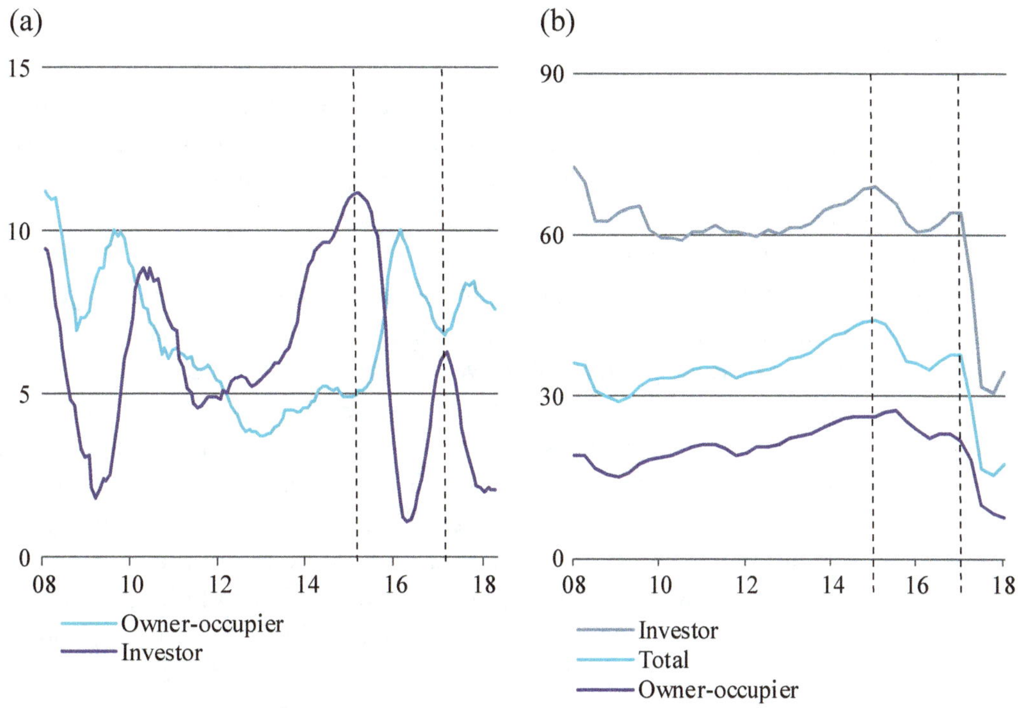

Source: APRA (2018); RBA (2018)

Fig. 17.5 (**a**) Housing credit growth (6-month-ended annualised) (**b**) Interest-only loan approvals share. Note: Dashed vertical lines in both panels of graph positioned in alignment with January 2015 and March 2017

Since then, risks in the housing market have again eased. The share of new housing lending that is on interest-only terms has declined to around 16%, well below the benchmark. There has also been less investor activity relative to owner occupiers and some signs of an increase in first home buyer activity. APRA has recently announced that the quality of new lending has improved to the extent that it will be able to remove the investor loan growth benchmark for individual institutions that meet certain requirements (APRA 2018). And while not a target in itself, growth in housing prices in Sydney and Melbourne has declined substantially, and in Sydney's case prices have even fallen a little in recent months.

4 Reflections

The Australian approach to addressing financial stability concerns has been heavily weighted towards setting appropriate prudential expectations, with relatively little use of prescriptive quantitative targets. While not an exhaustive list, there are four key issues that the recent experience has raised.

4.1 How Is Effectiveness Evaluated?

It is not always straightforward to measure the effectiveness of what have come to be known globally as 'macroprudential policies.' In Australia's case, the goal was to address financial stability risks by ensuring that banks and households were being appropriately prudent in their lending and borrowing decisions. But this broad policy goal is very difficult to measure with a high degree of accuracy. Instead, we can look to the specific impact of the measures taken—for example, the incidence of high-risk lending, pace of growth in investor loans and share of interest-only loans. By these metrics, the policies were apparently effective. But quantitative measures are difficult to calibrate and assess ex-post and in some cases have had only temporary effects, especially as other policies have continued to evolve. The benchmark on growth in investor lending introduced in 2014, for example, initially resulted in a sharp decline in the growth rate, but by early 2017 the growth rate was rising again. The 30% benchmark on the share of new interest-only loans introduced in 2017 was also materially overshot. But there appears to be continued demand for interest-only loans and there are signs that banks are looking to expand this category of lending again. More broadly, the global experience of the directed credit regimes of the 1960s and 1970s suggests that borrowers and lenders have an incentive to try to find ways to circumvent such controls. Noting this, the benchmark measures that have been used in Australia were always intended to be temporary while APRA put in place more permanent guidelines to address the associated concerns about lending standards.

Whether these measures had an impact on the growth of housing prices is unclear. Certainly, housing price growth in both Sydney and Melbourne eased substantially following the APRA and ASIC measures that were introduced. But loan approvals and price growth had already started to ease prior to the 2017 measures. And there is evidence that the price declines have been more evident in higher priced properties over the past year—a segment that would be expected to be least affected by the portfolio benchmark measures as investors are more likely to purchase cheaper apartments than detached housing.

4.2 Are Geographical Restrictions Helpful?

In Australia, we did not implement geographic-specific policies to shore up financial stability concerns, though some individual banks decided to restrict lending to certain postcodes. While it was mainly Sydney and Melbourne where housing conditions were most buoyant, APRA acted to improve mortgage lending standards across the board. One argument for implementing geographical restrictions could be that the banks would meet the new guidelines by restricting lending everywhere *except* for Sydney and Melbourne, disproportionally affecting (say) the Brisbane apartment market (that was not experiencing sharp price rises) and exacerbate the price falls in Perth. This has not turned out to be the case. But more broadly, we are sceptical about the value of geographic policies. Apart from the fact that it looks increasingly like directed lending, other countries' experiences suggest that there are difficulties in calibration and in implementation of geographic constraints over the longer run (Reserve Bank of New Zealand 2016). And as long as the large cities continue to grow, there will be a continuing demand for new housing and, if anything, a challenge for supply to keep up with that demand. This suggests that policies directed at lending in specific areas are likely to be successful in restraining housing price growth only in the short term.

4.3 Are There Undesirable Consequences?

An important challenge is to respond to systemic risks in a manner that strikes a reasonable balance between facilitating the ongoing provision of credit to the economy while managing the risks and other flow-on effects, including during the transition from one equilibrium to another (less risky) one. As seen in other countries, the use of quantitative restrictions to curtail the provision of credit to borrowers perceived to be systemically risky can have undesirable consequences. These include adverse effects on competition and distributional considerations. In Australia, some small and regional lenders have argued that the benchmark on the growth of investor lending has entrenched market shares (COBA 2017). Further, the various restrictions constrain the size of a loan marginal borrowers can get, including some first home buyers, and so have equity and distributional implications, although in doing so they make the debt more manageable for these households. Another group of borrowers that could be adversely affected by the tighter lending standards are investors that paid deposits on off-the-plan housing on the assumption that they would be able to get finance on prevailing credit terms, and now find that they are unable to do so.

4.4 How Are These Policies Likely to Evolve?

Like many other countries, the use of quantitative benchmarks to bolster financial stability does not have a long history in Australia and there are still many lessons to learn. In principle, these types of tools have the potential to contain a range of financial stability risks, and the early evidence is that they can be effective, at least for a while. But in practice, their use poses a range of challenges including calibration, selecting the most effective tool for the specific risk, containing potential leakages, ensuring on-going political support, and knowing how to effectively integrate them into the more traditional supervisory and monetary policy frameworks. These issues are a challenge for all countries (including Australia) and hence it is likely that their operational practices and governance frameworks will continue to evolve.

References

Australian Prudential Regulation Authority. (2014, December 9). *APRA outlines further steps to reinforce sound residential lending practices*. Media Release.

Australian Prudential Regulation Authority. (2017, March 31). *APRA announces further measures to reinforce sound residential mortgage lending practices*. Media Release.

Australian Prudential Regulation Authority. (2018, April 26). *APRA announces plans to remove investor lending benchmark and embed better practices*. Media Release.

COBA. (2017, September). *Submission to productivity commission inquiry into competition in the Australian financial system.*

Hsieh, W., Norman, D., & Orsmond, D. (2012, September 11–19). *Supply-side issues in the housing sector*. Reserve Bank of Australia *Bulletin*.

Kohler, M., & van der Merwe, M. (2015, September 21–30). *Long-run trends in housing price growth*. Reserve Bank of Australia *Bulletin*.

Reserve Bank of Australia. (2003, November). *Submission to the productivity commission inquiry on first home ownership*.

Reserve Bank of Australia. (2014, February). *Submission to the inquiry into affordable housing*.

Reserve Bank of Australia. (2017, October 27–30). Box B: Households' investor property exposures. *RBA Financial Stability Review*.

Reserve Bank of New Zealand. (2016, July). *Consultation Paper: Adjustments to restrictions on high-LVR residential mortgage lending*.

Graph Data Sources

Australian Bureau of Statistics (ABS). (2017). 5220.0 - Australian National Accounts: State Accounts, 2016–17. http://www.abs.gov.au/AUSSTATS/abs@.nsf/DetailsPage/5220.02016-17?OpenDocument

Australian Bureau of Statistics (ABS). (2018). 5204.0 - Australian System of National Accounts, 2017–18. http://www.abs.gov.au/AUSSTATS/abs@.nsf/DetailsPage/5204.02017-18?OpenDocument

Australian Prudential Regulation Authority (APRA). (2018). https://www.apra.gov.au/publications/quarterly-authorised-deposit-taking-institution-property-exposures

Bank for International Settlements (BIS). (2018). *Consolidated banking statistics*. Accessed June 1, 2018, from https://www.bis.org/statistics/consstats.htm

CoreLogic. (2018). *RP Data subscription*. https://www.corelogic.com.au/

International Monetary Fund (IMF). (2018). *Financial soundness indicators*. http://data.imf.org/?sk=51B096FA-2CD2-40C2-8D09-0699CC1764DA&sId=1390030341854

National central banks and statistical offices (various):

Bank of England. (2018). *Bankstats tables*. https://www.bankofengland.co.uk/statistics/tables

Statistics Canada. (2018). https://www150.statcan.gc.ca/n1/en/type/data?MM=1

Statistics Netherlands. (2018). *StatLine*. https://opendata.cbs.nl/statline/#/CBS/en/

US Federal Reserve. (2018). https://www.federalreserve.gov/data/mortoutstand/current.htm

OECD. (2018). *Household Debt*. Accessed June 1, 2018, from http://www.oecd.org/sdd/na/householddebt.htm

Reserve Bank of Australia (RBA). (2018). *Financial aggregates*. https://www.rba.gov.au/statistics/frequency/fin-agg/2018/

Chapter 18
Exploding House Prices in Urban Housing Markets: Explanations and Policy Solutions for the Netherlands

Christian Lennartz, Barbara Baarsma, and Nic Vrieselaar

1 Introduction[1]

Strong house price growth is by no means a post-crisis phenomenon but has been at the center of economic and societal transformations in almost all advanced economies since the 1980s (Aalbers 2015; Ansell 2014). For a given period it seemed that the global boom in house prices had finally come to a halt in and through the Global Financial Crisis (GFC) of 2008. Yet, 10 years after these events, housing markets are following a strong upward trend again, making the crisis years almost look like a glitch in the data.

However, the defining forces of house price appreciation have shifted substantially in recent years. Before 2008, price growth across the globe was largely carried by the easing of finance conditions, i.e. higher loan-to-value (LTV) and loan-to-income (LTI) ratios for individual borrowers, as well as the expansion of interest-only mortgages, mortgage guarantee funds, mortgage tax deductibility, and lower capital requirements for mortgage lenders (Cerutti et al. 2017; Schwartz 2012; Martin 2011; Schnure 2005). In the current boom cycle, other factors seem to have become more relevant.

Next to the extremely low (mortgage) interest rates, house price appreciation has become increasingly defined by fundamental demographic and economic parameters: the growth in the number of households relative to sluggish new supply, catch-

---

At the time of writing, Christian Lennartz and Barbara Baarsma worked at RaboResearch.

---

[1]Reprinted with permission of Rabobank. Previously published as Lennartz et al. (2018), Exploding house prices and imploding affordability in urban housing markets, Explanations and policy solutions for the Netherlands, Rabobank, June.

C. Lennartz (✉) · B. Baarsma · N. Vrieselaar
RaboResearch Rabobank, Utrecht, Netherlands
e-mail: Christian.lennartz@pbl.nl

R. Nijskens et al. (eds.), *Hot Property*, https://doi.org/10.1007/978-3-030-11674-3_18

up growth in jobs and job-related income, and the demand of (buy-to-let) investors pursuing high returns on housing property investments (e.g. Hekwolter of Hekhuis et al. 2017; Lennartz 2017). As a result of the rebalancing from a finance-driven towards a more fundamentals driven housing environment, market outcomes have become more regionalized, implying a growing divergence between *hot property markets* in major cities and less dynamic markets in more peripheral regions.

In this chapter we analyze these post-crisis developments for the Netherlands. Doing so, we establish a basis for a coherent policy discussion of how to mitigate the risks of extreme house price and excessive rent growth in urban housing markets. We propose five detailed measures to achieve this goal: [I] massively increase new housing production; [II] focus on affordable housing in the production of new homes; [III] increase the turnover rate of existing homes; [IV] better integrate housing and infrastructure/mobility policies; [V] penalize speculative housing investments.

2 The Specifics of Pre- and Post-crisis Housing in the Netherlands and Its Major Cities

Generally, house prices in the Netherlands have moved in line with the bulk of Western countries in the past 40 years. Starting in the early 1980s and ending with the Global Financial Crisis, the Netherlands experienced a sustained period of strong house price growth (see Fig. 18.1). This was followed by a prolonged market downturn between 2009 and 2013. Most strikingly, the recession on the housing market had—with the exception of Spain, Ireland and Denmark—run much deeper and for much longer than in most other countries.

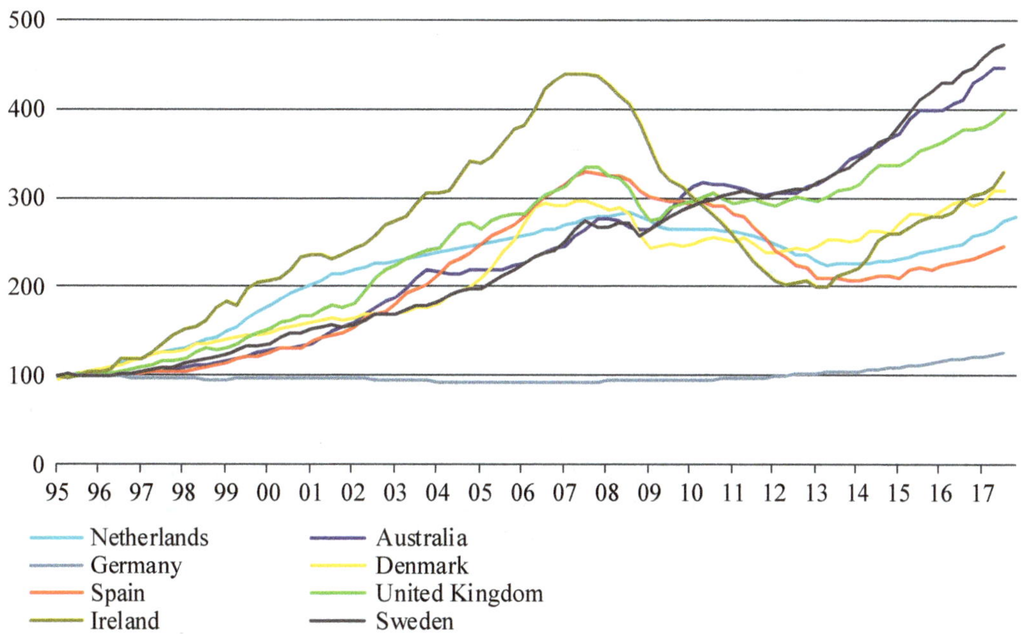

Source: Bank for International Settlements (2018)

Fig. 18.1 Nominal house prices

One explanation here is that due to high average loan-to-value mortgages a large proportion of mortgaged homeowners saw the value of their home decrease below their outstanding mortgage debt.[2] This meant that households had become more likely to repay their mortgage and less likely to consume, which in turn had a negative impact on the wider economy, implying lower growth and higher unemployment.

In reverse, the economic recession was further aggravated trough fiscal consolidation (see Heimberger 2017), which in turn had a negative impact on housing demand. Moreover, with high private (mortgage) debt having become a wearing factor for the stability of the financial system, the Dutch government implemented pro-cyclical macroprudential policies (lowering the maximum LTV, implementing binding LTI norms) in the early crisis period, which further suppressed demand for housing (Tu et al. 2017). Meanwhile, these patterns in price developments were also followed by national-level developments in housing affordability. Figure 18.2 illustrates that while the house price boom in the past 3 years has deteriorated affordability, relatively speaking housing costs in the owner-occupied sector still fall short of their 2008 levels.

Yet, the most noticeable feature of the post-crisis period is the way price recovery has differed across cities and regions. Even though the regulatory and institutional context is defined at the national level, local and regional housing markets have come to operate under different socio-economic and demographic conditions and

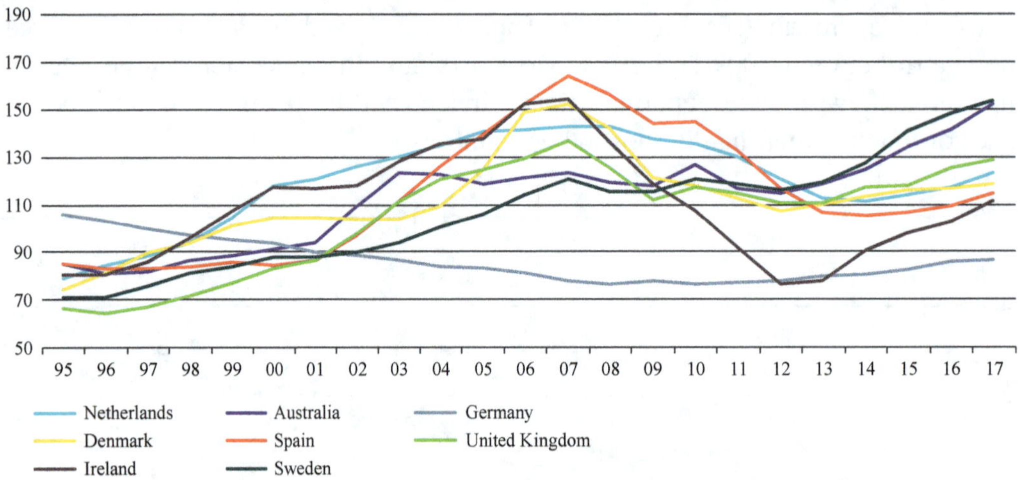

Source: OECD (2018)

Fig. 18.2 Price-to-income ratio. Note: Price-to-income ratio is defined as the nominal house prices divided by nominal disposable income per head. Net household disposable income is used. The population data come from the OECD national accounts database. The long-term average is calculated over the whole period available when the indicator begins after 1980 or after 1980 if the indicator is longer. This value is used as a reference value. The ratio is calculated by dividing the indicator source on this long-term average, and indexed to a reference value equal to 100

[2]For a good illustration of how severe the problem of underwater mortgages was, the reader is referred to Fig. 1 in Hekwolter of Hekhuis et al. 2017 (p. 33).

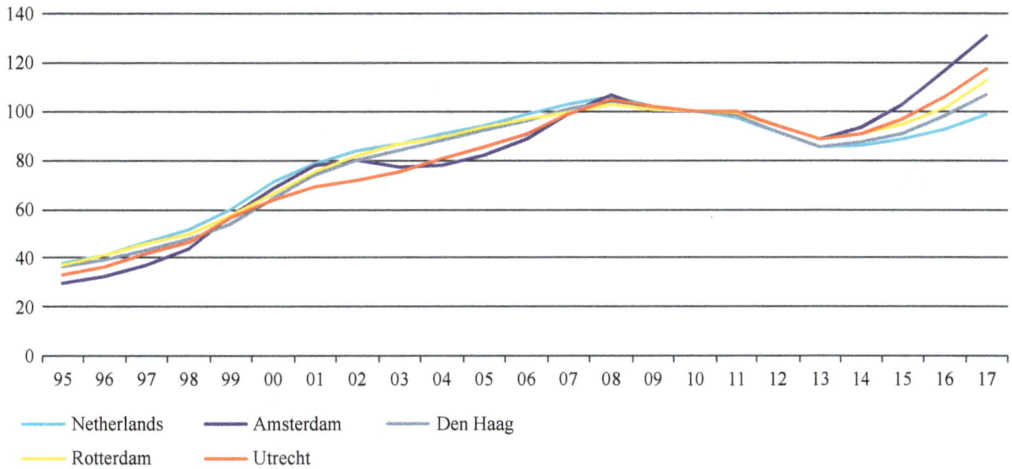

Source: Statistics Netherlands (2018)

Fig. 18.3 House price indices of the four largest Dutch cities

with varying price dynamics. To be more precise, regional house price data reveals a sharp and growing contrast between the major cities and city regions (Amsterdam, Utrecht, Rotterdam and The Hague inside the Randstad region (see Fig. 18.3), as well as Eindhoven, Groningen and Maastricht outside of it) and more peripheral housing markets.

Indeed, house prices in urban markets have long moved past their pre-crisis levels, with houses in Amsterdam as the most extreme case, now being 30% more expensive than in 2008 and a whopping 55% since they bottomed out in 2013. Meanwhile, house prices are still below their pre-crisis levels in more rural and less urbanized regions, particularly in those areas which are dealing with population decline and rapidly aging societies.

Secondly, Fig. 18.4 shows that in comparison to other major cities in Europe, the Dutch capital seems to be a particularly hot property market. While Amsterdam in absolute terms is on average (just like Dublin and Copenhagen) still relatively close to the national price level, the process of house price divergence since 2014 is only matched by the London/UK case.[3] Where in 2006 the average house in Amsterdam was only about 1.1 times more expensive than the average house in the Netherlands as a whole,[4] this ratio had increased to 1.5 by the end of 2016. Meanwhile, the price gap in Dublin, Copenhagen, and Stockholm had barely changed over the same period.

Whether the growing divergence between major cities and peripheral regions is a temporary phenomenon or a permanent structural shift in in the Dutch housing context is, of course, a valid question. Figure 18.3 reveals that Amsterdam experienced a major price correction in the mid-2000s after a period of unprecedented and unparalleled house price growth in the late 1990s. Accordingly, one could argue that

[3]For more capital/country pairs see IMF (2018).

[4]Admittedly, this does not control for differing compositions of the housing stocks.

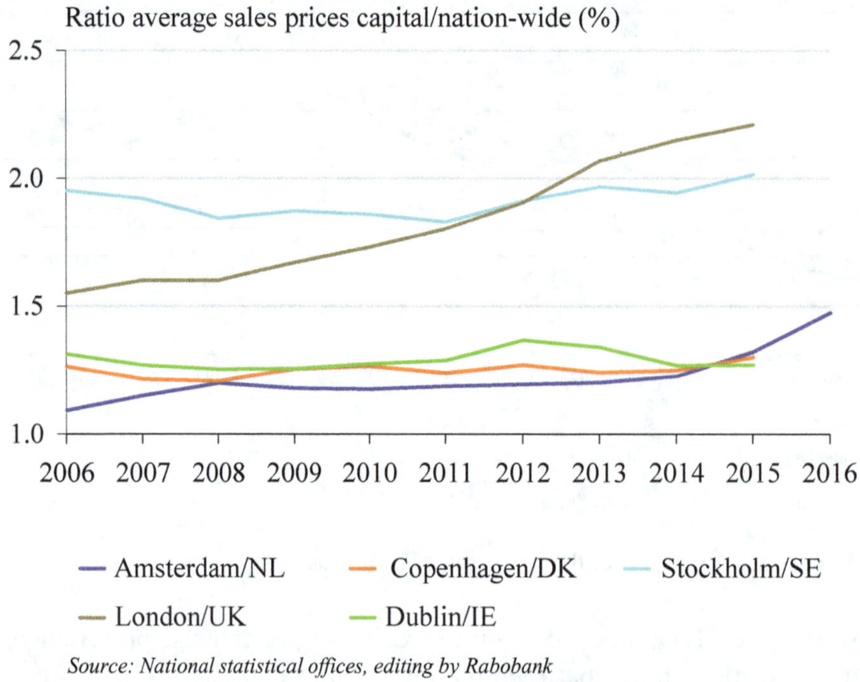

Fig. 18.4 Ratio of median house price in capital city to median house price in the whole country

in the current housing market cycle it is also a matter of time before house price developments in Amsterdam and other regions will level out again, be it through a relative fall in prices in Amsterdam (and other cities) or through faster growth in peripheral regions. In the following we will explicate why this is not the most likely outcome in the years to come.

3 Explaining the Emergence of Hot Property Markets

The emergence of hot residential property markets in the Netherlands can, by and large, be explained by three factors. Firstly, following the aforementioned economic and housing market downturn, housing production had fallen to an all-time low. Indeed, while in the years before the GFC the housing stock in the Netherlands had grown by more than 80,000 dwellings per year, this number dropped to 45,000 units between 2011 and 2014. Most strikingly, this drop materialized more rapidly and most strongly in urban regions (CBS 2018). Given that building land in these areas is scarcer and thus more expensive (See Fig. 2 in Hekwolter of Hekhuis et al. 2017), developers are seemingly more reluctant to keep investing in these areas, resulting in a relatively stronger backlog of new dwellings in relation to new households.

Secondly, following the restructuring towards a knowledge-based economy in the past decades, larger cities have increasingly become the economic powerhouses of the country. Even before the crisis this had led to positive (internal and external) migration rates of younger and highly-educated adults. After the crisis, this trend has accelerated considerably, also because knowledge-intensive sectors have fared better and recovered faster than more traditional and spatially less concentrated sectors as construction and retail. As a result, the demand of private households for rental and owner-occupied units in and around these cities has grown much stronger than elsewhere in the post-crisis period.

Finally, the housing landscape in the Netherlands has changed massively through the emergence of a new class of domestic[5] buy-to-let private investors.[6] Given the low borrowing costs and strong price appreciation since 2014, residential real estate has generally attracted increasing demand from small-scale (buy-to-let) landlords and more professional (and larger) investors alike. Here, investors specifically channelled their financial resources into urban housing markets such as Amsterdam, Eindhoven, and Maastricht, i.e. localities with the highest (possible) rent increases and price growth due to stronger imbalances between supply and demand (e.g. Hekwolter of Hekhuis et al. 2017). Within this process, buy-to-let investors have contributed to increasing prices in two ways. By turning owner-occupied units into rental properties they have significantly contributed to the scarcity of owner-occupied units in urban areas. Additionally, newly purchased buy-to-let properties were most often offered in the unregulated rental sector,[7] a sector which has seen tremendous rent increases, particularly in the larger cities (CBS 2017a).[8] This in turn has allowed for higher purchase prices by investors, which then were used to justify further rent increases to meet target returns—and so the cycle continued.

[5]Although this has become a topic of interest in the Dutch media, there is no clear evidence of increased activities of foreign buyers with the exception of international pension funds buying residential complexes of housing associations (Capital Value 2018).

[6]See Fields (2018) for a good overview of the forces behind this process.

[7]The Dutch rental market generally consists of two sectors: a regulated sector in which initial rents are stipulated by a dwelling quality and location-based point valuation system. Currently, the deregulation threshold stands at €710 net rent per month. Above this threshold initial rents are fully deregulated and freely negotiated between landlords and tenants. Likewise, rent increases are only regulated below the €710 threshold, where the central government determines maximum rent increases once a year. In the deregulated sector rent increases are not controlled, yet they can only be increased once per year. Furthermore, a specific trait of the Dutch rent regime is that access to regulated rental dwellings owned by non-profit housing associations is based on disposable household income (between €36,000 and €43,000 depending on household composition) and waiting time, while regulated units owned by private parties are not bound to this rule.

[8]Here, the specifics of the rent regime plays a key role. Since the point-based valuation system is partially based on house values, which in turn are based on current market values, rising house prices imply that rents can become deregulated much quicker.

4 Policy Solutions for Hot Property Markets

With house prices and rents increasing sharply in the past couple of years, and deteriorating affordability and accessibility becoming a threat to the stability of the Dutch housing market and the economy as a whole (see e.g. DNB 2018a), housing policy has become a central theme in local and national policy debates. In the following we seek to lay out coherent policy solutions to what were argued the underlying causes of the emerging housing crisis in the Netherlands.

4.1 Macroprudential Policy

It is necessary to first deal with the 'elephant in the room': macroprudential policy. In a country where the maximum mortgage loan still stands at 100% of home value, tightening mortgage lending might be the most obvious way of reducing demand of prospective house buyers, and through this lowering aggregate prices. Recent policy shifts in Sweden and Australia suggest that more restricted access to mortgage credit may indeed have a direct and measurable impact on house prices, at least in the short run (see Bloomberg 2018a; SMH 2018). However, we would argue that macroprudential policies are not the most useful solution to the problem in the current Dutch housing environment.

Firstly, tighter lending norms were already implemented several years ago. While the maximum LTV ratio has been reduced from more than 120–100% in 2018—which, admittedly, is still very high by international standards—it is particularly the more stringent LTI norms, which are becoming a limiting factor to exuberant mortgage lending and, accordingly, endless house price excesses (see also Tu et al. 2017). Secondly and related to this, the primary goal of macroprudential policy is to guarantee the stability of the financial system (Galati and Moessner 2017; and Kuttner and Shim 2012). Yet, in the recent boom cycle the growth in aggregate mortgage debt has lagged behind house price growth (see Fig. 18.5).

This brings up the question whether macroprudential policies would then not be utilized for targeting a problem which they are not designed for. In a similar vein, while macroprudential policies affect all prospective homebuyers, the problem of escalating prices is, as described, concentrated in the country's major urban areas. The fact that LTV and LTI limits are by design countrywide rules means that there is a risk of making the situation worse for first-time buyers in peripheral markets. And indeed, first-time buyers do borrow relatively more in these areas (average LTV is 95%) than first-time buyers in major cities (90%—see Hekwolters of Hekhuis et al. 2017).

Finally, macroprudential policies alone would do little to nothing about the problem of sharply increasing rents in the deregulated rental sector. In fact, given that buy-to-let properties are most often not purchased with high LTV ratios and do not fall under the current LTI regime, a further tightening of lending conditions

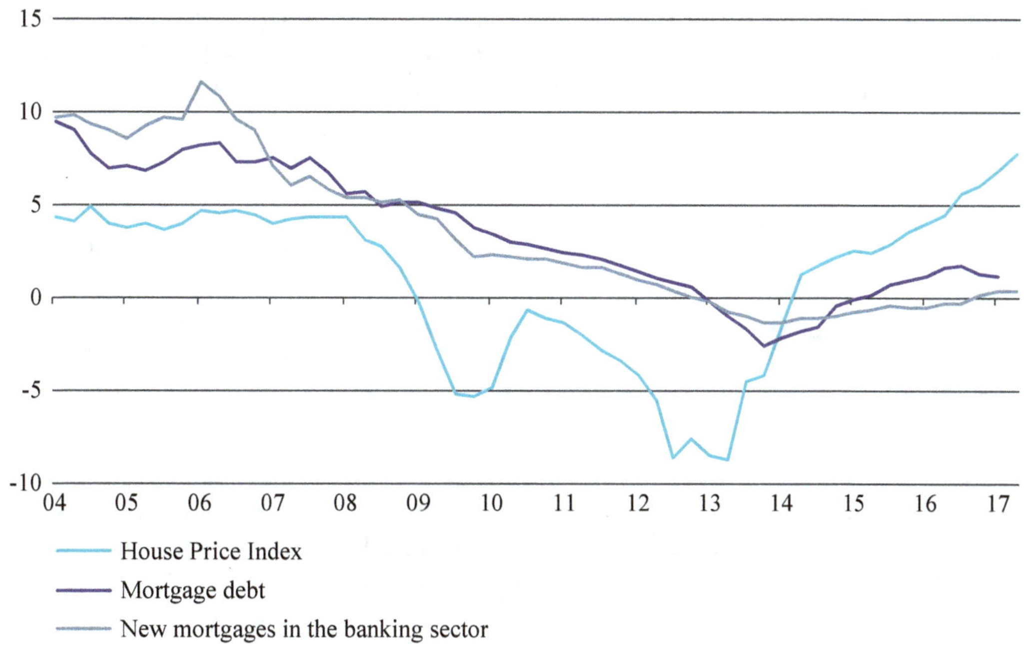

Source: DNB (2018b), Statistics Netherlands (2018)

Fig. 18.5 Mortgage debt versus house prices

would imply that first-time buyers fall further back behind the purchasing power of private investors.

4.2 Structural Urban and National Housing Policies

In short, although there is little doubt that macroprudential policies would lead, at least temporarily, to a fall in house prices, they are not effective in targeting the underlying causes of urban housing problems. From our viewpoint a mix of structural urban and national (housing) policies are much more suited for reaching this goal. These policies consist of five building blocks.

I. Massively Increase Housing Supply in Urban Areas

It was argued above that a shortage in new housing units is a key driver of the growing imbalances between supply and demand in the past 4 years. Yet, housing shortages are not a new phenomenon. In the second half of the Twentieth century, population growth and the demand for new housing was much stronger than in the current housing cycle. The solution to this specific problem at the time was a much more active role by the central government in the production of new housing through, for instance, bricks-and-mortar subsidies and a more direct role in urban and regional planning (see also Boelhouwer and Priemus 2014).

Currently, the Dutch government has given itself a coordinating part at best. However, the problem with this is that individual municipalities often lack the means and the willingness to spur production within their municipal boundaries (see also point IV). More precisely, since selling land at maximum prices is an essential source of income for local administrations (CBS 2017b), there is little incentive to sell many land positions simultaneously, since this would lower prices significantly. To overcome this blockade, the central government could reimburse city administrations either through direct subsidies on land sales or by rebalancing their income structure altogether, where the exploitation of land positions would receive a smaller role than it has now. Additionally, urban planners are increasingly dealing with voter backlash and Nimbyism against housing construction in inner-city areas (Hankinson 2018). By giving the central government a stronger role in issuing new housing locations, it could function as a scapegoat for the upzoning process. This would allow for taller buildings, greater densities and higher pace in land or building conversion projects (see also Metcalf 2018).

A final point here relates to the fact that potential building land, especially in outer-city locations, is not necessarily owned by public administrations but by private developers themselves. The underlying problem remains the same. While the willingness to build more housing appears to be high at the moment, private developers have little incentive to develop all of their locations simultaneously, as this would lead to a fall in sales prices and thus imply lower returns (Miles 2018). Since appropriation is time-consuming and costly, governments should address this problem by increasing property taxes on inactive land holdings.

II. New Production Should Match the Need for Affordable Housing

Where most newly constructed inner-city dwellings are small-sized apartments for single-person households or multi-person units in the high-end segment, it becomes increasingly apparent that just building a lot of new units is not enough. Rather, to keep urban housing markets diverse and affordable, planning authorities need to ensure that the new housing stock does not only satisfy the influx of higher-income households, but that it also covers the housing needs of (new) lower- and middle income households. Given the fact that in the two major cities of the country, Amsterdam and Rotterdam, regulated rental housing (<€710 net rent per month) already makes up more than 50% of the housing stock—and is thus significantly larger than the share of low and lower-middle income households,[9] this might seem a rather unnecessary prerequisite for housing policy. However, the crucial distinction here is between existing and readily available affordable units, where the former are abundantly available and the latter extremely scarce.

The main solution that is widely proposed for creating a more affordable and accessible rental housing sector is the expansion of the 'mid-level' market segment in the rental sector, which are deregulated dwellings with a net rent of between €710 and €950 to €1000 per month. While there certainly is growing demand for these dwellings, the discussion misses two essential points. First, rather than ensuring that

[9]For most recent numbers on the distribution of the housing stock the reader is referred to the report 'Housing in the Metropolitan Region Amsterdam 2017' (Booi et al. 2018).

these units are objectively affordable in relation to their occupiers' incomes, the 'mid-rent' segment only assumes affordable rents (see also Van Middelkoop and Schilder 2017). Second, there are no guarantees under the current rent regime that mid-level rental dwellings are not being pushed into the high-rent segment with the arrival of a new tenant.[10]

In our view, a more effective way of producing permanently affordable dwellings for middle-income households is through land policies and one new and coherent regulation regime that applies to the entire rental market. If municipalities for example sell land at reduced prices, or, alternatively, use ground lease arrangements to split the costs of land from the costs of building structures (see e.g. Kenny et al. 2018), developers should be obliged to (partially) construct new dwellings for lower- to middle-income single-person and family-households. Initial rents should take into account both dwelling properties as well as the income of its occupier, while annual rent increases should be controlled for a time-specific period, even in the case of tenancy change. The system of *local reference rents* to determine initial rents and rent increases as applied in Germany for instance, has proven to be an effective policy measure in that regard and could possibly be a leading principle in re-regulating the Dutch rental sector as well.

III. Increase Turnover Rate to Achieve a Better Allocated Housing Stock
Building new (affordable) homes is the key ingredient for a better balance between housing supply and demand. Nonetheless, prices and rents are, at least in the short run, more susceptible to changes in the stock for existing homes. One of the core problems of hot property markets is that they reduce the willingness and ability to move house because the additional utility of a new rental or owner-occupied unit most often does not justify its additional costs. Particularly in the rental market this tends to be a problem. While there is little incentive to move from a regulated to an unregulated rental dwelling per se, the growing divergence between the two sectors means that even if a move to a (better) or larger unregulated dwelling was desired, it has become more difficult to realize this wish. The solution to this problem most likely lies in a more balanced housing stock with a sufficient number of dwellings in all segments across the rental and owner-occupied spectrum, and thus will take many years to realize.

Nevertheless, governments could think about short-term solutions to achieve a more optimal allocation of the housing stock. A more penalizing approach would be the introduction of income-based rents and changing permanent into temporary contracts for tenants who, given their household income and household size,

[10]Similarly, critics of the sole focus on expanding the mid-level segment have proposed the alternative idea of increasing the current deregulation threshold (to €1000 per month). However, this proposal misses that this would further deteriorate the chances of newcomers and market outsiders to find accessible and affordable housing in cities—after all, the largest share of the deregulated housing stock is not only allocated based on household income but also on time accumulated on waiting lists. Moreover, it would, most likely, push investments by private developers further down the road, meaning that they would probably seek to establish a mid-rent segment that would start at much higher rents per month, e.g. €1000–€1200 per month.

severely overconsume social rental housing.[11] Since there are legal limitations to implementing such policies, incentivizing moves might be a more effective way forward. Amongst other options, local policy makers could think about setting up funds to cover the transaction costs of house moves or by giving rent credits to tenants and discounts on property taxes to owner-occupiers if they move to a more suited dwelling. In contrast, overcrowding as a coping strategy to avoid unaffordable rental costs could be averted by extending housing allowances to the deregulated sector.[12] This would mean that households who move to larger and often more expensive units would not lose their full subsidy automatically.

IV. Better Integration of Housing and Infrastructure Policies

In the current housing landscape in the Netherlands lower- and lower-to-middle income households are heavily concentrated in inner-city locations.[13] While there is an ongoing process of a displacement of poorer households to less desirable outer-city locations—in a recent study by Hochstenbach and Musterd (2018) this was dubbed as the suburbanization of poverty—there is still a case to be made for a more equal spread of different income classes across city regions.

On the one hand, this would require the production of new housing being set at the regional level. However, to guarantee that local planners do not seek to implement policies which would welcome higher-income but fend off lower-income households, oversight and coordination should potentially be given to national authorities. On the other hand, a regional approach would require better coordination and integration of housing and public infrastructure/transport policies.

In the Netherlands, commuting distances are strongly influenced by income and educational level (CBS 2016), meaning that the higher socio-economic stratum commutes significantly longer distances, while lower-income households tend to stay closer to their work places. If (public) transportation became cheaper, not living in inner-city locations would potentially become more attractive to all income classes. From a policy point of view this would not only include infrastructural projects that would particularly strengthen sustainable public transport projects but could also be achieved through partially replacing housing allowances with mobility allowances.

V. Penalize Speculative Buy-to-Let Investments but Incentivize Build-to-Let

Recent evidence shows that there is a relatively straightforward and effective way in limiting the influence of domestic and foreign investors in urban housing markets:

[11]These would be regulated rental housing units that are accessed through the income- and waiting-time based allocation system.

[12]Under current law housing allowances can only be obtained for regulated dwellings.

[13]See Booi et al. (2018) for the case of Amsterdam.

a substantial increase of stamp duty taxes on secondary property purchases.[14] Currently, the stamp duty tax (*overdrachtsbelasting* in Dutch) in the Netherlands stands at 2% of the purchasing price for all types of buyers. One possible avenue would be to increase it to the pre-crisis level of six per cent for the purchase of a second home and to-let dwellings. The rationale behind this measure is that it would make investments of speculative buy-to-let investors[15] and buy-to-leave buyers[16] much less attractive and would also tilt the level playing field back towards younger first-time buyers. However, long-term private investors who turn owner-occupied units into affordable rental units may be exempted from this rule. As it is often the first destination of younger newcomers in urban housing markets, affordable private rental dwellings serve a crucial function for spatial and economic mobility. This means that fending off private investors should not be a goal in itself; rather, policy makers should devise a system in which private investors do not solely seek to invest in the higher segment of the free rental market. As argued above this could be achieved through a system of a more comprehensive rent regulation regime that serves the interests of both landlords and tenants, as well as more targeted subsidies for new (affordable) housing.

5 Conclusions

Extreme house price growth and increasing unaffordability in the owner-occupied and private rental sector pose some of the greatest challenges in contemporary urban housing markets. While it has been argued elsewhere that hot property markets will cool off—to put it mildly—once interest rates rise to higher levels again, this contribution has argued that more coordinated policy interventions at both the local and national level are required. The potential problem with not acting quickly and decisively is manifold: It increases the risk of local bubble formations and severe housing market busts, it undermines the stability of the financial system and economic growth, it increases wealth inequality, and it weakens social cohesion within cities and across countries.

We argued that a coherent housing and planning policy approach would entail five key components. A massive increase of housing supply; the production and preservation of affordable housing; higher turnover rates to reach a better allocation

[14]Indeed, right after such a measure was introduced in London, prices started to fall relatively to the rest of the country (Bloomberg 2018b).

[15]That is private investors who purchase properties, refurbish and split them into smaller units, only to rent them out for high prices in the deregulated sector.

[16]That is buyers who do not seek to rent out the dwelling in the first place, but just use it to store their wealth.

of the housing stock; a better integration of housing and mobility/infrastructure policies; and finally, a significant reduction of speculative buy-to-let and buy-to-leave transactions.

We end this contribution on one specific qualification: While the policy details described in this contribution are specific to urban housing markets in the Netherlands, we would argue that the broader strokes also apply to hot property markets elsewhere. Recent studies have suggested that housing markets in major cities have become globally connected and thus increasingly function along the same basic premises (Aalbers 2015; IMF 2018). This then does not only suggest that policy solutions might even be sought at the supranational level, but it also means that international policy learning has become more meaningful in making national and local housing policies more robust and effective. This contribution hopes to be a testimony to this claim.

References

Aalbers, M. B. (2015). The great moderation, the great excess and the global housing crisis. *International Journal of Housing Policy, 15*(1), 43–60.

Ansell, B. (2014). The political economy of ownership: Housing markets and the welfare state. *American Political Science Review, 108*(2), 383–402.

Bank for International Settlements. (2018). *Residential property prices*. Accessed April 1, 2018, from https://www.bis.org/statistics/pp_selected.htm?m=6%7C288%7C596

Bloomberg. (2018a). *Sweden responds to worst housing slump with supply*. Accessed under https://www.bloomberg.com/news/articles/2018-03-12/sweden-responds-to-worst-housing-slump-since-2008-with-supply

Bloomberg. (2018b). *London house prices decline in stark division with rest of UK*. Accessed under https://www.bloomberg.com/news/articles/2018-04-15/london-house-prices-decline-in-stark-division-with-rest-of-u-k

Boelhouwer, P., & Priemus, H. (2014). Demise of the Dutch social housing tradition: Impact of budget cuts and political changes. *Journal of Housing and the Built Environment, 29*(2), 221–235.

Booi, E., de Graaf, L., & van Diest, M. (2018). *Wonen in de Metropoolregio Amsterdam* [Housing in the Metropolitan Region Amsterdam]. Amsterdam: MRA.

Capital Value. (2018). *An analysis of the Dutch residential (investment) market in 2018*. Utrecht.

CBS. (2016). *Hoogopgeleide man maakt meeste woon-werk kilometers* [Highly-educated men have the longest commuting distances]. Accessed under https://www.cbs.nl/nl-nl/nieuws/2016/25/hoogopgeleide-man-maakt-de-meeste-woon-werkkilometers

CBS. (2017a). *Laagste huurstijging sinds 2010* [Lowest rent increases since 2010]. Accessed under https://www.cbs.nl/nl-nl/nieuws/2017/36/laagste-huurstijging-sinds-2010

CBS. (2017b). *Het vermogen van decentrale overheden* [The wealth of decentralized government bodies]. Den Haag.

CBS. (2018). https://opendata.cbs.nl/statline/#/CBS/nl/dataset/70072ned/table?ts=1524665374837

Cerutti, E., Dagher, J., & Dell'Ariccia, G. (2017). Housing finance and real-estate booms: A cross-country perspective. *Journal of Housing Economics, 38*, 1–13.

DNB. (2018a). *Consumptie in Nederland hangt sterk samen met de huizenprijs* [Consumer spending in the Netherlands is strongly related to house prices]. Accessed under https://www.dnb.nl/nieuws/nieuwsoverzicht-en-archief/DNBulletin2018/dnb371605.jsp

DNB. (2018b) Statistics Netherlands. Accessed April 1, 2018, from https://statistiek.dnb.nl/downloads/#/?fq=%7Ctags%3Awoninghypotheken

Fields, D. (2018). Constructing a new asset class: Property-led financial accumulation after the crisis. *Economic Geography, 94*(2), 118–140.

Galati, G., & Moessner, R. (2017). What do we know about the effects of macroprudential policy? *Economica*. https://doi.org/10.1111/ecca.12229.

Hankinson, M. (2018). When do renters behave like homeowners? High rent, price anxiety, and NIMBYism. *American Political Science Review, 112*, 1–21.

Heimberger, P. (2017). Did fiscal consolidation cause the double-dip recession in the euro area. *Review of Keynesian Economics, 5*(3), 439–458.

Hekwolter of Hekhuis, M., Nijskens, R., & Heeringa, W. (2017). *The housing market in major Dutch cities* (No. 1501). Netherlands Central Bank, Research Department.

Hochstenbach, C., & Musterd, S. (2018). Gentrification and the suburbanization of poverty: Changing urban geographies through boom and bust periods. *Urban Geography, 39*(1), 26–53.

IMF – International Monetary Fund. (2018, April). *Global financial stability report*. Washington.

Kenny, T., Elliott, T., & Bicquelet-Lock, A. (2018). Better planning for housing affordability: Three approaches to solving the housing crisis in the UK. *Journal of Urban Regeneration & Renewal, 11*(3), 233–241.

Kuttner, K., & Shim, I. (2012). Taming the real estate beast: The effects of monetary and macroprudential policies on housing prices and credit. In A. Heath, F. Packer, & C. Windsor (Eds.), *Property markets and financial stability* (pp. 231–259). Sydney: Reserve Bank of Australia.

Lennartz, C. (2017). *Huizenprijzen Randstad zijn ontkoppeld van de rest van Nederland*. The Netherlands: Rabobank.

Lennartz, C., Baarsma, B.E., & Vrieselaar, N. (2018). *Exploding house prices: Five policy options*. The Netherlands: Rabobank.

Martin, R. (2011). The local geographies of the financial crisis: From the housing bubble to economic recession and beyond. *Journal of Economic Geography, 11*(4), 587–618.

Metcalf, G. (2018). Sand castles before the tide? Affordable housing in expensive cities. *Journal of Economic Perspectives, 32*(1), 59–80.

Miles, D. (2018). *Housing policy: Learning from the past and looking to the future*. Accessed under https://voxeu.org/article/uk-house-prices-looking-far-past-and-future

OECD. (2018). *Household debt*. Accessed April 1, 2018, from https://stats.oecd.org/Index.aspx?DataSetCode=HOUSE_PRICES

Schnure, C. (2005). *Boom-bust cycles in housing: The changing role of financial structure* (No. 5-200). Washington, DC: International Monetary Fund.

Schwartz, H. (2012). Housing, the welfare state, and the global financial crisis: What is the connection? *Politics & Society, 40*(1), 35–58.

Statistics Netherlands. (2018). Accessed April 1, 2018, from http://statline.cbs.nl/Statweb/

Sydney Morning Herald. (2018). *Sydney house prices fall for the first year since 2012*. Accessed under https://www.smh.com.au/business/the-economy/sydney-house-prices-fall-for-the-first-year-since-2012-20180301-p4z294.html

Tu, Q., de Haan, J., & Boelhouwer, P. (2017). House prices and long-term equilibrium in the regulated market of the Netherlands. *Housing Studies, 33*, 1–25.

Van Middelkoop, M., & Schilder, F. (2017). *Middeninkomens op de woningmarkt. Ruimte op een krap speelveld* [Middle-income households on the housing market]. Den Haag: Planbureau voor de Leefomgeving.

www.ingramcontent.com/pod-product-compliance
Lightning Source LLC
LaVergne TN
LVHW080047210926
848481LV00011B/3298